The Gothic Family Romance

POST-CONTEMPORARY INTERVENTIONS

Series Editors: Stanley Fish and Fredric Jameson

A Bloomsbury Family, by William Orpen
National Gallery of Scotland

The Gothic
Family Romance

Heterosexuality, Child Sacrifice,

and the Anglo-Irish Colonial Order

Margot Gayle Backus

Duke University Press   Durham and London   1999

© 1999 Duke University Press

All rights reserved

Printed in the United States of America on acid-free paper ♾

Designed by C. H. Westmoreland

Typeset in Minion with Oxford display by Tseng Information Systems, Inc.

Library of Congress Cataloging-in-Publication Data

appear on the last printed page of this book.

For Steve

Contents

Acknowledgments

I am extraordinarily fortunate to have received a vast amount of insightful and generous feedback and support from mentors, colleagues, staff members, and friends during my years of work on this project. Those listed below have made possible what no period of supported research in isolation could have. Everything that is good about this book is good because readers and others helped to make it so.

Elizabeth Butler Cullingford, Sharon Delmendo, Bonnie Blackwell, Maria Helena Lima, Ann Cvetkovich, and the members of Girl Group — Janet Foster, Susan Meigs, and JoAnn Pavletich — read many, many chapter drafts and provided invaluable guidance. I am especially indebted to Liz Cullingford for her tireless and exacting feedback at many stages of the book's production and to Sharon Delmendo for her help with final revisions of the entire manuscript. My work with the University of Texas Irish Interest Group and with Nathalie Frensley shaped my understanding of many issues in this book. Ann Owens Weekes and Mary Favret, readers for Duke University Press, and my editor, Reynolds Smith, provided indispensable help and encouragement in revising this manuscript.

Katherine Arens, Barbara Harlow, Wahneema Lubiano, Carol MacKay, Jane Marcus, Ramón Saldívar, and Kathleen Stewart enriched my understanding of literary criticism and theory, and read and responded to early articulations of these ideas. Mia Carter, Mary Jean Corbett, David Devereux, Laura Doan, Richard Haslam, Bill Harrison, Trevor Hope, Judiana Lawrence, Laura Lyons, Jane Marcus, Kevin McCarron, Beth McCoy, Lucy McDiarmid, Lisa Moore, Catharine O'Connell, John Roche, S. Shankar, and Dolora Wojciehowski gave valuable feedback on specific chapters.

I owe special thanks to those who have given me the gift of their friendship and with whom I have shared most extensively the joys and struggles that attended this work: Sharon Delmendo, Judiana Lawrence, David Sanders, and John Roche; JoAnn Pavletich, Ed Madden, and Bonnie Blackwell; Maria Helena Lima, Laura Doan, and Trevor Hope; and Liz Cullingford, Lucy McDiarmid, Lillian Robinson, and Constance Coiner, whom I miss.

I thank the following for providing materials, guidance, inspiration, and support: Nancy J. Raynor, Sanja Sefo, Lori Howard, Cole Bryant, Susan Fanelli, Marlene Mussell, Diane Lucas, Nancy Martin, Lin Mocejunas, Renée Locke, Steven Coleman, Laura Lyons, David Sanders, Alan Friedman, Martha McClelland, Pat Finnegan, Mary Condren, Katherine O'Donnell, Fintan O'Toole, Nicholas Grene, John Foley, Damian Doyle, Spurgeon Thompson, Mitch Harris, Esiaba Irobi, Joe Cleary, Jennifer Badot, Richard Sha, Kai Easton, Rachel Jennings, Katie Kane, Karen Steele, Purnima Bose, Susan Harris, Declan Kiberd, Helen Vendler, Roy Foster, Clyde Childe, Tony Roche, Guinn Batten, Frank McGuinness, David Lloyd, Luke Gibbons, Tom Staley, members of John Richetti's 1993 National Endowment for the Humanities seminar "The Rise of the Novel"—especially Nira Gupta-Casal, Patsy Griffin, Padmini Mongia, and Glen Colburn—Rivka Lahav, Susan Moore, Jan Carlson, Catherine Johnson, Tom Paul, Paul English, students, friends, and family members.

Grants and scholarships from the University of Texas, the National Endowment for the Humanities, and St. John Fisher College, a fellowship from the Austin branch of the English Speaking Union, and scholarships at the Yeats and Synge Summer Schools funded periods of intensive study in British and Irish literature. An earlier version of Chapter 5, "Irish Gothic Realism and the Great War: The Devil's Bargain and the Demon Lover," appeared in the *Canadian Review of Comparative Literature* (Spring 1994) in "Reading the Signs," a special issue on gay and lesbian literature coedited by Ross Chambers and Anne Herrmann, whose feedback enriched the current chapter. It is reprinted here with the permission of the *Canadian Review* and with thanks to journal editor Jonathan Hart. All quotations from Northern Ireland political propaganda, as well as the more general points I make about modes of political representation in Protestant propaganda, were made possible through materials from the Linen Hall Library's Northern

Ireland Political Collection. Librarians at the St. John Fisher College Lavery Library have been heroic in their support for my work.

I owe a special debt of gratitude to Steve Tennison—friend, partner, and computer wizard. Without his extended mental and physical exertions on behalf of a project he sometimes wished dead, this book would have been a goner.

I also thank the members of my decidedly nonnuclear family(s): Suzanne FitzGerald and Tom Morgan; Russell FitzGerald and Ron Kaake; Tom FitzGerald and Brad Hanson; Marjorie Peterson; Ellen Backus, Peg Backus, and the Backus clan; and the Community Now cohousing group. Without the myriad ways that your lives and experiences contributed to mine, this book could not have been.

Introduction

Behold, there are those near to thee, who though they no longer have a
tongue to speak, speak to thee with that eloquence which is stronger than
all the eloquence of living tongues.
— Charles Maturin, *Melmoth the Wanderer*

Glenn Patterson's first novel, *Burning Your Own* (1988), exemplifies the
basic narrative pattern that I examine in this book. In *Burning Your
Own,* Patterson depicts 1969 Belfast through the eyes of Mal, the pre-
adolescent son of troubled Protestant parents: an unemployed, alcoholic father and a distant, overwrought mother. Central to the narrative
are Mal's relationships to a predominantly Protestant gang of boys who
live on his family's new housing estate; to Francy Hagan, a Catholic
outcast who has taken refuge from the gang's persecutions in the town
dump, where he has created an autonomous kingdom of the imagination; and to his mother's sister, her abusive husband, and their daughter, Alex.

The novel is a semiautobiographical, expressionist depiction of transformations within a working-class Protestant community in the late
1960s as the Northern Ireland civil rights movement crumbled in the
face of anti-Catholic hatred.[1] To depict the position of children within
the contemporary Northern Irish social order, Patterson subversively
recycles gothic tropes originally established in eighteenth- and nineteenth-century English and Irish literature, embedding gothic conventions — the guileless protagonist, a forbidden liaison, secret pacts,
a labyrinthine interior space in which normative social values are inverted, and the return of the repressed — within a contemporary, realist
landscape. The novel's gothicism embodies family mechanisms that ensured the replication of a boundaried, unitary Protestant identity at a
crucial moment in Northern Ireland's history. The gothic-realist depic-

tion of Northern Ireland that results starkly foregrounds the autophagous, or self-devouring, aspects of Protestant domination in the North, casting the unionist power structure as an order that perpetuates itself through the destruction of its children.

While this book is not about the Troubles in Northern Ireland, it does represent an attempt to understand the interrelations between history and narrative that Patterson's novel depicts. A relatively unmentioned fact of colonial and postcolonial politics is that colonial rule, particularly where colonialism has taken the form of mass settlement, requires the production of children. As Patterson's novel illustrates, hundreds of years after spectacular dispossessions in the seventeenth century calculated to separate permanently English settlers from the native Irish, the maintenance of colonial domination in Ireland still requires the production of children, as well as the production within children of dishonest and confusing accounts of their own history. The collective psyche to which these processes give rise is shown, in *Burning Your Own*, ultimately to reproduce violence at both the familial and the national level. Like numerous tropes that traverse the history of gothicism in Ireland, the settler colonialist system against which Patterson's young protagonists struggle has a life of its own, independent of the individual subjects that generationally comprise it; like Dorian Gray's portrait, it is "worse than the corruption of death itself—something that [may] breed horrors and yet never die" (Wilde 273).

The novel explores the position of children within a transgenerational familial and national system that appropriates them into a priori patterns of loyalty and animosity. This system of appropriation, Patterson suggests, exploits children's innocence, effectively "killing" in them the capacity to think and act independently by ensnaring them within a dissembling and contradictory account of Irish history that treats Catholics as illegitimate interlopers. Most significant, for the purposes of my argument, is Patterson's figuration of the most dramatic risk to which the colonial project exposes children—the generationally deferred threat of retributive violence—via the gothic trope of the return of the repressed. This central gothic narrative motif is figured in the novel in the story of Sammy Slipper, a contemporary urban legend that turns on the paranoid gothic tropes of live burial and the living dead.

The story, a master metaphor for intrafamilial and community violence and the social order's repeated efforts to cover it up, recurs four times in the course of the novel. It is told twice by Michael, Mal's alcoholic father (29–32, 149), when he is on the brink of benders that will leave the family economically and emotionally devastated. In a pattern that emphasizes the transmission of misleading and destructive narratives from one generation to the next, the story is subsequently retold by children, once by the Protestant Mal and once by Francy, a Catholic misfit ostracized by the Protestant gang that orders the social life of Mal's housing estate. In the story, Sammy Slipper, a crafty Belfast ne'er-do-well, attempts to hide the body of his wife Sadie's beloved Pekinese, which he believes he has accidentally killed, by burying it in the garden. At a key moment in the story, the still-living dog is dug up, and its retrieval exposes Sammy as a liar and a perpetrator of abuse.

Central to this narrative pattern of involuntary recurrence, which itself "involuntarily" recurs within the larger narrative, is the theme of a hidden act of violence that is rendered, in the story's first three tellings, in a ludic mode which retroactively justifies both the perpetrator and the act. Crucially, only in its final telling by Francy, whose role throughout the novel has been to introduce Mal, the novel's innocent protagonist, to obscure and neglected aspects of Mal's own society, is the story's suppressed act of violence revealed to be at once more serious and more extensive than its earlier renditions acknowledged: the injury to the dog was indeed fatal, and the hidden nature of this fatality will inevitably precipitate further cycles of destruction.

The buried dog's "return" correlates with a pattern of return elaborated by Mal's older cousin, Alex, when she explains the dynamics of abuse that hold sway in her (more prosperous) family. Mal asks Alex whether her father is sorry after he hits her, to which she replies, "Sure he is . . . 'til the next time" (136). Mal asks why there must be a next time, and Alex tells him decisively, "Nothing's ever settled, just let drop for awhile. But it always comes back. Always, always, always" (136).

The helpless position of children as they are assimilated into the Protestant social order is dramatized through Alex's comments and behavior. After her father slaps her for asserting her right to autonomy by deflecting a question about where she has been, she tells her mother, who cautions her to stop "asking for it," "I'm the way I am because he's the way he is. . . . It's not me that's asking for it" (134). Shortly thereafter Alex connects the cycles of abuse that she suffers to her family's social context. In despair, she asks Mal: "Why did we have to get born here? Here of all places" (136). This question, with its focus on the relationship of familial reproduction, children's experiences within families, and colonial politics, is one that I have, in writing this book, set out to answer.

In this volume, I map out the formation of the nuclear family in relation to the emergence in British and Anglo-Irish literature of depictions of families and social orders that, like Patterson's fictional housing estate, covertly devour children.[2] In the book's early chapters I trace the institutionalization of the public, heterosexual man as the paradigmatic "citizen-subject," elaborating on the authorizations and protections provided by marriage and the production of children in early modern England. Chapter 1 delineates the violent elimination of alternatives to the heterosexual dyad through the persecution of sodomites, witches, vagrants, those deemed insane, the indigent, working women, sexually unconventional women, and members of communal religious and political sects. In Chapter 2 I explore the literary emergence of the gothic family romance and map ongoing changes within bourgeois family structure in Samuel Richardson's mid-eighteenth-century novel *Clarissa*. As my reading of *Clarissa* suggests, the persecutions that institutionalized the nuclear family continue to haunt it, in part through a fundamental confusion between the public and private spheres that the bourgeois family served to establish. Bound up with this structure's origins is its deployment of purportedly "private" sexual and parental relations as prerequisite to participation in a public economy. This paradox emerges at *Clarissa*'s center as a deadly double bind— Clarissa's fatal commodification—that allows me to read the novel as an unauthorized history of the nuclear family.

In *Burning Your Own*, the implications of the nuclear family's ambiguous positioning between the public and the private are figured in Mal's parents' endless fighting over what Mal's father fears is his Catholic-sounding name, Malachai. This fight over the significance of

Mal's name foregrounds both the parents' power to define the child and the child's appropriation by a system that neglects his legitimate needs while claiming that the ongoing hostilities that disrupt his life stem from a passionate concern for his well-being. This scene also makes explicit the powerlessness of Mal's parents over the larger system in which the family is embedded, and their inability themselves to negotiate the complex codes of their society. Their repetitive, compulsive dispute over Mal's name is counterpoised, in the novel's opening lines, against the disembodied voice of Francy Hagan as he ritually reassigns meaning to the world from the disorienting position of the estate dump: " 'In the beginning' — said Francy — 'was the dump' " (3). This introductory passage sets the stage for the novel's founding epistemological struggle, between the Protestant unionist perspective that dominates Mal's housing estate and his society and the alternative, notably grotesque worldview of Francy Hagan, "rebel bastard" (10), whose liminal world Mal grasps intuitively, through "his body, not his mind" (3).

In Chapter 3 I explore the means by which eighteenth-century writings by Jonathan Swift, Edmund Burke, and Maria Edgeworth negotiate a similarly drastic epistemological cleavage between English, bourgeois constructions of family life and the authors' own, corporeal life experiences. All three writers used irony to create a detached, ambiguous environment in which sensory and affective domestic experience may be apprehended, as it were, through the body rather than the mind, without allowing for any ownership of the experiences depicted on the part of the authors. Through ironic representations of (Irish, monstrous, Catholic) figures of alterity similar to Patterson's Francy, eighteenth-century Anglo-Irish authors found an idiom in which to explore the experiences of children born into the Anglo-Irish settler colony without having to acknowledge their own relationship to these experiences.

As processes of ideological production and transmission within the settler colonial order consolidated and intensified in response to the increasingly insecure position of the Anglo-Irish in the nineteenth century, the gothic family romance that the irony of Swift, Burke, and Edgeworth expressed and denied became autonomous, split off, and dissociated from the conscious mind of the individual writer and Anglo-Irish consensus reality. This development's purest expression was in the strand of "paranoid Gothic" (Sedgwick, *Between Men* 92) that emerged in Ireland during this period. Crucially at issue in this strand of literature are the themes on which I focus in this book: self-consuming systems, the living dead, the devil's bargain, questions of normative sexuality, and the sacrifice of children. In Chapter 4, I outline dynamics within the Anglo-Irish family and settler colonial order that account for the emergence of a fully autonomous gothic family romance in nineteenth-century Anglo-Irish literature. Through readings of persecution fantasies involving the sexual sacrifice of children in Charles Maturin's *Melmoth the Wanderer*, Sheridan Le Fanu's "Carmilla," and Bram Stoker's *Dracula*, I explore the workings of the Anglo-Irish gothic family romance. In each text the locus of persecution is situated in a geopolitical space of alterity (early modern Spain, Styria, Transylvania), and each of the persecutors is decisively divorced not only from the Anglo-Irish family but also from humanity itself through vampirism, extreme longevity, and, in two cases, homoeroticism. In these texts, the persecution of children, who are sexually and ideologically appropriated, cannibalized, and ultimately destroyed within literal or symbolic families, supplies an allegory for the experiences of the settler colonial child.

Burning Your Own repeatedly exposes the process underlying the formation of the paranoid gothic, whereby anxieties originating within the family are projected outside the family, perpetuating sectarian divisions. For instance, Alex, despite her insight into the repetitive, compulsive dynamics of abuse within her family, is unable to resist taking on the role of her bigoted, sexist father as a victimizer of socially vulnerable females when she picks a nasty fight with a Catholic waitress in order to release her pent-up grief and rage during an emotionally charged family "celebration" dinner. Alex loudly accuses a waitress of staring at her and then of "grinning"; it seems likely from the manager's exaggerated championing of Alex, whom he literally shelters with his body from the gaze of the unoffending waitress, that her irrational and vindictive outburst will cost the young woman a job that is, with Catholic unemployment at over 50 percent, irreplaceable.[3] Alex's parents enthusiastically endorse her displacement of familial anxiety outward, onto the Catholic Other. Her mother calls the waitress "a wee slatternly girl," in contrast, implicitly, with Alex, who for once discovers that she has found a way out of her accustomed position as the family scapegoat, while her father asks with pointed satisfaction, "Are you surprised? Name like Bernadette?" (145–46).

In this scene a link between familial and community systems of abuse is made visible to the reader as Alex learns that she can win the approval of her distant parents through expressions of hatred aimed at those outside their community. The function of these outbursts and the parents' motives for reinforcing them are clear: Alex's expressions of hostility toward the waitress provide an escape valve for growing tensions within her family, allowing family members momentarily to forget their mutual antagonism as they bond in a united show of hostility and contempt for a shared enemy.

The process by which the abuse and powerlessness that Alex suffers within her family paradoxically translates into loyalty to the Protestant order, and hostility toward Catholics parallels the narratives that I examine in Chapter 5, which explores representations of young Anglo-Irish men in the First World War in Frank McGuinness's play *Observe the Sons of Ulster Marching toward the Somme* and Jennifer Johnston's novel *How Many Miles to Babylon?* McGuinness's and Johnston's works exemplify the incorporation of the gothic within literary realism as a means to make visible the influence of a Burkean compact operating within Anglo-Irish history which requires the sacrifice of children. Both texts depict the intergenerational transmission of and collusion between homophobia and imperial warfare, focusing on the most extreme extension of the symbolic role of the child as the colonial order's "first line of defense." The most fundamental desires of the protagonists of these texts and, ultimately, their lives are sacrificed in defense of an order that has, via compulsory heterosexuality,[4] sentenced them to social death.[5]

Like many of the narratives I discuss in this volume, *Burning Your Own* associates homoeroticism with resistance to imperial control. In Francy and Mal's charged final meeting, the social atmosphere surrounding the two boys is growing increasingly chaotic. Francy tells Mal, who has by now completely internalized Francy's viewpoint, that Francy's version of reality is only another "pack of fucking lies" (230).

As Francy rails on, verbally rending the intimate world the two boys have built together, Mal registers an unfamiliar noise in the background: "the sound people had in mind throughout the year when they prophesied that any day now the guns were coming out" (230). Mal seizes Francy and kisses him on his open mouth as the sound of the Catholic families being driven from the estates swells in the background, in a final, powerful assertion of the dump's situation outside an increasingly violent and repressive social "order" (231).

Significantly, the novel's most intense and explicit expression of homosexual desire coincides with its greatest moment of political crisis. This simultaneity of transgressive sexual desire and systemic breakdown recurs throughout all the texts in this study. In early, paranoid gothic depictions of the Anglo-Irish colonial family romance, this breakdown is expressed in surreal, expressionistic terms as stemming from external, supernatural forms of persecution. In Anglo-Irish gothic realism's later, more distinctive critical form, however, collapse emanates from within the family. Starting around the end of the nineteenth century, in a process that commences with *Dracula* and *The Picture of Dorian Gray*, the inconsistencies between the internal and external historical circuits that the Anglo-Irish family serves to make congruent, and therefore to suppress, break loose: the family unit slowly but completely ruptures in response to pressures building up from within.

In Chapter 6 I trace the emergence and consolidation of this narrative pattern from Yeats's *Purgatory* through a particular strand of Big House novels by Anglo-Irish women that depict the disintegration of family structure in the face of growing opposition to the colonial regime. As in *Observe the Sons of Ulster* and *How Many Miles to Babylon?* gothic elements in Iris Murdoch's *The Red and the Green,* Elizabeth Bowen's *The Last September,* Molly Keane's *Two Days in Aragon,* and Rosamond Jacob's *The Troubled House* make visible the means by which the Anglo-Irish family has ordered social formation and political and economic allegiances within Ireland. These novels represent a suppressed tradition that specifies the position of women within the settler colonial order. They depict colonialism as a pervasive historical system that appropriates the sexuality and lives of Anglo-Irish children. In them, gender and sexual transgression, including lesbianism and reversals of historical patterns of sexual victimization, symbolize the overthrow of the colonial order, whereas anticolonial resistance, conversely, allegorizes transgressive sexual desire.

Abuse at the family, community, and national levels recurs inexorably in *Burning Your Own*. Repetitive patterns of abuse are, as Michael's story about Sammy Slipper suggests, maintained through attempts on the part of guilty parties to "bury" the past and to deny the past's relationship to the present. Mal's father's story presents a parodic version of this process, in which those who are injured within a system of recurring abuse are rendered in caricature, as are Sammy Slipper's wife and her Pekinese. Michael assures Mal, who is uneasily trying to ascertain the story's literal truth, that Sammy Slipper can still be seen walking the streets of Belfast "with his head down, duncher near covering his eyeballs, a big woman nagging at his back, a wee dog snapping at his heels, tormenting the life out of him and never letting him forget what he did" (32). Mal's confusion concerning the story's literal veracity emphasizes its twin themes of lying and denial, which it humorously legitimizes.

Mal's uncertainty about the Sammy Slipper story parallels his uncertainty about Francy. Throughout the novel, Mal searches for a way to justify the community's ostracism of Francy and his family. Ultimately, however, Mal learns the depth of his mistake in accepting the prevailing, comfortingly coherent rationalization of Catholic disenfranchisement, which suggests that Catholics simply do not want to fit in. From Francy's station within the dump, the well-ordered architecture of the estate is garbled, unrecognizable, as are the comfortable platitudes that Mal has internalized in the course of the novel. Francy tells Mal how he was chased into the dump by the housing estate's gang. Only desperation and mortal fear drove him into an unspeakable, taboo space he would otherwise never have entered, drove him finally to organize and inhabit this space and to tame and befriend the rats which are the dump's "rightful owners" and which will, he knows, soon reclaim it. Francy recalls that, once inside the dump, "I made myself a promise: never again would I be hunted by anyone; and I'd be looking after myself from now on" (227). Francy claims the dump as a sheltered space within which an alternate system, outside of societal repression, could temporarily be opened up. In so doing, he undergoes a transformation reminiscent of that of the Republican prisoners who, in the early 1980s, undertook a series of protests (the Blanket and Dirty Protests and the Hunger Strikes) that exploited their liminal social position as a means to promote a radically alternative vision of society. These prisoners used their marginal position to dramatize an alternate epistemology that constituted Northern Irish social dynamics as a Manichean struggle between an exploitative imperialist system and those who remain unassimilated into its objectifying modes of rationality. From within their isolated prison cells, the prisoners resisted British attempts to reconfigure them as criminals rather than prisoners of war by refusing to wear prison uniforms, confining themselves to their (resultantly filthy) cells to resist abuse by prison guards, and, in ten instances, starving to death.

Hunted like the woodkerns whose dispossession established Protestant hegemony in Ireland and simultaneously carrying out his own desperate Dirty Protest in the dump of a Belfast housing estate, Francy embodies the historical experience and latter-day political transformations of the native Irish. The ongoing proximity of the historical trauma Francy represents is dramatized when he tells Mal about burying the dump's rats when they die, and Mal thinks of the hundreds, maybe thousands of rats buried all around him as a collective manifestation of the living dead: "Dead and not dead. Like Bobo, Sadie's Pekinese" (228). He begins to tell Francy the story of Sammy Slipper, asking, in an awkward imitation of his father's opening gambit, "Ever heard of Sammy Slipper?" Francy has not, and

The tale tripped out of [Mal], like a spring uncoiling: the dog collapsed, Sammy took it for dead, panicked, buried it, and went off supposedly in search of it. And big, heartbroken Sadie was so ashamed at having done him down in the past that she got her father to do a wee bit to the garden as a reward. (228)

When Mal gets to the point in the story when he expects Francy to ask how the dog stayed alive underground, he is taken aback when Francy instead expostulates irritably, "That's not how it goes." He explains, quietly, "It's much simpler than that":

A family's dog dies and, for want of anything better to do with the body, they tie it in a binbag and bury it in the back garden. Years pass, the garden runs to seed and below, unseen in its polythene bag, the carcass rots. Eventually, the family sells up and another one moves in. First thing they want to do is build a greenhouse in the garden. When they're all set to begin, the father ceremonially stamps a spade into the ground—rips the dogbag and releases a stench so overpowering that one waft of it kills him on the spot. The End. (229)

"That's a disgusting ending," Mal exclaims, feeling nauseated. "It's a disgusting story altogether," Francy agrees. "Most stories people tell are" (229).

The disgust that Francy expresses for storytelling, for the production of comforting, coherent narratives, is understandable for readers who are, along with Mal, continually discovering that the power of narrative convention in the six counties of Northern Ireland has a tendency completely to overwhelm the facts. The inclination to subordinate events and individuals to narrative convention by twisting them into what, from the point of view of the dominant order, they "always already" are is shockingly illustrated at several key moments in the novel. One such climactic unveiling occurs when Mal first actually sees Francy's mother, in the novel's final pages, as Francy's family is being forcibly evicted from the estate. Disparaged frequently by the gang, Francy's mother is described early in the narrative by a gang member as a "greyhaired old hag" left "crying like a wee doll" when he and other binmen who dumped her garbage out in an act of anti-Catholic intimidation kicked a hole in her bin after she demanded they clean it up (67). Like Kathleen ni Houlihan, this old hag is transformed, when viewed through a gaze that has been jarred loose from its moorings within family and community conventions, into a beautiful image of "graceful dignity" and fertility. Mal is surprised that although her hair is gray, "she did not look old; her features were fine, unlined and very beautiful," and he wonders: "Was this the woman who—as Andy Hardy had told it— had yelled and squawked and cried like a wee doll the day the binmen kicked a hole in her bin? If it was, why had he not mentioned that she was a good many months pregnant?" (234).

A crucial difference between Mal's story and Francy's is that in Mal's version, in which humorous conventions "cover up" the violence committed against the parodically rendered Pekinese, the system repeats itself. Sammy's transgression, the burial, and the unearthing of the dog only intensify interactions within a fixed system. In Francy's story, on the other hand, as in Francy's account of his period of hegemony within the dump, systems are frail, malleable, subject to radical and even apocalyptic change according to the dictates of historical justice.

In Chapter 7, I explore similar dynamics in two incest narratives in which the protagonists grapple with the pleasant, socially acceptable accounts of their childhoods that are putting their lives at risk. This chapter presents similar depictions of the power of narratives to cover up and therefore perpetuate abuse, as well as a similar but more successful substitution of one narrative with another in two contemporary texts from the Republic that delineate the ambivalent relationship of Irish women to Ireland's colonial history as it remains inscribed within the Irish domestic sphere. I begin by reading Frank McGuinness's one-act play *Baglady* as a paradigm of the symbolic position of women within the Irish colonial family romance; I then consider Jennifer Johnston's depiction of contemporary Protestant/Catholic intrafamilial relations, reading her novel *The Invisible Worm* as an allegorical representation of neocolonial relations within the contemporary Irish Republic.

Both Johnston's and Patterson's novels end with scenes of immolation that represent, as do the fires that end two of the burning Big House narratives I discuss in Chapter 6, an image of past damage which can no longer be denied. Significantly, however, Johnston's novel, read as an allegory for the position of Irish women, ends on a hopeful note, whereas Patterson's reflections on his experiences as a Protestant child in Northern Ireland close on a scene of desolation, with Francy's family and other Catholic families driven out of the housing estate and with Francy's terrible, final act of self-immolation. In the novel's last scene, Francy publicly and spectacularly destroys himself, lobbing several petrol bombs into the Protestant ranks before setting his own body ablaze, thereby exiting an order that sustained acts of will and imagination can no longer hold in abeyance. Confronting the estate with its own trash, including a memorial urn that he has been using as a spittoon, Francy rails, "Youse never knew — what to waste — and what the fuck to keep" (246). The scene, like the literal, primal reenactment of founding colonial violence represented by the Hunger Strikes, stages the literal implications of the Protestant order's relationship to its own dead and to children — its own and those of the Catholic Others whose lives it continues to shape and constrict.

The Anglo-Irish Gothic

In this book I map out the Anglo-Irish narrative tradition that produced *Burning Your Own*, exploring this tradition in the light of a wealth of historical, theoretical, and critical research in British, Irish, and post-colonial studies. Critics working in these fields in the 1980s and 1990s have identified a complex network of constitutive relationships among gender, sexuality, capitalism, colonialism, and gothicism, producing a detailed account of the representational occlusion of "women and Black subjects," along with "certain states of being, such as madness, disease and criminality," that gave rise to the normative "eighteenth-century concept of the citizen-subject" (Azim 217).

A growing body of scholarship that takes as its object all the European Enlightenment pushed to the periphery is beginning to make tangible the distortions and exclusions through which an imperial, male perspective subordinated competing viewpoints. This body of scholarship has vast implications for an analysis of the gothic, calling our attention to the many guises in which dominant or authorized accounts are inevitably haunted by that which they exclude. For instance, in *Anomalous States,* a sophisticated analysis of "the hegemonic role of culture in the formation of citizen-subjects" (7), David Lloyd seeks simultaneously to make palpable and to contest the production of a hegemonic "modernity defined not so much by the erasure of the past as by the discrimination of those elements of the past which can be incorporated into a progressive narrative from those which must be relegated to the meaningless detritus of history" (10). Lloyd identifies prevailing standards of aesthetic taste as one crucial means by which elements of the past that persist within a dominant order incapable of accounting for them are relegated to the sphere of low or popular culture and thereby reduced to "meaningless detritus." Lloyd's work thus opens the way to a newly precise elaboration of subgenres — such as the gothic — as the historical residue that remains after the dominant culture has wrung from the real every detail for which it cares to account.

In *Ghostly Matters,* a project compatible with Lloyd's and equally stunning, Avery Gordon sets out to describe a sociological practice that "starts with the marginal, with what we normally exclude or banish, or, more commonly, with what we never even notice" (24–25). Gordon seeks to make visible "inarticulate experiences, . . . symptoms and screen memories, . . . spiraling affects, . . . more than one story at a time, . . . the traffic in domains of experience that are anything but transparent and referential" (25). Gordon pursues these nonlinear, inarticulate narratives to "follow the ghosts and spells of power" within a global capitalist economy that, like the fabled sorcerer, can no longer control the powers of the nether world it has conjured up. Gordon's guiding assumption, which I share, is that if we could change the collective lens through which we view our experiences, widespread social change would become possible. She seeks, for instance, to cognize, articulate, and respond to "the compulsions and forces that all of us inevitably experience in the face of slavery's having even once existed in our nation" (139). Her project thus crucially reenvisions the boundaries between what is constituted as the past and our present moment by postulating a new epistemology that enacts what Maggie Kilgour refers to as a "necromantic" function (*Rise* 221). By reconstituting the relationship between the past and the present, Gordon models a gothic methodology by which we may "tame this sorcerer and conjure otherwise" (28).

The specific applications for such a methodology in contemporary Irish studies have been concisely outlined by Barbara Harlow, who criticizes historical revisionism in Irish studies by pointing out that its goal is "to repress and deny both the history of colonialism and anything in the present that reminds us of colonialism."[6] I intend my readings of textual representations of English and Anglo-Irish families to contribute to a broader analysis of modernity's occluded, countervailing accounts, work that is already under way in projects such as Lloyd's. My discussions of an array of protogothic, gothic, and gothic-realist texts as allegorized histories of the Anglo-Irish family make visible a logic that runs through these texts, and chart changing relations between the family and the British state and between the Irish and the Anglo-Irish. These readings call attention to the family's production of a spurious political and national uniformity and an equally spurious, absolute division between an official public sphere and an unofficial and disavowed private sphere. By approaching these texts as allegorical enactments of the nuclear family's emergence in England and transplantation into Ireland, I counter the family's totalizing and atomizing effects, making visible elements that are hegemonically constituted as "past" as they continue to recirculate within the Anglo-Irish family.

As Judith Halberstam, Anne Williams, and Maggie Kilgour in various ways suggest, the gothic can be approached as a virtual compendium of the unauthorized margins of modernity's mutating dominant order. Insofar as the spaces of distortion or exclusion within Enlightenment epistemologies to which more recent research calls our attention correspond to the cultural spaces and subjectivities with which gothicism is preoccupied, gothicism in Ireland clearly affords a privileged site for an investigation into marginal, suppressed experiences that continue to haunt the Irish symbolic order. The Anglo-Irish gothic tradition, in particular, represents one of the cultural practices that, in David Lloyd's words, "appea[r] discontinuous, submerged, from the perspective of [institutional] discourses" (7).

In Ireland, as Terry Eagleton suggests, literary realism, which serves in this study as an approximate index of "the perspective of institutional discourses," can be divided into two discrete genres. Under the pressures of a Manichean colonial order, according to Eagleton, realism's aspirations "to a unity of subject and object, of the psychological and the social[,] . . . split into separate genres, with the naturalism of a Carleton or Lever aligned against the exotic fantasies of so-called Protestant Gothic" (*Heathcliff* 149). In this passage, Anglo-Irish (or Protestant) gothicism's "exotic fantasies" occupy a specific, mutually constitutive position relative to the naturalism that Eagleton posits as their antithesis. Whereas "naturalism," in Eagleton's terms, represents a scrupulously authoritative realism stripped of its subjective and psychological dimensions, gothicism's subjective and psychological forays lend a voice and a habitat to naturalism's unspoken detritus. Like Irish folklore, the Anglo-Irish gothic "discard[s] or transgress[es] realist conventions" and thereby winds up relegated to a subordinate position within a British imperial aesthetic and epistemological hierarchy (Eagleton, *Heathcliff* 154).

The subordinate position of Anglo-Irish gothicism, however, unlike the subordinated position of Irish folklore, serves to protect rather than discredit the political interests of the group whose "unofficial" perceptions it records. On the one hand, British imperialism counterfactually casts Irish culture as illiterate, framing all its productions, from Latinate manuscripts to speeches from the dock, as "colorful folklore." The Anglo-Irish, on the other hand, were granted a role in the construction of an official record, through the production of legislation, deeds, maps, histories, economic and social treatises, travel narratives, memoirs, commemorative statues, and architecture. The Anglo-Irish gothic tradition represents one concentrated strand of the perceptions and affect that had to be purged from this "official memory" for the Anglo-Irish to retain their privileged speaking role on the stage of the British colonial order. Anglo-Irish gothicism, like Irish folklore, thus represents British literary realism's "return of the repressed." In the history of Anglo-Irish literature, however, these repressed and unspoken themes have remained remarkably voluble, persistently returning to reconstitute and subvert the hegemonic realist tradition from which they were originally purged.

I have turned to the Anglo-Irish gothic tradition to retrieve accounts of that which has remained uniformly and transgenerationally unspoken within and about families, and in particular about the family form in relation to colonialism. Like those critics whose work I admire for making violence visible, the gothic itself uses the trope of visibility to make loss visible and felt and to remind us of that which we would otherwise forget. My reading practice places considerable emphasis on and extensively deploys tropes of visibility and invisibility, along with Eve Sedgwick's preferred unspeakability, to develop allegorical readings of opaque, baroque gothic textual elements. Through this process of visual and vocal remetaphorization, my readings retrieve elements of Irish history that have been "forgotten" and explore ways in which the constitution of families as "private" spaces, in which nothing of public or historical consequence occurs, has enabled certain forms of forgetfulness.

Family formation within modernity is, as Esther Rashkin suggests, haunted by "event[s] too painful to be absorbed by the ego" (42). As I have argued in an earlier article, traumatizing events retained within the family as "a gap in the unconscious" and "transmitted silently" to younger generations (Rashkin 27) are those which first institutionalized the public, heterosexual man authorized through his marital connection to a private, compulsorily heterosexual woman and through children.[7] This "private" familial arrangement was effected through the public annihilation of every alternative. Thus a constitutive confusion within the nuclear family between the public and private realms—and the transgenerational unspeakability pertaining to unauthorized sexual and social desires that masks this confusion—are structurally transmitted within families through, in Rashkin's words, "gaps and lacunae within the parent's speech" (27). As I will show, this intergenerational silence on the subject of family origins became particularly pronounced within the Anglo-Irish family. At the apogee of the Anglo-Irish gothic, to extend Rashkin's metaphor, the silences through which the families' traumatic origins become audible grow deafening. Indeed, in certain strands of Anglo-Irish literature those aspects of family life that dare not speak their name never shut up.

The Gothic Family Romance

Approaching the gothic specifically as a representation of marginalized and unspeakable experiences within families, however, requires additional justification. As Nina Auerbach has observed in *Our Vampires, Ourselves,* in their migration from the oral to the literary tradition, vampire narratives discarded "the traditional folkloric hell—and American heaven—of domestic confinement" and founded a tradition in which "vampires go everywhere *but* home" (17). My approach to the gothic as a form of family romance accounts for the familial significance of nineteenth-century gothic's pronounced aversion to the *heimliche,* laying the groundwork for my analysis of the gothic's return to the Anglo-Irish domestic sphere within Anglo-Irish gothic realism.

My use of the term "family romance" to specify the gothic's position in English and Anglo-Irish society is adapted from Freud's description of "the neurotic's family romance." According to Freud, the family romance represents a fantasy system through which a (usually male) child may resituate himself within society by replacing first both parents, through fantasies of adoption or orphanage, and later just his father, through fantasies involving his mother's sexual infidelities. Freud argues that such fantasies serve a surprisingly conservative function, preserving for the child "the happy, vanished days when his father seemed to him the noblest and strongest of men and his mother the dearest and loveliest of women" ("Family Romances" 241). Children's fantastic recastings of their parents may also, however, preserve them in another way: by projecting the threat posed to children's well-being by episodes of parental incompetence, negligence, or cruelty onto shadowy, persecuting outsiders. Like the aristocratic outsiders whom the child may imaginatively incorporate into the family, fantasized invasions of the household by menacing aliens are similarly "equipped with attributes that are derived entirely from real recollections" (240). It could be said that the family romance has two faces: an idealized image of the family that confers on parents the status and consequence of more highly ranked outsiders, and a converse demonic world emphatically external to the family, made up of the family's own dissociated experiences and conditions.

To ascertain the existence and widespread influence of such a gothic family romance, we need only reflect on the most common childhood fears — darkness, entities under the bed or in closets, liminal parts of the house such as attics, basements, and crawlspaces — and consider the close "family resemblance" between such primal fantasies and pop cultural horror. Some poststructuralists might claim that today's children learn to be afraid of the basement from watching television, but it seems far more probable that the myriad conventions of mass-produced versions of the gothic family romance represent traces of unspeakable childhood experiences in modern, isolated families in which, as Alice Miller writes, "the victimization of children is nowhere forbidden; what is forbidden is to [talk] about it" (190).

A particular unspeakability within Anglo-Irish families—the product of Anglo-Irish history—exacerbates the unspeakability that Rashkin identifies with the nuclear family more generally. As I will show, the Anglo-Irish settler colonial family relied on the suppression of its origins for its coherence. The Anglo-Irish gothic family romance therefore serves throughout the texts under consideration to make parallel and therefore natural and self-evident the external, political realm and the internal, intrapsychic realm and, hence, the past and the present. Through technologies of gender, sexuality, and maturation, the Anglo-Irish family romance posits a seamless coherence between intrapsychic and national subjectivities, extending and replicating settler colonialist symbolic relations by continually reinforcing Anglo-Irish settler colonialism's dominant obsession with the creation and maintenance of a national Other. The breakdown of this "costly but apparently stable schema" represents the central, obsessive theme of the texts that I explore throughout the book (Sedgwick, *Between Men* 198).[8]

In the chapters that follow, I trace the emergence, consolidation, and conscious politicization of a narrative pattern that offers extraordinary insight into the position of the nuclear family within an emerging capitalist and imperialist social order. The recurrence of elements of this pattern within *Burning Your Own,* a contemporary depiction of the social dynamics that perpetuate injustice and sectarian hatred in Northern Ireland, testifies to the continuing pervasiveness in Ireland not only of the gothic but also of the early modern social tensions that accompanied the genre's emergence. In particular, these recurring narrative conventions testify to the continuing cost that is being exacted from children born within a settler colonial order that prioritizes loyalty to an abstract national identity above local cooperation and identification. Although the vast bulk of this study deals with the past, the patterns that it identifies are significant to an understanding of the intransigence of sexism, homophobia, and sectarianism within the contemporary thirty-two counties of Ireland (and within other settler colonial societies such as the United States) and to the forms of abuse to which they give rise. As Francy's version of the story of the buried dog attests, secrets unaired grow more toxic with time; like dreams deferred, they are apt to explode.

Chapter 1
The Other Half of the Story

English and Irish Social Formations, 1550–1700

There is no such thing as society: there are only individual men and women, and there are families.
— Margaret Thatcher, *A Woman's Own Journal*

The political and social processes by which Western European societies were put in order are not very apparent, have been forgotten, or have become habitual. They are part of our most familiar landscape, and we don't perceive them anymore. But most of them once scandalized people.
— Michel Foucault[1]

In *Modern Ireland: 1600–1972*, R. F. Foster characterizes Irish society circa 1600 as it might have appeared to the colonizing English.

Though the Irish practice of fostering out their children had parallels in contemporary England, what struck observers was the exceptional depth of the bond created: foster brothers owed each other a deeper debt than natural siblings. The family could thus be extended in deliberate directions: another mechanism to this end was the custom of "naming" fathers, whereby a woman might claim paternity, often noble, for her child at any stage of his minority, binding him to a father he had not previously known. The convention of tanistry, the election of leaders, might be interpreted in this context, too, with the organization of the family group strengthening itself through redefinition in every generation. This symbolized the flexibility that was so characteristic of Gaelic institutions. Tenancies at will, chiefs living by levies and imposition, mobile pasture farming, were all instanced by the English as conducive to lawlessness. Partible inheritance, even subdividing and reapportioning the family castle from generation to generation, was equally shocking. . . . [W]here wealth was itself mobile in the form of cattle, rather than stable, in the form of land, such arrangements often benefitted the tenant. But in English eyes the whole system looked like a celebration of anarchy. (26)

Foster's analysis suggests that English colonial efforts in Ireland before 1600 were mitigated by the relational malleability that characterized Irish gender, kinship, and land-use patterns. Given this fluidity, the "stabilization" of the Irish within the Irish landscape logically became a priority for the English beginning in the mid– to late sixteenth century.[2]

When Charles Blount Mountjoy (whom Foster characterizes, curiously, as a "humane man" [34]) was appointed lord deputy from England in 1600, "his plan was to make Ireland 'a razed table' upon which the Elizabethan state could transcribe a neat pattern" (35). The "neat pattern" that England ultimately transcribed onto the "razed table" of Ireland clearly involved not only "stabilized" patterns of land use, measurement, and ownership but also extended deeply into the social realm, permanently and devastatingly realigning patterns of community formation, family formation, conjugality, sexual identity, and subjectivity.

A record of the devastation of Ulster that Mountjoy undertook in 1601 is preserved in documents containing "descriptions of starvation and cannibalism" that, as Foster concedes, "made unbearable reading even then" (34). But Foster's history of Ireland does not acknowledge that what happened to landownership as a result of Mountjoy's razing of Ulster only constitutes half the story. The other half of the story of Ireland's conquest is what happened to community and subjectivity in Ireland. Through the process of conquest, both were radically reconstituted: indirectly, through the process of dispossession, which ensured that the community, once broken up, had no material basis on which to reestablish itself; and directly, through murder, dismemberment, torture, internment, and starvation.

Setting the Scene
English Order and Stability in Ireland

Land use, family configuration, inheritance, and religious belief and ritual were regulated by externally imposed legislation such as An Act for the English Order, Habit and Language in 1537 (Jones and Stallybrass 157–58), the imposition of English property law in the early 1600s (Foster, *Modern Ireland* 65), and the Penal Laws, introduced in 1695 (McVeigh 15). A foreign language, English, was established as the language of law, learning, and trade. British imperialist encroachment and extraction, especially during the Penal Laws and the famines of the 1840s, also inadvertently established the Roman Catholic Church as the preeminent symbol of a martyred Irish national and spiritual subjectivity. Catholicism, once established as an absolute symbolic alternative to British governance, institutionalized many of the cultural changes that British imperialism was already promoting in Ireland: binarized gender norms, the regimentation and heterosexualization of sexuality, the privatization of property, and the normalization of class divisions.

The subjectivity and social relations of Scots and English settlers in Ireland were also radically reconstituted over the course of colonial conquest. Through the process of resettlement in Ireland, a large number of persons, themselves economically and socially displaced, achieved stable positions within *English* society. As colonizers in a foreign land, settlers were enabled to establish the nuclear families that signified full citizenship within their own society. The Anglo-Irish settler colonialist family therefore took on specialized meanings in terms of wealth and material security, along with a specialized relationship to national identity and social feelings of belonging. Paradoxically, only by remaining in Ireland could the settler colonialist participate fully in the national economic and political life of England.

While the settlement of Ireland was fueled by the quests of British and Scots Protestants for secure positions within their own national economies, Irish colonial subjectivity was forged through a process of violent physical appropriation explicitly designed to create a zero-sum relationship between the British colonizer and the native Irish.[3] The early chapters of Theodore Allen's *The Invention of the White Race,* vol. 1, represent an especially detailed and well-theorized account of the process by which the English ruling elite instituted an insuperable breach between settler and native through a strategic program of military dispossession and redistribution. Using abundant evidence drawn from letters and other contemporary sources, Allen demonstrates that the English systematically explored various means of establishing political control in Ireland. These included the establishment of an Anglo-Norman "Middle Nation" (the Old English); the policy of "surrender and regrant," a legal sleight of hand whereby the English offered to instate democratically elected tribal chieftains as permanent, hereditary rulers of their clans, granting them private ownership of the common lands under their stewardship; and plantation. Although Allen characterizes these policies as failures, he acknowledges that each individually yielded limited success, paving the way for the tactics that followed it. The legitimacy many self-interested chieftains granted to the English state under surrender and regrant, for instance, created a precedent that resurfaced in the subsequent establishment of the plantation system.

Nonetheless, until Mountjoy employed the tactic of mass starvation through the systematic destruction of crops in 1601, English ambitions to dominate Ireland were repeatedly undermined by the flexibility of Irish social relations. In the centuries before the Tyrone War (1594–1603), which I discuss in the next section, the heterogeneity and syncretism of Irish society consistently evinced a " 'nonracial' symbiosis" between the native Irish and their would-be overseers (Allen 48). The most well-known episode in this losing struggle against "hibernicization" among the Old English occurred in 1367, when an Anglo-Irish parliament at Kilkenny established the ineffectual Statutes of Kilkenny. This little-heeded legislation sought to stanch the flow of Old English settlers into the surrounding Irish population by forbidding English subjects to foster out children to Irish families, intermarry (under penalty of treason), "assume an Irish name, use the Irish language, or adopt the Irish mode of dress or riding, under penalty of forfeiture of all . . . lands and tenements" (55).

That the English victory in the Tyrone War in 1603 did not give rise to a system geared to co-opt Old English and Irish leaders into "an Irish buffer control stratum for the English" (47) is attributable to the Protestant Reformation's "recasting anti-Irish racism in a deeper and more enduring mold" (48). Instead, using mass starvation, Mountjoy and a small military force, well armed and unprecedentedly well sustained by an emergent mercantile economy (61), dealt a disabling blow to Irish society's seemingly infinite capacity for self-renewal. Thus did the English, realizing Edmund Spenser's prediction that "until Ireland be famished, it cannot be subdued" (cited in Allen 63), at last hit on the long-sought-for means to interrupt the relentless hibernicization of English agents in Ireland.

In her analysis of the emergence of nationalism in England, Liah Greenfeld situates Thomas More as the epitome of a religious, pre-nationalist epistemology that was superseded in England in the mid-sixteenth century by the post-Reformation, nationalist epistemology that mandated his death. This radical shift from a social identity predicated on a transnational, unitary Christianity to a narrowly construed Protestant national identity acted on the fortunes of the Irish elite (whether of Irish or English derivation) much as it did on the fortunes of More. The "full and final commitment of England to the Reformation" (Allen 47–48) obliterated the potential for a unitary or hybrid Anglo-Irish cultural identity. As Greenfeld's study suggests, a radical modification of an ostensibly religious identity gave rise in England to a national identity that remained dependent on absolute religious justifications for its very existence. Paradoxically, only when the Irish themselves became permanently and absolutely inassimilable into an emergent English national self-definition did the absolute appropriation of Irish lands, labor, and resources by the English become possible. Significantly, it was at precisely the moment when the continued existence of a hybrid Anglo-Irish identity within Ireland became impossible that the military, legal, and social annexation of Ireland as an extension of a newly self-defined English nation became inevitable.

This annexation of Ireland was pursued through the mass resettlement of human beings and an accompanying mass transformation of landownership from the tribal/communal/democratic forms of ownership characteristic of Celtic society to those characteristic of early modern capitalism. In the interest of supplying this newly secured territory with a resident "Protestant English settler militia," land appropriated in the course of the Tyrone War and the 1641–52 rebellion and war was used to repay investors whose funding underwrote Ireland's conquest, as well as the officers and soldiers who enacted it (Allen 67–68). Conversely, the Cromwellian Act of Settlement of 1652 sold defeated Irish soldiers by the tens of thousands to foreign powers as foot soldiers (50), a tactic designed to prevent the regeneration of Irish social forms and practices.[4]

A radical distinction between the first wave of English and Scottish Protestant settlers and the Irish and Old English was, therefore, predicated on the privileged relationship of the settlers themselves to England. Through the violence of colonial onset, itself an extension, as I will show, of the rise of capitalism and Protestantism within England, Irish Catholics were constituted as a demonic and subhuman Other. It was against this demonized Other that a heterogenous collection of displaced English subjects, along with significant infusions of Huguenots, Scots Presbyterians, and converted Irish and Old English subjects, forged themselves over time into a unified British- and Protestant-identified settler colonial order.

In retrospect, however, changes within Irish society in the centuries before Ireland's military conquest were already tending toward hierarchical new social forms. Although Allen neglects to explore this point, a more differentiated, binarized, and "stabilized" social order was already emerging within medieval Irish society through the growth of gender and status distinctions. These distinctions did not originate with but were exacerbated by the Catholic Church. Preplantation divisions are significant in that they provided an initial handhold for English colonizers and influenced the forms taken by colonization after 1600.

Irish Patriarchy before 1600
Symbolic Readings and Historical Repercussions

Through her symbolic readings of several crucial mythical and historical moments in *The Serpent and the Goddess*, Mary Condren has argued that Ireland became vulnerable to outside interference and manipulation only after patriarchal Christianity had begun to eat away at Irish social cohesion from within. As bonds of gender became synonymous with bonds of power and as both gender and power superseded bonds of community, Irish leaders grew more interested in establishing international alliances. No longer constrained by ties of kinship and mutuality, Condren suggests, Irish kings and religious leaders, like the mythical Cúchulainn, chose, in effect, to sacrifice Ireland's children in exchange for power. In a series of such devil's bargains, leaders within a new Irish patriarchal order bartered away the future of Ireland's people in return for personal influence, wealth, and prestige.

The symbolic relationship in modern Anglo-Irish culture between representations of child sacrifice and the emergence of both patriarchal alliances and capitalist social relationships will be explored in greater detail throughout this book. The importance of Condren's analysis for the current discussion is that she detaches the symbolic reading of Celtic mythology from an apolitical, mystical, and casually misogynist base, transforming it into a tool that complements my own reading method — that is, allegory.

Condren's strategy of linking the ills of colonial domination to the growth of patriarchal domination within Irish society through symbolic readings of history and myth powerfully counters the popular colonial originary tale that blames the arrival of the Normans in Ireland on the sexual misbehavior of an Irish woman, Devorgilla. In this story, which is best known to readers of Irish literature through Yeats's play *The Dreaming of the Bones,* Devorgilla, an errant wife, precipitates the arrival of Norman troops in Ireland through an act of sexual abandonment and betrayal that provokes her husband into seeking foreign allies. Condren meticulously traces a countermythology through an analysis of changes in Celtic myth that maps out the growing appropriation of women's and children's bodies within an increasingly patriarchal social order.

The growth of Christianity in medieval Ireland, as Condren's readings suggest, ushered in changes relating to the mother-child relationship and the position of children and women within Irish society. These changes made Ireland especially vulnerable to entanglements with the new forms of hierarchical power and control to which capitalism and the Protestant Reformation gave rise in England. Condren traces the fall of matrilineality in Ireland through a series of shifts, beginning with the pre-Christian subordination of the Goddess Macha. In the pre-amble to Ireland's epic saga, the *Táin,* male political leaders in Ulster force Macha to run a race against their fastest horses as she is going into labor. Having been forced to prove her mettle at her moment of greatest vulnerability, Macha is said to have cursed the men of Ulster, ordaining that they would become as weak as women in childbirth when hard pressed in battle. In this ancient story, Condren finds the initial symbolic transference of the creative capacities of childbirth from the bodies of women and a feminine godhead to the bodies of men, whose fundamental act of creative generativity would henceforward be enacted in battle, which the story literally equates with childbirth (33–34).

The Battle of Moytura, an early Celtic narrative, according to Condren, inscribes "the clash between matrifocal and patrifocal cultures" in ancient Ireland (61). In this narrative, the Goddess Brigit, "appearing as the wife of Bres of the Formorians, the mythical Irish invaders," originated keening in response to the death of her son, Ruadán, owing to conflicts between the maternal and paternal lines that produced him (61). Condren interprets Brigit's new form of lamentation ("the first time crying and shrieking were heard in Ireland" [61]) as emblematic of the unprecedented grief of Irish women at the symbolic ascension of patriarchal domination, symbolized by a new preeminence of patrilineality over and above matrilineal connections.

A threshold in the history of the fall of matrilineality in Ireland is also encoded in "a curious medieval Irish tale about an unmarried mother who asked the king to determine the father of her child," recounted in John Boswell's *Same-Sex Unions in Premodern Europe* (xviii). The secret to the child's paternity lies in the circumstances of the mother's impregnation, which occurred in the course of sex with a female lover, by the residual sperm of her lover's husband. "The king's perspicacity in thinking of this answer" (xviii) is the focus of the story, which could be read, according to Condren's model, as an allegory for the "discovery" of patriarchal lineage by a male ruler, despite the obstacles posed to its establishment by sexual bonds between women.

An eighth-century narrative concerning the greatest of Ulster's mythic heroes, Cúchulainn, and his killing of Connla, his son, "for the honor of Ulster" (Condren 182) figures the patriarchal state's appropriation of childbirth and children, both of which are sacrificed at the founding of an order based on patrilineal bonds and homosocial acts of loyalty. Condren perceives in these mythic narratives the symbolic rupture of a concrete ethics of maternality. Over time, the disenfranchisement of women and children, together with the concomitant emergence of powerful bonds between men that the new sacrificial position of women and children enabled, led to the growth of extended hierarchies of interest and appropriation arranged between men from widely different cultural and geopolitical contexts. This development, Condren suggests, would have been possible only after concrete ties of communal loyalty and caretaking had to some extent atrophied. Patriarchal bonds weakened clan ties and undermined the crucial social and symbolic roles of women, with which Condren especially identifies the figure of the Abbess of Kildare.

In 1132, the Abbess of Kildare was raped by the troops of Dermot Mac Murrough in a political strategy meant to render her unfit for office. This literal rape represented a strategic violation of what had arguably been the most important single position in all Celtic Christianity, the seat which, through the founding figure of Brigit, linked pre-Christian goddess worship to a Celtic Christianity that still, in the monastery at Kildare, retained positions of leadership and power for women and exhibited relative independence from Rome. By brazenly exploiting an already evident decline in women's prestige within Celtic society, Dermot Mac Murrough was enabled to introduce a female relative of his own into this influential position (Condren 107). In effecting this seizure of a ritually authorized site of power, Dermot took advantage of a specific weakness of the ritual objectification of offices, that "it is often a liability that so much authority is so loosely attached to the person, while being so tightly attached to the office" (Bell 212). The violation of the connection between person and office precipitated by Dermot's innovative use of new forms of patriarchal prerogative created a disastrous rupture within the Irish symbolic order. The *person* of the woman that upheld the office, with its crucial and culturally unifying links to the Irish past, its delicate articulation of pre-Christian and Christian belief systems, and its authorization of female forms of authority, was nullified. As Condren points out, subsequent to Dermot Mac Murrough's violation of an androgynous Celtic spirituality, Henry of London definitively severed the structures that Dermot's violation had covertly destroyed: "By 1220 the papal legate, Henry of London, felt confident enough of the demise of Kildare to order that the sacred fire, which had burned since the beginning of the monastery, be extinguished" (107).

As Foster notes and as Condren's account suggests, the colonization of Ireland first emerged as a "feudalization" that in fact seemed to implant into Ireland the very structures that England was energetically dismantling within its own borders (Foster, *Modern Ireland* 65). Two significant factors in Ireland roughly paralleled contemporaneous developments in England, however: the displacement of preexisting communities and the foreclosing of alternatives to heterosexual marriage gave rise to newly restrictive, atomized social forms during this period, and a "centralization of power on the part of both the church and state" was, simultaneously, being brought into being through "drastic ideological measures" (Condren 164).

The processes that underwrote the proletarianization of English peasants and the feudalization of the Irish created a spiral of social disorder and vagrancy the results of which are still being felt in Ireland today.[5] These processes include the enclosure or plantation of land, the religious persecution of witches or Catholics, the criminalization of nonheterosexually affixed women, and the restriction of women's ability to support themselves economically and to plan the size of their families. Central to these changes was the emergence of capitalism and an accompanying "reformation" of lay Christianity from a predominantly community-oriented cluster of benevolent magico-ritual beliefs into a political ideology, principally through the dissemination of a "pedagogy of fear" (Monter 212). Society, for those generations in England and, shortly thereafter, in Ireland that first encountered the new hunger for order which nascent capitalism ushered in, must have felt very much as Michael Taussig describes Chilean society under Pinochet's rule: "A society shrouded in order so orderly that its chaos was far more intense than anything that had preceded it—a death-space in the land of the living where torture's certain uncertainty fed the great machinery of the arbitrariness of power, power on the rampage—that great steaming morass of chaos that lies on the underside of order and without which order could not exist" (*Shamanism* 4). Originating in England, the chaos this new, orderly system created spun inward, into the heart of the patriarchal family, and outward, into the land and territories of disorderly Others in need of stabilization.

The Capitalist Symbolic Contract

The capitalist symbolic contract, the social convention that enables the radical transformation of the money-owner into capitalist and the possessor of labor power into worker, is the single most crucial distinction between capitalist and precapitalist social relations. The nature of the seemingly straightforward exchange that secures the bond between capitalist and worker is delineated by Marx in one of the most interesting figurative moments in volume 1 of *Capital.* In a passage that Ann Cvetkovich has compared with similar moments of revelation in the nineteenth-century sensation novel (180–82), Marx crosses a symbolic threshold into the "hidden abode of production," over which hangs the notice, "No admittance except on business" (279–80), to observe and report on the mysterious transformation that takes place at the closure of the capitalist symbolic contract. This transaction, which appears to the reader on one side of the threshold as a contract between equals, is revealed on the other side of the threshold as a devil's compact. As Marx's dramatic scenario suggests, the worker is "always already" consumed, whereas the capitalist is "always already" the rightful, transhistorical owner of surplus value. In attempting to secure his biological existence, as Marx shows, the laborer is forced to exchange away everything he (for Marx, always a man) has in a single stroke. A strange transformation has taken place in the course of a seemingly innocent transaction between the possessors of equivalent values: "He who was previously the money-owner now strides out in front as a capitalist; the possessor of labor-power follows as his worker. The one smirks self-importantly and is intent on business; the other is timid and holds back, like someone who has brought his own hide to market and now has nothing else to expect—but a tanning" (280). Marx uses the metaphor of one who takes his own hide, his sole marketable commodity, to market and who is left, having sold it, with nothing forthcoming but a beating; conversely, the capitalist is empowered through the anticipated consumption of the worker's vitality. Capital, in this equation, is seen as a transhistorical vampiric force capable of consuming limitless numbers of lives. Conversely, those who are, within the capitalist economy, placed in a position such that they must barter away their very bodies and lives in return for a biological existence which is parsimoniously handed back to them in judicious increments, have no choice but to empower the force that consumes them through the ceaseless contribution of their own labor.

In his book *The Devil and Commodity Fetishism in South America,* Taussig describes the radical conversion from the belief in a universe governed by beneficent forces to the terror-filled belief in a world governed by the devil and his minions, who must be continually propitiated, that took place in two South American cultures in the course of proletarianization within a (virtually) preindustrial context. Significantly, the preindustrial peasant cultures of Europe and the British Isles also underwent a radical conversion to obsessive fear of and preoccupation with the devil on the eve of proletarianization.[6] There is a striking simultaneity, in these cases, between the onset of capitalist exploitation and dispossession and the emergence of a new religious ethos. In Europe, the community was broken up into competing, fearful and mutually distrustful individuals through a new obsession with the devil that swept western Europe over the course of the Reformation and Counter-Reformation, while in South America, newly exploited and alienated peasants appropriated the European figure of the devil in order to make sense of their condition. In both cases, the devil represents the terror of possession, of a bodily appropriation that has always already taken place. The devil, in figuring the "perfect evil" on which Manichean systems of meaning are predicated, figures precisely the horror of, to use Althusser's term, "interpellation," the state of being possessed by discourses that are hostile to one's own best interest and of being helplessly spoken by them (170–76). As Lawrence Stone writes, during a period when "the unity of Christendom had been irreparably shattered by the Reformation . . . [and when] no one could be completely certain [what beliefs and practices were] right and which [were] wrong . . . , [t]he first result was extreme fanaticism" (*Family* 146). The Reformation "destroyed the social and psychological supports upon which both the community and the individual had depended for comfort and to give symbolic meaning to their existence" (103), leading to a new socialization of children, who were taught "at a very early age, to be afraid of death and the possibility of eternal damnation" (124). An emphasis on the obligation to combat the devil by any means necessary gave rise to "a suspicious and inquisitorial society, constantly on the watch to spy out the sins of others and to suppress all deviations from the true way" (152). As communities underwent "the drastic elimination of sacred ritual by Protestant zealots," subjects once bound together through bonds of interdependence were atomized. As a result, they became more vulnerable to exploitation within a new and hostile socioeconomic order. This ideological atomization and re-formation of society both accompanied and enabled the "growth of more commercialized bonds between man and man" and "the rise of 'possessive market individualism' " that further eroded "old communal affiliations" (100).

The Anglo-Irish devil's compact and the figure of the living dead, the gothic literary tropes on which my textual readings in subsequent chapters focus, emblematize the capitalist symbolic contract as it has played out within Ireland under and in the wake of British colonial rule. Both embody the crucial connection between capitalist social relations and religious forms inscribed within individuals and the nuclear family in the crucible of Reformation-era ideology. The devil's compact embodies both the capitalist symbolic contract that alchemically transforms a "free" owner of labor into an empty skin awaiting a tanning, and the ideological disavowal of the constitutive acts of violence and dispossession out of which this contract emerged both in England and in the course of Irish settlement.

In the capitalist contract elucidated by Marx, the worker must barter his life's substance in return for an unsatisfactory and contingent extension of his biological existence. The transhistorical, demonic forces of capital with which the worker is obliged to traffic are, for their part, empowered to consume all subjectivity that exceeds that worker's most meager biological existence. The symbolic threshold of Marx's own analysis stops, however, at the factory, so that other, even more carefully "hidden abodes of production," the family and the colony, remain invisible even to Marx. But as rapid changes in the representation and treatment of women and the Irish suggest, the central symbolic contract around which industrial capitalism configured itself (that the subject must contribute to the production of profits or starve) also radically reconfigured social relations beyond the factory. I am especially interested in the ways in which that contract became integral to the production of gender and sexuality, to the symbolic organization of the family cell, and to the national and international constitution of colonial relations.

While the process of proletarianization in England set about alienating "filthy" peasants from their "disorderly" landholdings so that they could be transformed into workers — sterile, abstract labor fueling capitalism's "dark satanic mills" — and their land could be converted into orderly and exchangeable units of real estate, English women and the colonial subjects at the periphery of this process were assimilated into the system on an even more ambivalent basis. For dispossessed English women and for the Irish, bouts of mass extermination alternated with bouts of internment, as both groups were gradually battered into social and intrapsychic shapes congenial to the new dominant mode of production. These violent processes of subject formation not only accommodated English women and, over time, the Irish to the dominant mode of production, but they also situated women and the Irish within the English symbolic order, permanently marking them as occupying a specialized relationship to "nature." Outside the officially acknowledged realms of industrial production arose two shadow spheres, realms of production on which the capitalist order relied but which it encoded not as abodes of production but as abodes of nature: the family cell and the colony.

The Capitalist Family Cell

Social change during the early modern period oscillated between rounds of intensifying order and outbreaks of perceived social disorder that legitimated increasing repression. During this period, a newly acute interest in the containment, legislation, and stabilization of bodies was expressed in the English metropolis through vagrancy laws, internment, and such royal speech acts as Queen Elizabeth's 1597 proclamation "reiterat[ing] a national dress code . . . listing clothing and materials that must be used according to rank, degree and proximity" (Armstrong 70). As Luther himself boasted, " 'Among us,' there was now knowledge of the Scriptures and also of 'marriage, civil obedience, the duties of father and mother, father and son, master and servant' " (Stone, *Family* 111). Meanwhile, the same stabilizing impulse, expressed most blatantly in the enclosure system and in Christianity's newfound interest in regulating the beliefs and doings of the weak (Monter 212), undermined rural community at the material and ideological levels.[7]

It is significant to note that many of the most overtly brutal moments in the subjugation of Ireland by England came during this decisive period. The strategy of plantation in Ireland, which conceived of Irish community as a messy obstacle to English order, mirrored the logic and method that governed the formation of capitalist hegemony in England as well. The period's characteristic oscillation between the aggressive imposition of order and repression in response to ensuing disorder is described by Christina Larner as the means by which the hybrid religio-political Protestantism that she characterizes as "the world's first political ideology" gave rise to a newly cohesive national order: "It was not possible (and it is, indeed, difficult now) to put a barbed wire fence around newly acquired or consolidated borders and police them. Instead, you built churches on your borders, sent priests and ministers to instruct your subjects and stamped out heresy and witchcraft, false belief and apostasy—with particular ferocity in those vulnerable border areas" (124).

The displacement of a "mystified feudal order" in England by a "mystified capitalist agrarian order" took place, according to Raymond

Williams, over two centuries. From the outset of the sixteenth century, Williams writes, "a more settled and centralized order—a system of social and economic rather than directly military and physical control" —gradually consolidated (38). The "stabilizing" devastation of Ulster undertaken by Mountjoy in 1601 can be interpreted as an exaggerated repetition of the punitive "stabilizing" measures against vagrants and displaced persons of all sorts through which a new order was brought into being within England. The increase in vagrancy to which such punitive measures responded, in turn, reflected the mass dispossession that flowed from land enclosure and "the rapid development of new kinds of capitalist landlord."[8] Owing to this new breed of landlord, rural dwellers' access to the land of their ancestors became contingent on their ability to pay in money rather than in labor or shares of a landholding's production. As land became "property" through which a landholder could amass a greater and more fluid surplus, "more and more of the population [became] propertyless" (Stone, *Family* 416). Ideological and repressive intrusions into the agrarian community proceeding from what William Monter has characterized as "the Protestant and Catholic Reformations" (204) also contributed to the psychic and affective conditions under which "the village neighborhood [gave] way to the floating urban migrant mass" (Stone, 415).

Central to the establishment and maintenance of a new economic, social, and symbolic order in England, as well as the subsequent extension of that order into Ireland, was the emergence of a new and specialized social formation. Foucault refers to the family formation that emerged during this period as "the family cell" (*History of Sexuality* 108). Lawrence Stone designates it as "the closed domesticated nuclear family" (149-297). I have chosen the term "the capitalist family cell" because this family formation is intimately associated with the emergence of capitalist social relations and because the term "family cell" calls attention to the hermetic, detachable, and self-replicating qualities on which I focus.

Measures to control and "stabilize" the landless and desperate subjects left wandering aimlessly in the wake of massive economic and social changes were, throughout Europe, directed especially at indigent women. According to Merry Wiesner, vagrant or simply "unaffixed" (unmarried or widowed) women were perceived by both Protestant and Catholic authorities as posing a serious threat to "public order, propriety, decorum and morality" in "a world that appeared [to the authorities] to be becoming increasingly disorderly" (227).

This official uneasiness in response to a growing perception of civil disorder *within* England is closely correlated with English representations of the Irish as disorderly. As Jones and Stallybrass have shown, women bore the brunt of English charges of disorderliness against the Irish (168). Spenser, for instance, fretted that Irish women were continuing to evade proper forms of "howse-wiverye" (166). Fynes Moryson, for his part, bridled at Irish women's transgression of accustomed class boundaries. These women, he angrily alleged, would rather yield their " 'fruites of love' " to " 'an Irish horsboy, then to any English of better condition' " (166). As is evident from these complaints, early modern authorities viewed disruptions to their ideals of domestic and colonial order through a single lens, believing disturbances in either sphere to be susceptible to one common solution: the containment and subordination of women.

Spenser's investment in the containment of Irish women within families and Moryson's in the subordination of women's sexual desire to national and class hierarchies exemplify a more general interest in the "stabilization" of women during this period. While early modern authorities embraced the nuclear family as an indispensable means for maintaining stability in a rapidly altering world (Wiesner 227), a spate of emerging laws, regulations, and social attitudes and practices fueled what Larner has called a mass criminalization of women between 1550 and 1700. This trend was manifested in patterns of legislation and prosecution that correlated closely with outbreaks of witch persecutions (86). Throughout sixteenth-century Europe, Larner observes, "certain activities of women were made into crimes for the first time":

While older women were coming into the courts for witchcraft offenses (including unofficial healing) and for keeping disorderly houses, younger women were being prosecuted for infanticide and prostitution. The criminalization of younger women came in the wake of new punitive attitudes to sexual activity. Women with children, lacking the male escape routes of mercenary fighting or urban labouring, were also particularly vulnerable to the new laws against vagabonds. There is much to suggest that in the law-and-order crises generated by the new regimes of early modern Europe, women were a prime symbol of disorder. (86)

Clearly, new legal and social standards governing women's sexuality and gender roles lent extensive support to the individuated family unit. Simultaneously, as Wiesner observes, the rise of capitalism brought about changing definitions that pushed women out of the world of public work and simultaneously compelled their unremunerated labor within the family:

During the Middle Ages, work was defined as an activity performed to support and sustain one's self and one's family. Domestic and productive tasks were both considered work, and all women, except perhaps those from very wealthy families, could be called working women. With the development of capitalism, work was increasingly defined as an activity for which one was paid, which meant that domestic tasks and childrearing were not considered work unless they were done for wages. Women's unpaid domestic labor freed men for full-time wage labor but was no longer regarded as work. (224)

The growing importance of wage labor, Wiesner suggests, rapidly altered the legal and social definition of women's labor, which previously had been undifferentiated from the labor of their male counterparts. This transition, like changing legal standards, had the effect of coercing women into maintenance roles within families.

The social changes that occurred during this period brought into being the social arrangements and intrapsychic associations described by Carole Pateman as "the sexual contract." In her essay "The Disorder of Women," Pateman points out that within modern western societies:

Women are direct mediators between nature and society . . . because [they] face nature directly, and because, in giving birth and in other bodily functions, they appear as part of nature. . . . Women impose order and foster morality . . . but they are also in daily contact with dirt and with natural processes only partly under their control. They cannot escape being tainted by this contact or completely transcend the naturalness of their own being. Hence they represent both order and disorder, both morality and boundless passion. (25)

Underlying this account of the symbolic position of women in the modern social contract is a binary schism between nature and society in which "nature" is cathected through the bodily, the dirty, the disorderly, and the unremunerated, and society is cathected through the abstract or intellectual, the clean, the orderly, and the production of surplus value. The values underlying such a division are conditioned by the commodity and the alienation of labor and thus could have come into being only after capitalism was established as the dominant mode of production.

Surplus value constitutes the ordering metaphor in the above symbolic arrangements: by virtue of having been alienated from its origins within the "natural" (that is, dirty) processes of production, the abstract, refined exchange value is constituted as a social value. Women, like workers and colonized subjects, are structurally positioned as mediating between the social and the natural. They can never themselves fully transcend the natural, can never be wholly cleansed of their association with "natural" or unremunerated forms of labor. Women, in fact, perform a crucial role in the production of alienated "civic" subjectivities. The nature of this role, however, can never be formally acknowledged within the capitalist order.

At the same time that women were being coerced into housewifery, men were also under pressure to conform to increasingly restrictive social and sexual norms. Michel Foucault, in *Discipline and Punish;* Orlando Patterson, in *Slavery and Social Death;* Jonathan Goldberg, in *Sodometries;* and Klaus Theweliet, in *Male Fantasies,* vol. 1—all note that changing laws in the sixteenth and seventeenth century also brought into being new, rudimentary subject positions governing the position of men, both as workers and within the family. Patterson, in making the connection between legislation and the extension of the condition he terms "social death," argues that waves of criminalization explicitly shaped a new male workforce, suited to the growth of urban, industrial forms of production. During this same period, England was also distinguishing itself as "the first country to consider placing the insane (in other words, from the sixteenth and seventeenth centuries on, people who were not working) in institutions" (Theweliet 1: 310). "The first internments," as Theweliet suggestively calls the incarceration of the indigent, "occurred in 1575" (310).

Men were also being pushed into families as a form of social control. In his work on sodomy, Goldberg identifies the regulation of sodomitical acts as a means by which sexual acts "that d[o] not promote the aim of married procreative sex" were conjoined with social identities — "traitors, heretics or the like" threatening to "the social order that . . . marriage arrangements . . . maintained" so as to produce new juridical subjects (19). Surveying early modernity, Goldberg proclaims that "marriage is the social institution whose regulatory functions ramify everywhere" (19). Theweliet concurs, concluding that "any sexuality that survived the attempts at its extermination" during the early modern period "was to be encoded anew" (310).

Dating from the early to mid-sixteenth century, then, and continuing through the seventeenth century, significant representational or symbolic trends included the differentiation of women and the emergence of new forms of criminality and insanity correlated to a subject's failure to fulfill rigidly defined familial and economic roles. These factors both contributed to and conditioned the emergence of a more highly differentiated family. All these changes, moreover, were connected to the growth of wage labor and industrial capitalism.

The shift in English policy toward Ireland away from assimilation and in favor of annihilation during this period was also fueled by the privatization of property in England. As Jones and Stallybrass show, an important point raised in favor of changes in English policy toward Ireland was that the Irish would never claim proper "ownership" of the land, because they did not "build houses, make townships or villages," as Sir John Davies complained in 1610 (158). Davies' assertion that the Irish failed to approach their land as *property* provided sufficient support, without further rationale or evidence, for his central argument: that "it stands neither with Christian policy nor conscience to suffer so good and fruitful a country to lie waste" (cited on 159). Like English women, male vagrants, and sodomites (who "emerge[d] into visibility" only when they also in some way "disturb[ed] the social order" [Goldberg 19]), the Irish were criminalized through their precarious relationship to an emerging capitalist economy. In each case, the failure of a subject position to produce surplus value was invoked to provide support for institutional controls via extermination or internment or via containment within nuclear families.

Compulsory Heterosexuality

Over the course of early modernity, Europe annihilated within itself a broad range of subjectivities through the destruction of individual subjects who were, regardless of their actual proclivities, made to represent forbidden subject positions. The newly enforced heterosexual, monogamous, childbearing dyad was pushed to the center of the social order as all available alternatives to it were symbolically destroyed, legislated against, or, later, representationally made to disappear.[9] In order not to disappear themselves, those early modern adults that survived rapidly organized themselves into the sole sanctioned social unit: the capitalist family cell. This they did, in areas dominated by Protestantism, even if they had formerly been Catholic nuns or monks, great numbers of which were dumped en masse into society in the wake of Protestant-decreed closings of monasteries and convents (Wiesner 228). As the conjugal unit became nothing short of a life raft, the emotional ties that initially bound members of this unit to each other were necessarily of the most extreme, violent, and compulsory nature.[10] During this period, kinship bonds and community bonds in general atrophied. Needless to say, this was hardest on the poor and socially disenfranchised. As Stone observes, without commenting on the relationship of this change to the emerging capitalist economy, extended relations gradually came to be "regarded more as a potential burden than a potential opportunity" (108). As more affluent members of society became less dependent on family connections for prestige and promotion and as the poor became dependent on wages, rich and poor alike grew increasingly anxious to concentrate resources within the most narrowly defined family unit possible. In such an environment, ties of familial or neighborly obligation that ranged beyond the nuclear family's narrow confines grew increasingly risky and unsustainable. Stone observes that as community bonds disintegrated, "wives maltreated by their husbands [became] less able to turn to kin for support and defense," while "the kin could no longer so readily serve as mediators between the parents and the children in the case of a direct clash between the two on the issue of the choice of a spouse" (107). By the same token, daughters, and children in general, would have become more vulnerable within families.

With the breakdown of prior bonds of mutuality, kinship systems that had stabilized local patterns of "sexual access, genealogical status, lineage names and ancestors, rights and people—men, women, and children—in concrete systems of social relationships" (Rubin 88) gradually collapsed. Wally Seccombe, for instance, observes that suitor desertion, paternal desertion, and informal cohabitation "bec[ame] widespread in the midst of full-fledged proletarianization" (50). This disintegration of premodern kinship systems on the road to modernity is a phenomenon that has been in various ways bracketed off from theoretical discussions of kinship systems and the incest taboo. Most relevant in "The Traffic in Women" is Gayle Rubin's evasion of any direct discussion of the impact of capitalism on the modern sex/gender system by conflating two arguments: that without capitalism there would be no sexism, and that without sexism, there could have been no capitalism. By decisively refuting the former she seems to refute the latter, which she substitutes for the former when she equates arguments seeking the genesis of women's oppression in capitalism with attempts to "locate the oppression of women in the heart of the capitalist dynamic by pointing to the relationship between housework and the reproduction of labor" (76). Through this sleight of hand, she creates a schematic division between sex/gender systems and the economic realm that produces a synchronic, more or less transhistorical "traffic in women" that she usefully theorizes. Yet the transhistorical identity that this model produces between the work of Lévi-Strauss and that of Freud ultimately glosses over a significant rupture between the premodern and the modern. Rubin draws compelling conclusions based on the similarities between Lévi-Strauss's model of societal exchange and the Freudian account of the psychological development of male

and female heterosexuality, but she never asks how the externally regulated "traffic in women" that Lévi-Strauss situates at the heart of all
civilization became internalized as the Freudian Oedipal complex. It is
this transformation—from the external and the overtly economic and
repressive to the internal, the familial, and the psychological—that I
seek to disentangle.

As Rubin explains, kinship groups and the sex/gender systems they
underwrite are brought into being by the incest taboo, which, "by forbidding unions within a group, . . . enjoins marital exchange between
groups" (85). As Lévi-Strauss and Rubin agree, the (premodern) incest taboo exists to compel the sexual circulation of women and hence
the creation of bonds between males; its prohibition against the sexual
appropriation of females within a kinship group is contingent and secondary (85). Typically, the premodern, nonnuclear kinship groups on
which Rubin bases her conclusions include multiple adult males. Men
within such a group, like Penelope's suitors, watch each other to make
sure each is upholding the group's central, constitutive pact. Thus the
paradigmatic kinship structures that led to the elaboration of a universal incest taboo are regulated by an externally imposed prohibition
against the sexual appropriation of female group members.

Family structures during the early modern period were subject to
pressures that eventually disrupted existing kinship systems: the at-
tenuation of bonds beyond the biological family, a concomitant tightening of affective bonds within the family, and the concentration of
responsibility for the maintenance of the incest taboo in the hands
of individual fathers. With the nuclearization of the family, the incest
taboo, heretofore a communal project to ensure the growth of bonds
between groups, came to depend on the contingent goodwill, integrity,
values, and self-discipline of individual fathers and brothers. Within the
privacy of the nuclear family, the sexual appropriation of female family
members no longer imperiled the process of circulation that the incest
taboo once ensured. This is especially true because the larger kinship
system, made up of multiple kinship groups, was itself breaking down.
Just as men no longer acted as checks on the sexual impulses of other
men within families or groups, newly atomized families no longer felt a
compelling stake in the sexual conduct of other families.

The narrowing, eroticizing pressures that began to build in the family in the early modern period are perhaps most dramatically and memorably figured in Edgar Allan Poe's "The Fall of the House of Usher." In Poe's story, a brother and sister, the last of their line, undergo an incestuous *Liebestöd;* they are buried alive within an inherited architecture that ultimately devours them. Poe's imagery provides an apt template for the powerful centrifugal forces that economic and ideological changes within early modernity unleashed within the family. The emergence of the capitalist family cell sexualized familial relations regardless of whether children were literally sexually violated within the family, since enhanced paternal autonomy concerning the sexual disposition of children would have heightened incestuous intrigue and tension within all families. But the breakdown of localized systems of kinship exchange also emphasized the ultimate sexual fate of children, which was now conceptualized as a gendered abstraction within an anonymous national community. Situated within an abstract heterosexual teleology stripped of any localizing particularities, within families that made gender and sexuality central, children during this period would have been the first to internalize the normative drives that Freud later identified with preordained male and female psychological trajectories.

As localized kinship systems broke down, an abstract, universal system of compulsory heterosexuality emerged as the symbolic residue of premodern systems of marital exchange. Through a collective shift in emphasis, the paramount sexual taboo that had regulated sexual exchange between kinship groups was replaced by a paramount injunction situating the subject within a vast, sexually binarized, imagined community. The premodern incest taboo was thus displaced into the realm of the publicly verifiable, so that compulsory heterosexuality replaced the prohibition against incest as the cardinal index of the communal sex/gender system. Within contemporary society, the remnants of Lévi-Strauss's universal incest taboo are to be found not in prohibitions against the sexual exploitation of children (which may or may not exist within a given family) but in prohibitions against any discussion of intrafamilial sexuality and in the overwhelming and tireless project that is the thoroughgoing imposition of heterosexuality on children.[11]

Thus, as the forces of capitalist expansion exerted pressure on family structures, the family cell, during a period characterized by an apparent shift away from civil repression in favor of ideological subjection, internalized the forces of repression that had originally shaped it. This internalization allowed for the growth and valorization of civic freedom from state-authored repression that has characterized Enlightenment and post-Enlightenment industrial capitalism. Compulsory heterosexuality was the system of regulation by which formerly external guidelines for the disposition of one's sexuality came to be internalized and naturalized. Gender was the category through which this transformation was mediated. Emerging in place of traditional sex/gender systems, which locally ordained whose daughters were to be given in marriage to whom, was a far more extensive national marriage market ordering the fate of the gendered child as, in effect, an "exchange value" within an abstract teleology: the formation of future heterosexual dyads. By setting children in symbolic relationship to an imaginary system of gendered exchange that was no longer apprehendable as a whole, the family cell reduced children to their gender in new and all-pervasive ways, taking to heart the repressive, policing functions that were, during the crucial pre-Enlightenment period, still being exercised by the state.

This account, at least insofar as it encompasses families in the upper social strata, deviates dramatically from Stone's view of a bourgeois "closed domesticated nuclear family" in which bonds of trust and affection replaced the cool indifference characteristic of the aristocratic family of alliance and respect for the individuality of the child superseded an earlier, more instrumental view of children (254). Although Stone sees the bourgeois family as embracing the repressive characteristics that I emphasize for the period 1550–1700, he contends that patriarchal domination, binary sex/gender distinctions, and the objectification of children began to recede among the middle class in the eighteenth century (254). Stone depicts eighteenth-century bourgeois families as islands of nurturance and calm floating on an ocean of seething social chaos; he preemptively dismisses the possibility that the brutal logic of emergent industrial capitalism could have structured early modern bourgeois family relations and affect beyond simply providing them with the material abundance that underwrote intensified parent-child bonding and affective warmth. In a telling moment, Stone dismisses a seventeenth-century social theorist's crude assertion that "children are so much the goods, the possessions of their parents, that they cannot, without a kind of theft, give away themselves without the allowance of those that have the right in them" (128), as a failed attempt to reconcile theories of the family with emergent theories of economics. In light of the literature on which I focus, the crudity of this attempt to theorize family relations and children's sexuality according to the laws of capitalism appears to me to lie not in its anomalousness but in its surprisingly open articulation of an emergent bourgeois ideology that conceived of children as a new kind of property. This ideology did not, as Stone suggests, fail. Rather, the writings of subjects raised within the bourgeois nuclear family Stone celebrates betray ample evidence that the early modern ideology that conceived of children as property, while usually left unstated, flourished and spread within modernity.

Stone's focus on the growing awareness of the individuality of bourgeois children excludes from consideration the commodifying (and thus standardizing) aspects of the new affective parent-child bonds he records, bracketing out the sense in which the child, as she or he came to provide new forms of parental gratification, became a form of luxury item for the parent. He also ignores the ways in which the enhanced bonds of solidarity and trust that he discovers between parents and children beginning in the mid–eighteenth century parallel the conversion from repressive to ideological domination which was simultaneously taking place throughout the public sphere. An exclusive focus on the undoubted benefits of parental attention and tenderness for bourgeois children in Stone's work ignores the ways in which such bonds afforded increased parental and, by extension, societal leverage over children, as well as the sense in which a new investment on the part of the bourgeoisie in securing the loyalties of its children to itself signaled a significant closing of ranks on the part of the ruling classes.

Early modernists have tended to focus exclusively on either repressive or institutional forms of control in a manner that is class-correlated, using a lens that views classes in relative isolation. They discuss repression predominantly in relation to the poor, generally exploring ideological modes of control as they operated among the bourgeoisie; seldom are institutions inspected closely as cross-class phe-nomena. For instance, in his early work, Foucault focuses on repressive forms of social control as a means of exploring the world of the urban poor and peasantry during the early modern period, whereas in his later work on institutional power, he focuses on the middle class. This class-based disjunction disallows consideration of the ways in which the modern industrial working and ruling classes were formed in response to the same historical traumas and the ways in which each class's historical experience in various ways marked and defined the other's.

While the accommodation of the families of the poor and property-less to the requirements of capitalism documentably occurred under conditions of massive societal trauma and terror, the bourgeois family also bears traces of this trauma and terror as it differently but acutely beset the emergent bourgeoisie. In the following chapter, situating Samuel Richardson's *Clarissa* in relation to Foucault's account of the family, I explore the relationship between repressive and institutional forms of control as they underwrote gendered and sexed subject for-mation within the English bourgeoisie.

Chapter 2
"Does She Not Deserve to Pay for All This?"
Compulsory Romance
in the Constricting Family Cell

Force, indeed, I abhor the thought of; and for what, thinkest thou, have I taken all the pains I have taken and engaged so many persons in my cause but to avoid the necessity of *violent* compulsion? — Richardson, *Clarissa*

Samuel Richardson's *Clarissa* dramatizes the incorporation of the feudal, repressive ancien régime that Clarissa Harlowe's friend Anna Howe mockingly calls "Old Authority" (331) into the welter of lateral social relations that Foucault describes in volume 1 of *The History of Sexuality*. This transmutation is figured most saliently in the gradual transformation of Clarissa's family into a penitentiary, replete with unannounced inspections, frisking, surveillance, censorship, the confiscation of writing materials, and solitary confinement. The progressive regimentation and constriction undergone by the Harlowe family suggest provocative interconnections between Foucault's earlier and later analyses of power in *Discipline and Punish* and volume 1 of *The History of Sexuality,* respectively. The family's transformation strikingly resembles the metamorphosis of the eighteenth-century family of alliance into the "family cell" in *The History of Sexuality.* Similarly, the novel's other central transformation—Clarissa's progressive corporeal decline as her writings expand in volume and agency—seems to parallel what Nancy Armstrong reads in *Desire and Domestic Fiction* as Pamela's evaporation into discourse in the midst of her attempted rape by Mr. B. In

Clarissa, however, transforming family structures and gendered subjectivity are brought about not, as Foucault and Armstrong have it, exclusively through the generation of discourse but through a dialectical relationship between discourse and the modes of repression associated with Foucault's earlier work.

In *The History of Sexuality,* Foucault's laconic dismissal of silence as "only the counterpart of other discourses, and perhaps the condition necessary in order for them to function" (1: 30), demarcates an interpretive horizon beyond which his own analysis cannot penetrate. Foucault dismisses the question of silence in the above passage even as he calls attention to its peculiar, foundational significance for the study of discourse. But in *Clarissa,* the extraordinarily dynamic relations between discourse and silence reflect powerful forces that were in the process of shaping bourgeois subjectivity in the mid–eighteenth century.[1] To produce a historicized reading of *Clarissa,* Foucauldian discourse analysis as set out in *The History of Sexuality* must be firmly reconnected to the material roots of discourse which that volume elides. The discursive "analytics of power" for which Foucault polemicizes brilliantly account for the novel's burgeoning discourses of romantic intrigue through which, in Anna Howe's words, "curiosity begets curiosity" in pursuit of an elusive sexual secret. Yet this novel repeatedly exposes the roots of power, privilege, and educated speech in the soil of deprivation, disenfranchisement, abjection, and enforced silence.

In *Clarissa,* physical repression stimulates discourse, which in turn stimulates further repression. The novel's representation of crude material techniques of surveillance and physical coercion correspond to Foucault's earlier emphasis on discipline and punishment. Incestuous encroachment, domination, violent rape, and murder sporadically intrude into the narrative, kindling and inflaming in the novel's two main characters an early prototype of bourgeois romantic love. In such a reading, the insights of *Discipline and Punish* are always implicit in and prerequisite to those of *The History of Sexuality.* Thus to honor the insights *Clarissa* affords into the discursive mechanisms of power that Foucault describes, I will read Foucault's work, in a sense, against itself and with an ear to the sacrificial silences that the discursive production of decentralized power required and rationalized.

The discussion of *Clarissa* that follows calls attention to the role

of repression, confinement, intimidation, silencing, and sexual violation in the production of the modern nuclear family. I am particularly
interested in *Clarissa*'s figuration of a daughter consumed retroactively
by an internalized family romance. In approaching *Clarissa* from this
angle—as the story of a daughter who is destroyed by a family system
from which she ostensibly escapes but which devours her by remote
control—I in many ways reinstate Clarissa Harlowe's own account of
her fate. My aim in so doing is to instate *Clarissa* as a primal scene
that makes scandalously visible the uses to which children's, particularly daughters', sexuality was put as families constricted in response
to a dramatically shifting economic and social order. The figure that
emerges from such a reading—a family romance, born of the conver-
gence of capitalism, imperialism, and compulsory heterosexuality—
blurs the constitutive boundaries between the internal and the external, the past and the present, the living and the dead, victim and
persecutor, and frequently the female and the male. This recognizably gothic family romance aptly embodies mid-eighteenth-century
changes in family structures, the new interrelationship of the bourgeois
family with the state, and the interpenetration of the intrapsychic and
the public introduced by these changes.

Similar patterns of self-consumption, or "autophagy" (Maud Ellman's term, which I have salvaged and recycled for new purposes), are
implicit in a number of gothic conventions, from the self-consuming
text that crumbles away to dust to the internally devouring qualities
of the devil's compact. Largely unexplored by theorists of the genre, I
believe that an examination of autophagous dynamics within the constricting, privatizing bourgeois families of eighteenth-century England
as they relate to gothic conventions simultaneously emerging within the
mainstream of literary realism offers an opportunity to pull together
heretofore competing readings of the gothic which variously privilege
changing class, gender, or sexual relations during this period.

Clarissa's multivalent allegory, which registers both the objective repression of daughters and the subjective impact of a growing commodification of children, strikingly resembles the Anglo-Irish gothic allegories that I explore in subsequent chapters. The connections between

the nuclearization of the family and emergent gothic conventions that my reading elucidates establish a link between British society and the Anglo-Irish gothic narrative patterns on which I focus. I am not interested in claiming an intertextual relationship between *Clarissa* and later Anglo-Irish gothic works; rather, I wish to establish a concrete relationship between the social changes that *Clarissa* encodes and later Anglo-Irish gothic narrative patterns that reflect similar processes, which I take to have been for various reasons ongoing and, in a particular, traumatic way, intensified within Anglo-Irish families. *Clarissa*'s inclusion within the purview of this book is crucial because, unlike the later gothic allegories I explore, Richardson's novel emerged both temporally and spatially in the midst of or within the cultural memory of specific historical changes that this allegory encodes. As I will argue, the novel allegorizes the nuclear family's role in an early modern redistribution of discipline and punishment away from the public and into the private sphere, as well as in the growth of confessional discourses and practices of self-surveillance that accompanied the emergence of compulsory heterosexuality and bourgeois ideologies of romantic love and choice.

Gothicization

Richardson and the Exorcists

Clarissa's monumental position within the history of the novel has largely occluded its equally foundational position relative to the novel's subgeneric inheritors. Ian Watt acknowledges this dual lineage when he claims that the novel can either expand readerly sympathies or serve as a "purveyor of vicarious sexual experience and adolescent wish fulfillment," observing that Richardson "initiates both these directions" (*Rise of the Novel* 202). Although Watt does not explicitly mention the gothic, he associates Lovelace with the later gothic antiheros Heathcliff and Rochester, and *Clarissa*'s plotline, with the Victorian imagination's "haunted" preoccupation with "perpetual attacks on pure womanhood by cruel and licentious males" (231). In these and other passages, Watt points to an affinity between *Clarissa* and the gothic without explicating the connections his terms imply. More recently, Terry Eagleton, in a Freudian reading of a dream in the novel, tacitly affirms the novel's gothically involuted structures of meaning (*Rape of Clarissa* 63), and Terry Castle also indirectly acknowledges *Clarissa*'s gothic affinities.[2] Conversely, critics of the gothic can seldom forebear to cite *Clarissa* on one or another pretext, although rarely as a founding text within the genre.

Clarissa's pivotal position in the history of the gothic is, however, recognized in David Richter's analysis of the reception of the gothic novel in the 1790s, in which he traces "the emotional sources" of empathetic reading practices associated in the 1790s with gothic literature to the publication of *Clarissa* and other unnamed sentimental novels at midcentury (126–27). *Clarissa* has also been persuasively linked to the gothic in an incisive article by Leila May, who situates the novel within a distinctive strand of gothic literature: *Frankenstein, Wuthering Heights, The Mill on the Floss,* and "The Fall of the House of Usher." Like each of these later fictions, as May argues, *Clarissa* expresses the "seditious effects of repressed feminine desire" (31).

The historical origins of the repression to which Clarissa Harlowe's desire is subjected are encoded in the novel through recurrent figurations of the demonic, often accompanied by depictions of autophagy or, in Raymond Hilliard's terms, ritual cannibalism. Building on the work of Eli Sagan, Hilliard locates cannibalism in

cultures where prolonged oral dependency (nursing) exaggerates the weaning process, most typically in cultures making a transition from a social system based on close kinship ties to one based on insurgent forms of individualism. He traces the cannibalistic impulse to a . . . struggle against maternal dependency [that] requires violent assertions of autonomy on the part of males in particular . . . from an accent on male identity . . . to self-conscious forms of male solidarity based on the denigration and degradation of females, to cannibalism itself, a type of "assertive action" that symbolically recapitulates the infant's original break with the nursing mother. (1087)

Hilliard's reading of *Clarissa*'s cannibalistic imagery as a sublimation of infantile desires is sparsely historicized with an abbreviated argument "t[ying] cannibalism . . . to the competition over property in the world of *Clarissa"* (1091). Yet despite Sagan's discovery of transforming kinship bonds at the root of cannibalistic impulses, Hilliard's analysis lacks an explicit historical framework with which to identify specific changes that may have given rise to the image patterns he brings to light. In this chapter I will add a historical dimension to Hilliard's excellent and suggestive essay by arguing for a connection between the novel's representations of a demonic, devouring family and the long-term processes that gave rise to the capitalist family cell.

In his essay "Shakespeare and the Exorcists," Stephen Greenblatt argues that exorcism in early-seventeenth-century England was driven out of society's "central zone" and into the cultural borderlands of the theater (104). Greenblatt suggests that the diabolistic rituals and beliefs surrounding exorcism kept alive "pockets of charisma" that challenged the centrality of the Church of England. The importation of these elements into the theater, where they appear in *King Lear* as fraudulent spectacles enacted before a complicitous rather than a believing audience (115), constituted what amounts to an ideological decommissioning of outdated ideologies too powerful to leave in force, yet too deeply embedded within a distressed and plague-ridden society to banish (107).

Greenblatt's essay is significant for my work because it specifies an early moment of transmission from the cultural and institutional center of English society into the representational margins of the numinous, uncanny, and demonic matter that would, in a parallel moment of transition in the eighteenth century, emerge as the gothic. Also significant is Greenblatt's description of the institutional negotiations whereby a supernatural sphere that could be neither banished nor safely retained was partly absorbed into and partly expelled from the state apparatus into the liminal realm of representation so that its powers could be fully claimed by the state.

Certain similarities between *King Lear* and *Clarissa* are immediately evident. Both works revolve around a female Christ figure sacrificed at the hands of an earthly father who comes too late to a full understanding of his solipsism and its fatal consequences. Each father has three children—two greedy, one loving—and in each case the father sides with the greedy children against the good child. In each, familial conflicts are engendered over questions of inheritance. The parallels between the two texts to which Greenblatt's essay serves to call attention, however, transcend narrative or thematic considerations. Just as Greenblatt posits *King Lear* as a historical site of reception for a cluster of beliefs that were expelled from the religious, political, and judicial realms and were reinscribed into the liminal, intermediate realm of the theatrical, *Clarissa,* I contend, represents a similar site of inscription, marking the transition of folkloric and Reformation-era diabolism into the literary-realist novel, an eighteenth-century form as central to its epoch as was the Renaissance theater to its own.

Significantly, while Shakespeare retained the rituals associated with exorcism but emptied them of agency, Richardson rationalized the rituals, stripping them of the rigmarole of ceremonial magic but restoring to demonic invocations, curses, and witch accusations the magical and juridical efficacy of which Shakespeare and (more recently) the English judicial system had divested them. These recurring diabolistic images are downplayed in the text, where they manifest largely as image patterns rather than narrative events, but they perform a crucial function as figures for an ineffable causality within a complexly overdetermined web of social interactions.

Thus in the figure and fate of Clarissa, contemporary material changes combine with earlier beliefs and rituals that were pushed to the literary margins as religion and state authority merged. Clarissa experiences her family as a "worse than Moloch-deity" (242) seeking to sacrifice her to a "diabolical" suitor (153); her sister, Bella, accuses her of (figurative) witchcraft (194, 195); her father curses her; and her confidant, Anna Howe, concludes that Clarissa's family members are possessed by diabolical spirits sent to test her spirit (579). Clarissa is, as the result of these events, like an accused witch of the previous century, cast out, incarcerated, interrogated, stripped, sexually tortured, and eventually destroyed by the "diabolical" (1014) treatment she receives at the hands of the novel's proto-Byronic villain, Richard Lovelace. The entire process of familial replication and nuclearization that Clarissa seeks to bypass but is paradoxically compelled to reenact is, in fact, figured as sorcery.

In a letter to her uncle Antony, Clarissa argues that her repellent suitor, Solmes, is demonic precisely owing to his personification of the entrepreneurial individualist who jettisons extended family members to create a restrictive and imprisoning domestic sphere suited to the most expeditious and extravagant accumulation of wealth:

> Does not his own sister live unhappily for want of a little of his superfluities? And suffers he not his aged uncle, the brother of his own mother, to owe to the generosity of strangers the poor subsistence he picks up from half a dozen families? You know, sir, my open, free, communicative temper: how unhappy must I be, circumscribed in his narrow, selfish circle! out of which, *being withheld by this diabolical parsimony, he dare no more stir than a conjurer out of his; nor would let me.* (153; emphasis added)

Unlike allusions to devils, demons, and pagan gods in *King Lear,* the diabolist vocabulary and imagery that recur throughout *Clarissa* are not taken literally by the novel's characters. Conversely, the heated words, feelings, and wishes connected to *Clarissa*'s diabolism *do* have far-reaching effects. The nature of these effects is overdetermined: Clarissa is accused, interrogated, and cast out like a witch, but the demonic, "worse than Moloch-deity" that has possessed her family appears to follow her and enact her family's will, so that the powers that ravage her seem simultaneously human and inhuman, contemporary and historical. In this her fate is similar to that of Cordelia, but the novel resituates the performance of cultural problems that theater had maintained in a liminal space, both within and outside of public consciousness, within the private, interior space of the novel. *Clarissa* thus reincorporates at the psychosymbolic level the ideological conflicts that Shakespeare externalized, neutralized, and offered up as the objects of collective grief through the rantings of Poor Tom and the death of Cordelia. As the complex bearer of both secular and metaphysical, historical and contemporary forces, Clarissa takes her place, in effect, as the first gothic protagonist.

The obscure forces that determine Clarissa's fate and for which the novel's characters employ a diabolist vocabulary are emphatically sublunary, if unspecifiable, from within the realist epistemology the novel helps to establish. They also, however, represent the resurgence of diabolistic matter that was originally banished from consensus reality in

the early seventeenth century. In *Clarissa,* these decommissioned ideologies are resurrected and redeployed to stand in for the overdetermined forces that changing class and gender relations and economic
structures were coming to exert on the middle-class family. Recurring
throughout the novel is a discernible textual preoccupation with such
overdetermined processes and with thresholds at which contingent factors once set in motion combine to spawn inexorable consequences. In
a particularly remarkable passage, Clarissa metaphorizes her brother's
campaign against her as a sort of Frankenstein's monster that, having
been taken up by their father, "will *walk alone* without needing his
leading-strings" (96). Later, Clarissa's betraying suitor, the aristocratic
Lovelace, observes that "a small spark falling by accident into a powder
magazine has sometimes done more execution than a hundred cannon" (709).

Richardson's figuration of Clarissa's destruction as a witch hunt
undertaken by a family of demoniacs bears witness to the unspeakable power that the witch trials (which had ended officially only in
1736 with the repeal of the Witchcraft Act) and diabolistic beliefs continued to assert within the eighteenth-century unconscious. It also
suggests the ongoing influence that the early modern criminalization
of women still exerted within the confines of the eighteenth-century
bourgeois family. Like Shakespeare, in my reading Richardson empowered his work with cast-off ideological materials that retained a
numinous charge within the social unconscious of its period. And, like
Shakespeare's play, Richardson's novel ties these ideological materials
directly to specific, painful transformations in subjectivity within contemporary society. As Clarissa's dilemma illustrates, even though the
surveillance of women for signs of witchcraft or possession was now a
thing of the past, polarized and exacting conceptions of female purity
and pollution were actually intensifying at this time. Punctilio, the
complex code of honor governing women's and girls' maintenance of
their (literal and symbolic) sexual purity, represents the elaborate care
with which females were obliged to observe and uphold solidifying
boundaries between the domestic and public spheres. At the same time,
children, especially daughters, found themselves caught within increasingly demanding and intrusive families. Thus several of the most well-

known gothic themes, with their autophagous implications—imprisonment, sexual and epistemic boundary violations, interlocking regimes of parental and institutional coercion, the evacuation of agency, and double-binding devil's bargains—all have parallels in the historical experiences of bourgeois children during this period.

Embourgeoisment

"Sprung up from a Dunghill within Every . . . Remembrance"

Early in the novel Clarissa reflects, "The world is but one great family; originally it was so; what then is this narrow selfishness that reigns in us?" (62). The narrative that follows could be read as an answer to her plaintive query. As Ian Watt has argued (*Rise of the Novel* 220–28), Clarissa's sufferings emblematize the ordeal of bourgeois daughters during an extended period of public and private transformation. The late seventeenth century had witnessed "a subordination of marriage to the increase of landed wealth" as "the eldest son came to occupy a unique position of authority" in ruling-class families scrambling to move upward or to retain their position within a shifting social order (Hill 102–3). During the eighteenth century, as the middle-class family was publicly sentimentalized and representationally universalized, bourgeois women grew more dependent for their social authority and the safety of their persons on their status as daughters, sisters, wives, and mothers. Simultaneously, according to theorists of the family, the interiors of such families were becoming increasingly affectively saturated and intrapsychically intrusive.[3] Moreover, an attendant middle-class valorization of childhood, which constituted immaturity and innocence as aesthetically and psychosexually gratifying, rendered children, especially girls, more vulnerable to sexual and emotional exploitation both within and outside their families.[4] Within the emergent nuclear family, daughters found themselves trapped between affectively demanding and appropriative families and more potentially explicit and permanent forms of sexual exploitation within a market economy in which female sexuality was, like everything else, commodifying apace.

Clarissa reflects the impact of these forces within a family of the lower gentry that seeks, through intrusive, coercive, and ultimately fatal measures, to consolidate and augment its wealth and status by exploiting a daughter's sexuality. Clarissa's misfortunes begin when she inherits her grandfather's estate, which her family members believe should rightfully have gone to the Harlowe's eldest son, James. The inheritance provokes a series of sadistic maneuvers on the part of the family which are aimed at wresting the estate from her through a forcible marriage to the repulsive Solmes.

Clarissa's grandfather's transmission of his estate to the most trustworthy of his grandchildren, without regard for gender or birth order, represents the last act of an archaic order still capable of apprehending the best interests of the family as a whole. Among subsequent generations of the Harlowe family, however, expanding economic and social horizons and growing competition with a fluid and upwardly mobile middle class exert new pressures. As a lower branch of the gentry, with such family members as Clarissa's Uncle Antony (her father's youngest brother), who announces that his "very great fortune" is "all of [his] own getting, or *most* of it" (624), the Harlowes are becoming hard pressed to distinguish themselves from their middle-class neighbors. Ironically, their strategies for reinforcing their distinction from the middle class are paradigmatically middle-class. In seeking an alliance with Solmes, they pursue an infusion of money that they naïvely believe will be assimilated to the family as a whole, as land would be, on the event of Solmes's marriage to Clarissa. This influx of wealth will, they believe, qualify James for a title. Thus the Harlowes are seeking, by means of enforced marriage (a lapsed prerogative of the old regime) to raise cash (a tactic associated with the middle class) to reinforce their male heir's position within the aristocracy. The Harlowes' deluded conviction that Solmes's wealth can be securely affixed to James through Clarissa's enforced marriage reveals the speed with which their society's economic structures and its tacit rules governing caste are transforming, for it shows the family's complete ignorance of the crucial differences between landed and commercial wealth.

Whereas Clarissa's grandfather saw his estate as the collective property of an extended, intergenerational family, bequeathing it in stewardship to the family's most prudent member, Clarissa's parents would prefer to concentrate resources in the hands of their eldest son, despite the manifest dangers posed to the family's long-term fortunes by James's short temper, impulsiveness, vanity, and greed. James, as the head of the newest generation, greatly exceeds his parents in his own pronounced preference for the accumulation of capital in the hands of a single male figurehead. The marked generational differences among the Harlowes chart the emergence of bourgeois individualism within the British gentry in response to the new forms of wealth and power, as well as the fluid, dynamic class structures to which industrial capitalism gave rise.

During the eighteenth century, the British aristocracy and bourgeoisie were, as E. P. Thompson puts it, "cross-fertilizing" (455) to an unprecedented extent. The two classes were not merely intermarrying; they were also in various ways mimicking, competing, and cooperating with each other. As Christopher Hill has pointed out, new pressures on the landed aristocracy from the middle class led to growing vigilance concerning female chastity as a means of maintaining control over inherited wealth (103). Thus, as volatile and appropriative relations within the Harlowe family indicate, the eroticization of relations within nuclearizing families accelerated as competition for wealth and position in a fluid economy gave rise to a growing obsession with the sexual biddability of daughters.

In many ways, the Harlowes' simultaneous competition and collusion with the aristocratic Richard Lovelace therefore resemble the ambivalent attractions and hostilities that characterized relations between the owners of commercial wealth and those of landed wealth at this time. Certainly Lovelace seeks to "put the Harlowes in their place" as the product of new or commercial wealth when he dismisses Harlowe Place as having "sprung up from a dunghill within every elderly person's remembrance" (161). Indeed, his obsessive efforts to seduce Clarissa represent an explicit form of class aggression by which he seeks to reduce the Harlowe family to the status of the middle-class families on whose daughters he has typically preyed.

Lovelace's sexual predations literalize (and counter) the cross-class defenses implicit in the new regimentation of bourgeois women. The class hostilities underlying Lovelace's sexual conquests are made explicit in a letter to John Belford, his increasingly reluctant partner in crime, in which Lovelace scrupulously explicates the class and theological implications of the sexual transgressions he single-mindedly pursues. In a passage that classifies children as possessions and as the vehicles by which class rank and property are maintained, he argues for a direct correlation between the interests of capital accumulation, patriarchal domination, and divine morality: "since the wife by a failure may do much more injury to the husband, than the husband can do to the wife, and not only to her husband, but to all his family by obtruding another man's children into his possessions . . . [i]n the eye of heaven therefore, the sin [of fornication] *cannot* be equal [for both sexes]" (429).

The Harlowe family's mania to control Clarissa's sexuality, particularly James's conviction that control of his sister's body is tantamount to control over his own economic and social future, recapitulates the assumed identity between the interests of patriarchy and capital for which Lovelace argues, but in grotesquely magnified and sadistically magical form. If women are, for the ruling classes, geese that might lay either authentic or inauthentic golden eggs, the Harlowes seek a course of absolute control over the goose's ovulation by breeding her and eviscerating her simultaneously. For his part, Lovelace reflects the ethos of the Harlowe family and the period when he demands, after enumerating the emotional and psychological discomforts to which his ardent pursuit of Clarissa has subjected him, "Does she not deserve to pay for all this?" (401).

The Harlowe family's transformation over the course of fifteen hundred pages from an extended and translucent, semipermeable social network in which power and resources circulate to a closed, opaque, and bounded hierarchy reenacts the social history of the nuclear family. The family's central priority remains constant throughout: to sustain or augment its status by concentrating all wealth and power in the hands of a single patrilineal line of succession. Male power and the sexual subordination of women within the family are, in the minds of the novel's male characters, naturalistically associated with wealth and prestige. Yet the motivating connection between the sexual deployment of daughters and the retention or acquisition of resources nonetheless takes on a symbolic, incestuous charge within the Harlowe family that far exceeds its basis in material fact. Male and senior family members express a current of unconscious eroticized aggression through their obsessive desire to control and dominate the body of the daughter with whom the family as a whole most closely identifies.

Sexual Binarization
"Every Well-Dressed Man, I Think to Be Him"

The aggression directed against Clarissa within her family allegorically enacts what Ruth Perry has called the mid-eighteenth century's "colonization of the female body for domestic life" (208). According to Nancy Armstrong and Leonard Tennenhouse in their account of the economic and cultural forces that led to the cross-class domestication of women in the course of the eighteenth century, "men of opposing classes [came] to agree that economic dependence was desirable in a woman" (232). This moment of male cross-class consensus is connected, in their analysis, with the disavowal of national shame at the brutal exploitation of workers more generally, especially children, that accompanied industrial capitalism. In this account, the ruling classes forwent the extensive use of women and children and accepted the necessity of paying higher wages to a largely male workforce in exchange for a cross-class alliance between men that excluded women from the world of waged labor. For workingmen, such an exclusion meant higher wages and less competition for jobs. For owners, this exclusion offered the appearance of moral scrupulousness and headed off a more general and, for them, dangerous debate concerning the exploitation of workers as a class.

The effect of erasing class differences among women, as Perry points out, was "to universalize the meanings and purposes of the female body and to reduce the degrees of freedom in interpreting women's sex roles" (208). Thus through the reification of a maternalized, asexual (but exclusively heterosexually appropriable), middle-class womanhood, the British state, as Perry argues, colonized women's bodies, thereby inducting biology into the service of ideological and social production and reproduction. One effect of these changes, as Clarissa's situation once outside her family makes clear, was representationally to demote or exclude female sexuality within the bourgeois domestic sphere in a manner that dangerously hypersexualized all girls and women outside that sphere.

As Felicity Nussbaum contends, "The cult of motherhood disguise[d] the way that middle-class Englishwomen, formerly producers of things as well as of life, [were] encouraged to limit themselves in the newly emergent money economy to producing life" (165). The experiences of daughters of the emergent working classes, as they were shaped by the iconization and privatization of the middle-class family, are more difficult to assess. On one hand, the same forces that nuclearized and gendered bourgeois families and bourgeois space, making the capitalist family cell synonymous with *the* family, materially atomized, degendered, and representationally effaced working-class family and community cohesion, incrementally reducing members of working-class families to their roles as laborers. On the other hand, in the figure of Richardson's first protagonist, Pamela, we see that women who labored for wages were explicitly invited to embrace the growing commodification of women in general within an intensifying marriage market as an opportunity for upward mobility. Simultaneously, as in *Pamela,* middle-class women were offered up the image of the servant girl, armed only with her insurmountable ethics, as an objective correlative for their own bereft condition. The differing conditions of daughters of the laboring and ruling classes were, in short, conflated and universalized, but each was also made available to the other as a fantasy object. Servant girls' fantasies of becoming bourgeois wives, and middle-class daughters' romantic identification with such protagonists as Pamela, would have provided both groups of readers with momentary relief from the painful conditions that must have characterized the experience of women of all classes during this period.

Ian Watt's contention that the extreme vulnerability of women in the mid–eighteenth century offered opportunities for the emergence of new forms (ideological as well as aesthetic) is confirmed in principle throughout Richardson's novel, as Clarissa's feelings or purported feelings are repeatedly appropriated to hostile ends. Clarissa's harsh treatment at the hands of a cross-class male alliance bent on "coloniz[ing] the female body for domestic life" generates emotional reactions on her part (real and imagined) which are themselves appropriated to produce what Eve Kosofsky Sedgwick has called "the modern terms of the social articulations of male homosocial desire" (*Epistemology* 67). In one such instance, Clarissa's unwanted suitor, Solmes, leeringly intimates to Sir Harry Downeton that "terror and fear . . . looked pretty in a bride, as well as in a wife" [238]. This repellent bit of homosocial bonding is initiated by the socially liminal Solmes toward a character of whom we know nothing except that he has a title and thus is Solmes's social superior. Through his sadistic invocation of Clarissa's terror on their wedding night (and thereafter), Solmes fuses terror and erotic appeal in an attempt to forge bonds of cross-class intimacy based on a shared sensation of masculine invulnerability. Here, as elsewhere in the novel, Clarissa's real or fantasized emotional responses to sexual threats are appropriated by men within and outside her family to form pleasurable eroticized bonds with other men.

The intersection of middle-class and aristocratic male interests during this period and the binary and absolute schism between the genders which this alliance underwrote is also reflected in the novel through the interchangeability of bourgeois and aristocratic male characters. This is particularly clear in the novel's equation of Clarissa's brother, James, with her two suitors, Solmes and Lovelace. Early in the novel, for instance, Clarissa remarks that "my brother pretends to court me as [Solmes's] proxy" (62). An example of a similar but more extended and explicit identification between James and Lovelace occurs in Lovelace's characteristically ironic and homosocial remark to Clarissa that "he wished that the man who took such pains to keep up and inflame the passions of [her] father and [her] uncles were not at the bottom of [a further stratagem of Lovelace's] too" (460). Clarissa believes Lovelace is referring to James, and James has indeed inflamed the passions of her father and her uncles. As readers, however, we are aware that the (other) man to whom Lovelace refers is himself. The pleasure he takes in conflating himself with James and in titillating himself with the thrilling thought that he has "inflamed the passions of Clarissa's father and uncles" calls attention not only to the two men's parallel positions relative to Clarissa but also, more generally, to the homosocial bonds between men that extend throughout the novel. These bonds, which James and Lovelace forge with others through acts of cruelty toward women, eroticize the interchangeability of middle-class and aristocratic men that transforming class relations and the binarization of gender are bringing about. Clarissa herself thus learns to conceptualize the world in terms of masculine interchangeability, as when, after her escape from Mrs. Sinclair's, she tells Anna Howe that "every well-dressed man I see from my windows, whether on horseback or on foot, I think to be him" (756).

Heterosexualization
"All the World Gave Me to Him"

As indicated by the myriad bonds between men both within and out-side the Harlowe family which were formed through Clarissa's sexual and emotional persecution, the commodification of women and chil-dren and the ascendance of binary gender relations brought into being new possibilities for sexual relations within the eighteenth-century imaginary. This new dispensation, which Carolyn Woodward has termed the "heterosexual contract" (855), constituted women in eigh-teenth-century England as a new kind of sexual property both within and beyond the domestic sphere. Significantly, the novel represents the sexual appropriability of women as affording new discursive powers for Bella, Mrs. Sinclair, Mrs. Howe, and Anna, as well as the novel's male characters. As we have already seen, not all the eroticized bonds made possible by this emerging regime are heterosexual in nature. Within the confines of Richardson's families, the heterosexual contract mani-fests itself as a series of incestuous heterosexual and homosexual en-croachments.

The growth of cross-class bonds between men at a time when affec-tive bonds within the family were also intensifying makes the work-ings of the incest taboo, which purportedly compensates fathers and brothers for the sexual "loss" of female family members through the extension of reciprocal bonds between men, shockingly explicit in *Clarissa*. In the novel, the power struggle over Clarissa's sexual deployment serves as a self-evident pretext for the gratification of incestuous drives churned up by the family's rapid physical and emotional constriction. For example, the overt aggressions unleashed in the controversy over Solmes's courtship afford James, through his identification with Solmes, new, distinctly sexual prerogatives. In one instance, shortly after Clarissa notes that he is courting her as Solmes's proxy, he responds to her entry into a room by "measur[ing her] . . . with his eyes . . . from head to foot" (63).

A generalized obsession with the sexual control of female family members is dispersed throughout the novel, in recurring instances of family members engaging each other erotically by proxy. Anna's mother, Mrs. Howe, (more or less flirtatiously) uses Anna's unwanted suitor, Hickman, to engage Anna erotically, just as James and Mr. Harlowe use Solmes and Lovelace to engage Clarissa. This pattern of "incest by proxy" is represented in a comic mode in Mrs. Howe's erotic engagement with Anna through the lackluster but comparatively enviable Hickman. Anna repeatedly rejects Hickman in favor of Clarissa, whom she finds superior to any man; she fends off her mother's attempt to place herself, via Hickman, between Anna and Clarissa by suggesting in a knowing and playful misreading that Hickman must be the object of her mother's erotic intentions (279). James and Mr. Harlowe, in a more complicated homosocial parallel of Mrs. Howe's comic seduction of her daughter, entrap Clarissa between Solmes, a man who repulses her, and Lovelace, whom they claim to hate but whom they systematically isolate as the only possible route out of an enforced marriage with Solmes.

The point of this marital jockeying is only purportedly the control of profit and family status. Instead, in both the Howe and Harlowe households, eroticized parent-child or brother-sister bonds are, in effect, consummated through the sexual deployment of children. This impulse is depicted as relatively benign in the case of Mrs. Howe, who occupies a uniquely fortunate position as a middle-class widow with her property at her own disposal. Free to make reasonable, if not actually appealing, choices on her own and her daughter's behalf, she marries Clarissa's wealthy Uncle Antony, a shipping magnate who yearns for someone with whom to count his money in his old age, and triangulates with Anna via Hickman. In the Harlowe family a parallel libidinal current manifests itself in a series of escalating eruptions of incestuous rage.

That this drive to dominate through the exercise of sexual control over family members exceeds and indeed undermines the Harlowe family's financial and social interests is one of the novel's central points. Clarissa and others repeatedly point out that Solmes's chief attraction for Clarissa's family members seems to be his thoroughly repellent *person* rather than his convoluted and improbable promises of restoring to the family an inheritance that could be more effectively secured by retaining Clarissa in her preferred unmarried state. As Anna observes, Clarissa's family members, overstimulated by enticing new forms of wealth and social status within society, as well as new technologies of gender, subjectivity, and power within the family, are comparable to a body in which "all the senses" unite in "a confederacy against that which would animate and give honour to the whole" (475).

Anna Howe strikingly conveys the impact of changing economic structures on the constitution of families when she likens the Harlowe family to an autophagous body in which the senses are no longer constrained by the interests of the whole but whose organs ultimately devour themselves in a heedless competition for gratification. In addition to reflecting a growing concern among the aristocracy and middle class with the consolidation of resources in the hands of eldest sons, insatiable appetites were also kindled during this period in response to social technologies of difference that led to new distributions and concentrations of power within smaller and more autonomous social units. Moreover, the unbridled appetites that drive the novel's characters are also undoubtedly stimulated by new economic, social, and geographic horizons opened by this period's growth in mercantile trade and consumption.

Central to the novel's action, but simultaneously subordinated to it and peripheralized by it, is Clarissa's romantic friendship with Anna Howe.[5] The two young women repeatedly and explicitly express the central utopian wish that the novel both invokes and nullifies—that they might find a means to live together in peace (133). As the novel's events graphically illustrate, however, their friendship's salvific power is contingent on the goodwill of a heterosexist social order which ordains—paradoxically—that only through marriage or, at minimum, the goodwill of an amiable suitor can Anna even temporarily extend to Clarissa the protections that a bourgeois man could extend at any time.[6]

In an early, ongoing dispute with Clarissa, Anna, like Lovelace, emphasizes the advantages that Clarissa might find in accepting terror as an erotic trigger by reframing her blushing, palpitating responses to Lovelace's encroachments—responses she understandably interprets as fear and shame—as love. Anna's rather breathless contributions to these discussions also appropriate Clarissa's imagined emotions as a means of forming new bonds and ideologies. Her heated probings of Clarissa's libidinal reactions to Lovelace—an object charged within a web of coalescing social relations with the numinous appeal of romantic love—create the context for a great deal of intensely erotic flirtation and the fragile beginnings of a discourse of lesbian bonding (355–56). Thus although Anna, like many of the novel's characters, also exploits Clarissa's disempowered position to generate new discourses and previously unassertable bonds, her arguments in favor of a rapprochement between terror and sexual attraction are motivated very differently from those by James, Solmes, and Lovelace.

A third discourse, also predicated on the eroticization of terror, emerges in the internal articulation that Clarissa herself is pushed to engender by her circumstances. In an early letter to Anna, Clarissa recounts Lovelace's schematization of her predicament in terms of the reproduction of familial power relations. As Lovelace points out, a forced marriage (her family's proposed resolution to her current confined and reviled state) would only replicate and indeed reaffirm the conditions she might be tempted to marry Solmes to escape. Lovelace's suggested solution to the dilemma he expertly frames is romantic love, with its promise of erotic and epistemic liberation. Clarissa recounts his arguments to Anna: "The terms Solmes had proposed were such as would have involved me in the same difficulties with my relations that I now laboured under. [Lovelace] therefore took the liberty to say, that my favour to him, far from increasing those difficulties, would be the readiest way to extricate me from them" (167). As Lovelace's arguments make explicit in this and other passages, and as his manipulation of Clarissa's material conditions within her family illustrates, Clarissa is, as Charlotte Sussman has observed of her working-class counterpart Pamela, "hemmed in by the threat of physical punishment" (97).[7] Under such circumstances, as Lovelace argues, an ardent allegiance to ideologies of romantic love and the freely chosen companionate marriage this ideology implies represent the only pathway by which a daughter of the middle class might tenuously hope to realize her own social, affective, and sexual desires and might fend off the economic and physical threats that teemed about her. In effect, as Lovelace tells Clarissa, recapitulating what he claims to be the general public sentiment, "all the world . . . gave [her] to [him]" (168).

Terrorized by her family's "final solution," a plan to remove her to an isolated, moated estate where she would have "but little hope, if carried thither, whether sensible or senseless . . . but they will endeavour to force the solemn obligation upon me" (290), Clarissa is tricked into fleeing with Lovelace. The scenario of sexual violation at the hands of her family that Clarissa foresees and flees to evade tragically foreshadows her fate at Lovelace's hands. For once under Lovelace's control, Clarissa's fate proceeds smoothly along the lines her family originally ordained: confining Clarissa within an isolated sphere, Lovelace, unable to seduce Clarissa "sensible," renders her "senseless" and rapes her. Clarissa's father invokes and indeed mandates this violation by disowning her and cursing her, figuratively participating in her projected violation by himself vowing to "*treat [her] . . . like a common creature . . . and doubt[ing] not that this will be [her] fate*" (509; emphasis added).

Through Lovelace's machinations, Clarissa's attempts to evade sexual violation within her family are elaborated beyond that family's borders into a number of contingent subject positions, including that of bourgeois beloved and betrothed, prisoner, prostitute, housewife, rape victim, madwoman, imprisoned debtor, and corpse. It is one of the novel's central points that this last category is the only one that does not afford Lovelace, acting as the agent of the wishes held by Clarissa's father and brother, a means of either interrupting or distorting Clarissa's words, appropriating her body, and abrogating her freedom of movement.

Thus, as Clarissa discovers through a series of ever worsening revelations, Lovelace's purported alternative represents only a further level of entrapment within the same system of familial replication. Lovelace's complicity not only with the Harlowe family but also with the family structure itself is made clear in his ardent wish that he might be "a father, uncle, brother, and . . . husband to [Clarissa], all in one" (377). The structure of Lovelace's wish figures the process by which male dominance and encroachment within the domestic sphere perpetuate themselves by way of romance and marriage, a figuration that derives a subversive frisson from its incestuous implications. Lovelace's implicit equation of himself to Clarissa's male relatives suggests that she will be as safe with him as she would be with any of them, which, given her ultimate fate at his hands, suggests a deliberate double entendre on Richardson's part and an express allusion to the air of erotic aggression that imbues Clarissa's relations to her male relatives. Clarissa and Lovelace's drama of mutual distrust, seduction, shame, and rage reenacts emotional dynamics that originated within a family that is devouring her by proxy. Seen as an extension of dynamics internal to the nuclearizing family, the bonds that hold Clarissa and Lovelace together in a painful and ambivalent thrall dramatize in distinctly gothic terms the clumsy, violent, and consuming emergence of the bourgeois discourse of heterosexual love.

At the rational level, Clarissa's serial transformations from devoted and well-loved daughter to corpse are wrought through the dialectical interactions of an unnaturally hard-hearted family and the unscrupulous manipulations of a rake and a libertine. At the irrational, magical level, however, the sexual contract by which Clarissa is originally bound through her family's attempts to shackle her to a repulsive suitor gains agency beyond the Harlowe domestic sphere via her father's curse. This curse thus figuratively enacts the unification of domestic and national patriarchal orders. Such a unification historically occurred during the mid–eighteenth century through the increasing synchronization of private and public patriarchal values, as the middle-class family became emblematic of British national identity, values, and society. This growing identification of the British state with the bourgeois family had the paradoxical effect of both heightening and disguising a growing cleavage between a feminized and private bourgeois domestic sphere and an increasingly masculinized public realm.

Clarissa's fate, as Leila May contends, reflects the daughter's evolving role within an interpenetrating imperial state/family system that constitutes her as "the repository of familial values, hence of social values themselves in a civilization which promulgates economic violence as a way of life, and whose self-justification is the protection of the family — and particularly of its purest, most delicate, vulnerable member" (30–31). Like the gothic narratives of devoured daughters to which May connects it, *Clarissa* "portrays . . . a universe where the calm surface of repressive convention and ingrown hypocrisy is . . . threatened by the irruption of the secret violences which it provokes but conceals" (Watt, *Rise of the Novel* 211).

Watt describes repression and resistance in *Clarissa* in terms that anticipate Foucault's account of power within the family in *The History of Sexuality,* but he fails to specify that the "secret violence" which Clarissa's universe both "provokes" and "conceals" is, in the last instance, familial violence, and that far from being threatened by this violence, the forces of nuclearization indeed *feed* on the violent but doomed resistance they provoke. Within an imperial social order that cultivates the sexual vulnerability of daughters as the central justification for ongoing imperial aggression and appropriation, as May argues, "sisters must," like Clarissa, "be taught to will their own self-negation" (31).

Interiority, Confession, and Autophagy
"The Principal End of Our Pious Cares Is Attained"

Like many subsequent gothic protagonists, Clarissa responds to an erotic threat by instituting a system of internal surveillance. Such a strategy defends the boundaries of an imperiled self, seeking to seize control of self-definition by emphasizing the ontological boundary between the interior self and external observers and privileging the self's epistemologically advantaged position. Clarissa's subjectivity is thus repeatedly refined according to a characteristic pattern: eroticized encroachment gives rise to an intensified interiority, which incites further encroachment, thereby subjecting Clarissa, through her ever keener perceptions, to ever more eloquent pain. *Clarissa* depicts modern interiority as emerging in response to, but also as itself enabling, new forms of intrapsychic intrusion and epistemic pain. Clarissa's eroticized interiority, which the Harlowe family and Lovelace persistently violate, is thus itself brought into being in the course of the family's constriction.

To defend herself against the humiliating and unfounded allegation that she secretly desires Lovelace, Clarissa zealously gathers evidence to support an alternative account of her own internal state. This self-scrutiny partakes of the lacerating, compulsively repetitive compact that Sacvan Bercovitch detects at the heart of Puritan subjectivity: a "narcissistic *Liebestöd,*" in which the individual identity is affirmed "by turning against [the individual's] powers of self-affirmation" (20). Clarissa's practices of self-interrogation are undertaken with good reason, however, because her family bases its demand that she marry Solmes on the claim that her supposed yearning for Lovelace must be foreclosed at all costs.

Clarissa's continually demonstrated and commented upon excellence at self-surveillance contributes to her accounts a certain dangerous authenticity that her family members fear. As her internal surveillance proliferates and circulates as discourse, the family closes ranks and solidifies its boundaries in an attempt to restrict and silence her accounts. Clarissa's foreclosed attempts to express her internal experiences are used to justify the emergence of a constricted, univocal, and "impenetrable" (169) patriarchal family, unified and ideologically homogenized under the Law of the Father. This process reenacts at the level of discourse the pattern that René Girard has described in his analysis of the role of the scapegoat in Western culture. Clarissa's uncle Antony, for instance — one of several family members who initially side with Clarissa in her aversion to Solmes — turns against her when he determines that her refusal to be "made a sacrifice" (Richardson 411) to the will of her father threatens "the good of the whole" and thereby risks "set[ting] one part of [the family] against another" (158). Such an act of projection allows an imperiled community to reconsolidate itself by expiating inassimilable emotions through a culminating, unifying act of communal violence. In this case, such an act of ritual expiation (initially) takes the form of Clarissa's isolation and silencing (50). Such scapegoating also, although Girard is somewhat ambiguous on this point (113), allows for the consolidation of newly hierarchical and totalitarian social orders. As Clarissa's cousin Dolly Hervey points out, Clarissa's mother and aunt are demoted within the family when they try to speak up for Clarissa. She reports that Clarissa's male relatives have silenced the voices of the senior women in the family, who had ordinarily had a say in domestic matters. This silencing of maternal voices is dramatized shortly after Dolly departs, when Clarissa overhears "a confused mixture of voices, some louder than others, drowning, as it seemed, the more compassionating [female] accents" (309).

Clarissa's detailed descriptions of her processes of inner surveillance are undertaken in self-defense, to fend off her father's and brother's misappropriations of her interiority to consolidate their power within the family and augment the family's economic and social position. These descriptions also, however, partake of a certain *jouissance*—the liberatory release of giving voice to that which has been repressed or misrepresented—in which the reader also participates. These initially liberatory acts of self-scrutiny, however, actually incite the Harlowe family to drastic measures aimed at containment, control, and retaliation. This progression reconfirms Foucault's representation of confession as simultaneously pleasurable and reinforcing of a priori power dynamics. It also, however, points to a significant dialectic between coercive silencing and the "pleasurable" compulsion to speak which operated within eighteenth-century bourgeois society. Clarissa's letters repeatedly conjure up appalling images of a hostile inner eye that conducts interrogation sessions, sometimes accompanied by searches that, in their zeal and intrusiveness, rival family members' "violent" searches of her boudoir (482). In this imagery, a crisis that results from conflictual impulses to silence and mortify the self, as well as to protect an imperiled self that throughout the novel remains poised on the brink of annihilation, gives rise to episodes of ecstatic release into speech. This dynamic resembles the "incitement to discourse" that Foucault enshrines as the fundamental impulse underlying the proliferation of discourse during the eighteenth century. It also, however, reinstates that proliferation of discourse within the history of material repression that Foucault sought decisively to banish with his contemptuous dismissal of the repressive hypothesis.

As Maud Ellman observes in *The Hunger Artists,* her extraordinary meditation on the sociocultural underpinnings of hunger: "Clarissa, like the modern anorectic, starves in private; and although she indulges her taste for words as vigorously as she stints her taste for food, she never articulates the reasons for her hunger. Indeed, her body's protest wildly exceeds her speech, racked with meanings too ferocious to enunciate" (72). These unspoken meanings are connected to the nature of the changes that were occurring in family structure at the time of the novel's writing, and with the constitutive relationship between silence and discourse for which Foucault was understandably reluctant to account. These changes are encoded in the novel's representations of Clarissa's silences, in its representations of a continual pattern of attempted restrictions on and appropriations of her words, and in the book-long enactment of the premandated rape and death toward which her entire family incessantly drives her.

Clarissa's fate dramatizes the narrow and dangerous path faced by bourgeois daughters in the mid–eighteenth century. The novel makes explicit the symbolic sexual sacrifice implicit in the transition from the early-eighteenth-century "family of alliance" to a more affectively charged, nuclearizing bourgeois family by depicting the daughter as a scapegoat onto whom is projected responsibility for the uncontrollable economic and Oedipal desires that are breaking loose within her family. Lovelace's repeated demands that Clarissa love him—and love him in a particular obsessive, self-abandoning way—reveal this novel's prototypical position within the emergence of the ideology of bourgeois romantic love. The novel's popularity, especially with female readers, seems related to its powerful evocations of both fear and attraction with respect to romance as a potential means of escape from the family cell.

But the novel's narrative trajectory also structurally reveals the bankruptcy of romantic love by positing Clarissa's relationship to Lovelace as the product and mirror image of the Harlowes' incestuous intrusion into Clarissa's inner life. Far from offering an actual means of escape, Lovelace inflicts on Clarissa the ultimate violation of her trust, agency, and selfhood that she had sought to evade, and he does it in a manner that places the blame for that violation, as in literal scapegoat rituals, on his victim. Thus through the production of a publicly legible female interior—a project to which *Clarissa* itself contributed enormously—women of all classes were constituted, through their purported inner "attachments" to desires that preemptively justified their violation, as "always already" guilty of their own ruin. Perhaps the cruelest paradox of this paradoxical novel is that it is simultaneously so brutally revealing in its depiction of the process by which affective reserves building up within the middle class during a period of massive transformation were diverted onto middle-class daughters, and so effective in compelling readers' investments in the emergent cult of romance through which this transmission was accomplished.

Chapter 3
"Something Valuable of Their Own"

Children, Reproduction, and Irony in Swift,

Burke, and Edgeworth

The gentry are no doubt philosophers enough to bring up their bairns like sheep to the slaughter, and despatch them like cadies to Bengal and the Cape of Good Hope. — David Moir, *The Life of Mansie Wauch*

As Elizabeth Bowen recalls in *Seven Winters: Memories of a Dublin Childhood,* disorientation was fundamental to the Anglo-Irish child's emerging self concept: Anglo-Irish children learned young that they were "not Irish" and, only slightly later, that they were also "not English." In the late seventeenth and eighteenth centuries, children of the newly cohering Anglo-Irish were born into families that presented them not only with the familiar double binds of binary gender norms and heteronormativity but also with a parallel dispossession at the level of group identity. In an often-quoted formulation, Bowen calls attention to parallels between Anglo-Irish national and sexual subject formation when she refers to the awkwardness of "English-Irish interaction" as "a mixture of showing-off and suspicion, worse than sex" (cited in Foster, *Paddy* 31). It is important to bear in mind, however, that the identity crisis facing settler children of the seventeenth and eighteenth centuries would have greatly exceeded that which Bowen was, by the early twentieth century, able to shrug off with a characteristically defanging bon mot.

Often raised away from their parents by Irish nurses, the children or grandchildren of English settlers would have been all the more emphatically "not Irish" in a world governed by penal laws that did not "suppose any such person to exist as an Irish Roman Catholic."[1] The cultural life around them would have been off-limits, which might explain why toward the end of the eighteenth century some Anglo-Irish men and women "awaken[ed] a new historical consciousness" (Trumpener 24) through antiquarianist scholarship that (in true melancholic fashion) both preserved and mourned the folkloric traditions forbidden to them as children.[2] Venturing further afield in search of a secure identity, these children of reluctant immigrants would inevitably have been mortified to learn they were also (unlike their parents) "not English."

While colonizing and colonized groups are by definition diametrically opposed in their material aims and political interests,[3] Anglo-Irish literature nonetheless evinces a fascination with patterns of representation that parallel or conflate the positions of the Anglo-Irish and native Irish, particularly as children. Parallel or oscillating representations of the colonizer and the colonized in Anglo-Irish writing seem to represent vestiges of the Anglo-Irish child's ambivalent identification with the native Irish. Anglo-Irish children understandably craved a secure national identity, and this desire would have fueled a covert attraction to the unambiguous position of the native Irish. Moreover, owing to their own subtly exploited position as the involuntary perpetuators of the colonial system, such children also ineffably identified with the subjugated native Irish, toward whom they still, as adults, expressed passionate fellow feeling, frequently in their writing and sometimes in their political allegiances.

The near mythical uncertainty that surrounds the familial and national affiliations of the eighteenth-century Anglo-Irish writers Jonathan Swift, Edmund Burke, and Maria Edgeworth exemplifies a larger set of cultural uncertainties that concern nationality and family bonds in eighteenth-century Anglo-Irish society. The children of the Anglo-Irish were epistemologically disempowered by virtue of their cultural displacement; the narrative that the logic of colonialism required — a prescriptive attachment to Irish property accompanied by an absolute alienation from Irish society — precluded their acquisition of a coherent cultural identity. When, like Swift, they remained in Ireland as the by-product of settler families that did not settle after all, their national surroundings would have felt not only alien but anathema as well. When, like Edmund Burke, they were raised in families that externally conformed to Protestantism yet covertly maintained Irish Catholic traditions, bewilderment would have ensued when rituals and sentiments customary in one setting were dangerous and forbidden in another. When, like Maria Edgeworth, their childhood passage out of and back to Ireland was messy, entailing long periods of separation from their parents, they would have felt desperate to secure their connection to Ireland and (hence) to their family at any cost.

Narrative, formal and informal, authorized and unauthorized, has served as a staging area on which these authors and their biographers have claimed and repressed an array of nationally nuanced identities. The biographies of Swift, Burke, and Edgeworth all encompass apocryphal or repressed narratives that conspicuously seek to redefine the author's group or national origins. Jonathan Swift claimed to have been kidnapped by his Anglo-Irish nurse and taken to England for three years during his early childhood. Edmund Burke, it was remorselessly rumored, had a "Jesuit past" (Kramnick 52); he was typically pictured in contemporary English cartoons in Jesuit garb, with a potato and whiskey bottle in the foreground (C. O'Brien 50). When Maria Edgeworth's father returned to Ireland upon the death of his first wife to marry his second, the seven-year-old was sent to boarding school in England for two years. Paradoxically, in her father's memoirs, which she completed after his death, Maria's English affiliations are repressed, along with all memory of her mother (Gonda 210). Each of these authors was shaped by and in turn inscribed in his or her work aspects of a politically and economically constituted Anglo-Irish family romance.[4]

Settling the Anglo-Irish Family

The same economic and social dynamics reflected in the Harlowe family's expulsion of Clarissa into its own devouring mirror image — Mrs. Sinclair's brothel — fueled the capitalist family cell's disorderly spilling over into Ireland. Ireland's chaotic and contested landscape, however, delayed the advent of either literal or figurative Anglo-Irish counterparts to the Harlowes. English subjects displaced into Ireland in their search for a secure economic niche did not uniformly configure themselves into new-style nuclear families upon receiving their land grants from Cromwell. Rather, the process whereby the dispersed, often nationally and religiously heterogenous seventeenth- and eighteenth-century Anglo-Irish family of affiliation reconfigured itself into a boundaried and "pure" Protestant, unionist Anglo-Irish family cell was gradual, ambivalent, and messy.[5] During the course of this transformation, Anglo-Irish authors typically confined themselves to representations of less politically fraught English, Irish, or (as in Burke's philosophy) unmarked "generic" families.

Throughout the eighteenth century, many established Nua-Ghaill, or New English, families resembled the Foucauldian family of alliance, differing from Old English families only insofar as their religion, the Penal Laws, and their possession of large tracts of freshly expropriated land discouraged the emergence of common sympathies between themselves and their compatriots. Social relations during this period were the product of massive military and ideological transformations that deprived most sectors of the Irish population of basic protections, subjecting them to social death. Despite an array of repressive laws designed to discourage intermarriage and crystallize the bitter internecine feelings created by Cromwell's brutal subjugation of the Irish, however, the New English (as opposed to the pre-Cromwellian Sean-Ghaill, or Old English) only intermittently spoke or acted as a unified, self-conscious group. Throughout much of the eighteenth century, settler families remained diffuse and hybridized in composition. Often these families cut across religious and national identities, and individuals sometimes invented their family's religious or national identities anew, as did Edmund Burke's father, apparently with little ensuing outcry (C. O'Brien 3–14).

The inherent ambiguity of this group's national identity was exacerbated by numerous and variously motivated waves of English immigration to Ireland during the seventeenth century. The rapid, historically nuanced sedimentation of English immigrants into Ireland during this period is vividly delineated by Peter Somerville-Large when he describes Dublin as incorporating "another spurt of immigration" after the Battle of the Boyne (1690), so that "more newcomers joined the earlier groups of Old English, Elizabethan, Cromwellian, Restoration and Hugeonots [*sic*]" (155). Among economically insecure newcomers in the late seventeenth and eighteenth centuries, marriage and the establishment of a conventional, bourgeois family would have helped to establish the aura of security and belonging that land grants had provided their predecessors. Like the redistribution of land, this transposition of English social forms into Ireland on the part of newcomers eager to obtain a margin of security they had lacked in England contributed to the establishment in and around Dublin of, in Declan Kiberd's words, "a new England called Ireland" (*Inventing Ireland* 9–25).

Children of the *Nua-Ghaill* thus grew to adulthood in a social landscape that was simultaneously volatile and convention-ridden. The writings of Swift, Burke, and Edgeworth inscribe the ambivalent political and national position of children born into the emergent Anglo-Irish settler colonial order. Further recourse to their biographies bears witness to the political and social upheaval that characterized this purported "golden age" of Anglo-Irish rule. Jonathan Swift fled his studies at Trinity as part of a mass exodus of Protestants in 1688–89, when "the troubles closing James II's reign upset any sort of orderly business" (Ehrenpreis 85). As an adolescent, Edmund Burke observed around him and recorded in his journals the appalling images of mass starvation to which Luke Gibbons attributes Burke's early interest in the sensory apprehension of horror in his *Philosophical Enquiry* on the sublime.[6] (Later, as a member of Parliament (MP), Burke felt unable to intervene to save an Irish Catholic cousin threatened with death under the Penal Code [C. O'Brien 50–51].) On their way from Dublin to Edgeworthstown during the 1798 rebellion, Maria Edgeworth's father and his wife passed "a carriage turned; a man hung in between the shafts, murdered by insurgents" (Harden 13). Nostalgic latter-day representations of this epoch notwithstanding, as these details suggest, the eighteenth-century Anglo-Irish were frequently confronted with disturbing reminders of their contested position in Ireland.

Irony provided the crucial, self-protective stance by which eighteenth-century Anglo-Irish authors could indirectly explore experiences associated with the emergent Anglo-Irish social order by projecting their contemporary concerns and preoccupations onto families carefully designated as other than their own. English families, like Gulliver's family of origin and his much-fled wife and children, adapted easily to an ironized or satirized stance because as the representational norm they could readily be reduced to ahistorical cyphers or caricatures. The generic or "natural" (nuclear, heterosexual, patriarchal) family from which Burke derives his model of the state seems — like the proverbial virtuous nation and woman — to have no history and thus authorizes the adoption of a disinterested "objective" stance. Temporal distance allowed Maria Edgeworth to assume a similarly detached, ironized position relative to the Rackrents.

Unlike the nineteenth-century paranoid gothic that I discuss in the following chapter, the ironic mode always retains traces of that which it suppresses. The texts that I examine in this chapter both own and disclaim all knowledge of the subject matter that necessitates their ironic stance; in them, irony simultaneously asserts and denies elements of an emergent Anglo-Irish gothic family romance. These texts therefore represent a sort of median point en route to the paranoid gothic, which achieves its effects through a complete displacement of its subject matter.

As Peter Stallybrass and Allon White observe of Swift's paradigmatically ironic "excremental interest," Anglo-Irish ironic strategies were notably disingenuous. These writers' "sole avowed reason" for contemplating repellent objects, "in all bad faith," is to steer clear of them and "to come out as cleanly as [they] may" (109). But just as Swift's ironic depictions of excrement allowed him to expose his own anal preoccupations even as he used these excursions as occasions to chastise others for their vulgarity, depictions of the abhorrent, the grotesque, or the morally dissolute within (other people's) families and nations afforded these writers the chance simultaneously to reveal and disavow unauthorized aspects of Anglo-Irish family life and social dynamics.

British settler colonialism's dependency on the production of English-identified children and the incoherence of New English children's position within the emerging Anglo-Irish settler colonial order are inscribed in ironic eighteenth-century representations of familial corporeality and sexuality, reproduction, and intergenerational relations. The texts included in this chapter chart the struggle of eighteenth- and early-nineteenth-century Anglo-Irish colonial elites to position themselves within a chaotic environment in which a clear and stable set of ethnic or culturally based class divisions had yet to emerge. Writing while pitched battles over Irish land rights sporadically burst forth within miles of their doorsteps, Swift, Burke and Edgeworth used irony to gain definitional power in an uncertain social milieu.

"A Modest Proposal"
Allegorizing Settler Colonial Reproduction

Swift's "A Modest Proposal" offers a suggestive template for all subsequent gothic and gothic-realist representations of the Anglo-Irish family. The essay exposes in the crudest terms the mechanisms by which externally imposed economic mandates pervade familial relations and indeed human corporeality within an imperial economy. In it, Swift schematizes in bold, certain strokes the colonial order's transformation of social, familial, and affective relations within Ireland at a time when these pervasive effects were not yet transparent or safely relegated to the realm of the ideological. In later Anglo-Irish gothic literature, children are frequently associated with guilty secrets that must be forcibly suppressed for the good of the larger order; here Swift uses the spectacle of an overt traffic in children to expose a guilty secret concerning the role of familial reproduction in maintaining a dependent relationship between the English and Irish economies.

The nuclearization of the English family had a significant impact on early Anglo-Irish literature because early Anglo-Irish writers were acutely aware of themselves as both within and outside such families. In his discussion of Jonathan Swift in *The Origins of the English Novel,* for example, Michael McKeon calls attention to the parallel that Swift continually draws between "second sons" disenfranchised by primogeniture, and dispossessed English subjects forced into "aimless mobility and exile," who, "unsettled," could ultimately *settle* their affairs only as "strangers in strange lands" (338–39). More generally, Warren Montag attributes "the complexity of Swift's work, its often paradoxical and self-subverting character," to "its inscription in the uneven and contradictory development of English society (and its Irish colony) during this time [1688–1714]" (2).

Jonathan Swift was born in Dublin into a middle-class, Anglican family in 1667, eight months after the death of a father who had "settled in Ireland, taking advantage of the opportunities afforded by the Cromwellian occupation" (Montag 6). His mother straightaway relinquished him to a wet nurse and departed for England with his elder sister in tow. She spent brief periods in her son's company only "during the first year of his life, and for a year or two before he entered school" (Ehrenpreis 32). Thus Swift, to an extent surpassing that of most middle-class Anglo-Irish children of his time (who may have been handed off to wet nurses but usually inhabited the same country as their parents and siblings), grew to maturity outside the auspices of anything remotely resembling a nuclear family. Notably underconditioned by the conventional taboos and priorities of bourgeois family life, Swift would later characterize his family members as "of all mortals what I despise and hate" (3).

In private conversations and correspondence, Swift situated his own nativity at an autophagous intersection between the corporeal and the economic. For instance, he often observed that he "came time enough to save his mother's credit" (Ehrenpreis 27). This remark reveals a striking and bitter awareness of his mother's dependence on his birth to validate her sexual conformity and hence to uphold her "credit," which puns on the way in which a new widow's presumed sexual continence can be translated into buying power. A symmetrical but opposing set of economic-corporeal images inheres in Swift's description of his parents' marriage, which was "very indiscreet," for his mother brought his father "little or no fortune," and his father died "before he could make a sufficient establishment for his family." "His son," Swift remarks "hath often been heard to say that he felt the consequences of that marriage not onley [*sic*] through the whole course of his education, but during the greatest part of his life" (28). Here again, Swift is linked to his parents through bonds in which the economic and the physical commingle in an exploitative manner. In this instance, Swift's parents are driven to rob their child of his birthright by "indiscreet" impulses in which the sex drive and the drive to maintain class position converge. The hungry, impulsive "indiscretion" to which Swift attributes his parents' coupling partakes of economic as well as sexual motives, as it was economics, not eroticism, that drew English settlers to Ireland in the first place. Moreover, the need to establish himself within the Anglo-Irish community may have pushed Jonathan Swift Sr., who upon his arrival in Dublin rapidly wed a native-born Anglo-Irish woman while waiting to be called to the bar, to prioritize marriage ahead of economic security (27).

Swift's representations of his own vulnerability relative to his parents' powers of sexual reproduction and their simultaneously engulfing economic lack recur, magnified, in "A Modest Proposal," as a national system that eats children. If in *Gulliver's Travels* the relationship between imperialism and the gendered body is explored indirectly through an emphasis on bodily grotesquerie,[7] in "A Modest Proposal" Swift foregrounds the relationship between English imperialism and an all-consuming system of sexual reproduction. In this essay, Swift's representations of children as consumable commodities produced to buoy up a flagging colonial economy are, of course, inspired by his firsthand observations concerning the impact of English colonialism on the Irish.[8] But the satire's autophagous logic also reflects the international traffic in human flesh, English as well as Irish, that governed his parents' union and his subsequent birth. For instance, the essay's introductory frame links a sensational scene of colonial deprivation — an explicit depiction of Irish beggars in the streets — with another undefined stratum of human misery that resembles Swift's own life experience. Swift's opening paragraphs employ the spectacular image of Irish mothers forced into beggary. In the third paragraph, however, Swift's "lethally rational economist" (Deane, *Short History* 41) extends his proposal to encompass an unspecified class of parents who are, as were Swift's, as ill-prepared to support their children as the native Irish (203).

Swift was and understood himself to be the product of economic forces that inexorably pushed the disenfranchised offspring of the English middle class to the colonial periphery. His bitter resentment of his parents' Irish marriage, his own Irish birth, and the imperial economic and cultural forces that mandated it gave rise in his writing to a particularized, high-voltage revulsion toward familial relations, which are figured, above all, as nauseating in their physicality. Swift's familiar grotesque renditions of bodies and of all functions relating to reproduction and nurture are carried to their outermost extremes in "A Modest Proposal," in which parental relations to children are conflated with the rearing of animals for slaughter, so that each act of nurturance is reframed as an act of exploitation.[9] The underlying contempt for his own parents—and the colonial system that exploited them—which fuels this bleak parodic vision is registered in the insouciance with which his economist adds to the pile of colonialism's casualties an Anglo-Irish underclass "in effect as little able to support [their children], as those who demand our charity in the streets" (208).

Swift's satirical proposal advocating the breeding and rearing of children for profit thus covertly inscribes a critique of settler colonialism's exploitation of Anglo-Irish children—even while bleakly literalizing colonialism's impact on the children of the native Irish. Anglo-Irish and native Irish children are obliquely compared throughout the essay. Indeed, even the essay's most overtly sectarian passage suggests indirect parallels: Swift's narrator assures his readers that his proposal "would greatly lessen the number of Papists, with whom we are yearly over-run, being the principal breeders of the nation, as well as our most dangerous enemies" (213). The death of Catholic children, in this dystopian passage, serves the same political purpose as does the birth of Protestant children—to equalize bitterly opposed political constituencies.[10]

The economist goes on to argue that by turning children into commodities, "the poorer tenants will have something valuable of their own, which by law may be made liable to distress, and help to pay their landlord's rent, their corn and cattle being already seized, and *money a thing unknown*" (213; Swift's emphasis). This passage brilliantly enacts the double-binding effect of commodification, which seems, in assigning market value to a thing already possessed (land, labor, time, bodies, health, relationships, emotions, values), to extend subjects' resources—offering to provide the economically disenfranchised with "something valuable of their own"—only to render previously inappropriable resources newly liable to seizure.

English and Anglo-Irish children were, as Swift's own childhood attests, already bound up within a capitalist economy that required the formation of nuclear families to secure subjects' sexual/economic "credit," and simultaneously commodified within a larger colonial economy in which settler colonial populousness secured England's political and economic interests overseas. Native Irish children, on the other hand, born predominantly outside a wage economy (with "*money a thing unknown*"), had yet to be transformed into civil subjects confirmed through marriage and childbirth as viable economic units within a heterosexist cash economy.

The calculation by Swift's economist of the savings per annum to be gained by the nation through the mass sacrifice of "an hundred thousand children, from two years old, and upwards" (213) draws its inspiration most directly from shifting contemporary attitudes toward disenfranchised children in England. As Linda Colley has observed of England during this period, the quest to "compete in terms of cannon fodder" was increasing "along with the scale of European warfare" (240). In response to the pressures of rampant militarism and burgeoning industrialism, a new patriotic rhetoric "encouraging women to breed, urging the benefits of maternal breast-feeding over wet-nursing, [and advocating] rescuing foundlings and orphans" (240) constituted children as a new form of public property. Social theories representing the lives and bodies of children as a legitimate means to advance the political and economic ends of their betters gave rise to the orphanage system that Blake would memorably indict in *Songs of Innocence and Experience* as England's own "modest proposal" for the conversion of child flesh into political and economic capital. Most significantly, Swift's economist enthuses that his proposal will be

a great inducement to marriage, which all wise nations have either encouraged by rewards, or enforced by laws and penalties. It would increase the care and tenderness of mothers toward their children, when they were sure of a settlement for life, to the poor babes, provided in some sort by the public to their annual profit instead of expense. We should see an honest emulation among the married women, which of them could bring the fattest child to the market, men would become as fond of their wives, during the time of their pregnancy, as they are now of their mares in foal, their cows in calf, or sows when they are ready to farrow, nor offer to beat or kick them (as it is too frequent a practice) for fear of a miscarriage. (Swift, "Modest Proposal" 214)

This passage reenacts the institutionalization of heterosexual marriage in England and Ireland through a system of severe social and juridical punishments and more dubious rewards, as well as the commodification and increased affective focus on children that ensued from it. The parodic image of maternal competitors vying to bring the fattest child to market prefigures the maternal pressures that nation-states would learn to mobilize to enlist young men during times of war. Conversely, Swift's narrator's rapt vision of increasingly solicitous fathers within a newly cohesive, economically mandated family unit corresponds to (and parodies) the sentimental rhetoric of bourgeois paternity that replaced (and supplied an alibi for) flagrant wife and child abuse.

The essay's culminating image occurs in the narrator's assurance that *here* at last is a domestic industry "whereby we can incur no danger in disobliging England" (215–16)—a pointed allusion to England's suppression of Irish industries—because the children's carcasses could not be exported, "the flesh being of too tender a consistence to admit a long continuance in salt" (216). The horrific imagery that this passage evokes, of children's carcasses salted and nailed into barrels for export (a contingency hampered neither by law nor economics but only by the regrettable fragility of child-flesh), is revealed to be less abominable than the reality of "a country . . . which would be glad to eat up our whole nation" (216). It is significant that this essay, which opens on a scene of Irish immiseration but hints at a penumbra of English dispossession and misery that surrounds and fuels the system of Irish colonialism, closes with an appallingly concise image that literalizes colonial expropriation—dead children's bodies being shipped away—and the even more horrific revelation that the English are devouring the Irish without any such implicating traffic ever leaving the dock. This image also, of course, points to the importation and exportation of bodies—a covert traffic in which Swift himself was bound up throughout his life, through his father's emigration to Ireland, his mother's departure to England, his own relocation to England, and his subsequent forcible resettlement in Ireland—as a "guilty secret" that is crucially implicated in the ongoing, correlated production of power and death in Ireland.

The essay's outrage concerning levels of exploitation that make the slaughter and consumption of children humane by comparison, imposed by an unnamed country "which would be glad to eat up our whole nation without [salt]" (216), derives much of its heat from Swift's own former position as a child reared within the Irish settler colonial order. Swift's fury at the exploitation of Anglo-Irish children, who retroactively legitimize the colonizing presence by reflecting back to their parents their own sense of natural ownership and belonging, is expressed in an image pattern that would become conventional in Anglo-Irish literature. In this pattern, children are figured as expendable commodities through which the British state may both extend its agency and legitimate its position. As in much of later Anglo-Irish gothicism, the native Irish child in "A Modest Proposal" embodies both the abject status of the colonized Irish and also the guilty secrets of colonial domination.

In Swift's satire, the human is transformed into an object that, purified through the process of commodification, may be consumed acceptably as food. This cannibalistic logic reenacts Maggie Kilgour's account of the rise of individualism in seventeenth-century England. Kilgour points out that during this period, "terms previously held in a more flexible relation to each other became consolidated as binary oppositions" (*Communion* 167). This tightening of the symbolic order allowed for the emergence of "the individual, a unified and coherent being defined by and against others: . . . women, social and religious deviants, cannibals—whose very existence threatens the unity of the individual" (4). The menace that individualism poses to itself through the creation of fragmentary Others against which the individual is defined is endlessly defended against, according to Kilgour, via a cannibalistic/capitalist epistemology within which "what is different . . . must be appropriated and consumed" (167). This epistemology itself, however, poses an ongoing threat, because the "apparent firmness of [the] opposition" on which it is based is deceptive. "The idea of incorporation depends upon and enforces an absolute division between inside and outside; but in the act [of consumption] itself that opposition disappears" (4).

As "A Modest Proposal" illustrates, the constitution of the native Irish as incoherent Others against which a settler colony's autonomous subjects may be defined was an especially precarious project during a period when a clear opposition between colonial objects and subjects had yet to be established. The unstable and volatile conjuncture out of which "A Modest Proposal" emerged greatly exacerbated the dangers that Kilgour identifies as operative in seventeenth-century England. In the settler colony, which exists at the periphery of the symbolic economy Kilgour describes, this cannibalistic economy appears shockingly literal, and its potential reversibility poses a literal threat. In entering a colonial economy, settlers more or less voluntarily risk their own deaths (which are frequently metaphorized in terms of consumption by cannibals). By extending the colonial order they have helped to establish into the future through procreation, however, they also impose the risks inherent in appropriating the land and resources of others onto their children. Moreover, the "delicate balance of simultaneous identification and separation" through acts of incorporation by which groups or individuals maintain their coherent identity within the modern, individualist economy can, in such a setting, easily go awry. Raised, as Elizabeth Bowen puts it, "under the strong rule of the family myth," the Anglo-Irish child is responsible for upholding an irrational belief in the legitimacy of the family's claim to land and power in Ireland (*Bowen's Court* 18). It is through the maintenance of this myth that ancestral guilt is held in abeyance; through their belief, in effect, children symbolically protect their parents from responsibility for an unpayable debt. Saddled with the responsibility of endlessly rationalizing the ongoing consumption of native Irish resources, Anglo-Irish children are ensnared within a symbolic order in which the Other could, all too easily, "go down the wrong way" and be consumed not as a tasty, commodified morsel but as that prerequisite but occluded by-product of the British imperial economy: the rotting corpse.

The Social Contract as Devil's Compact
Edmund Burke and the Gothic Family Romance

Edmund Burke was born in 1729, the year that Swift wrote "A Modest Proposal," into a heterogenous and diffuse Anglo-Irish family alliance. Although his mother was an Irish Catholic from a venerable Old English family, his father, a lawyer, converted to Protestantism to circumvent the Penal Laws, thereby casting the family's lot with the diverse political and sectarian constituencies that would, toward the end of Burke's lifetime, consolidate into the Protestant Ascendancy.[11] For Burke's family, as for the emerging Anglo-Irish as a whole, social and epistemological coherence was predicated on the repression of origins, a dynamic that Burke would later elaborate as a political philosophy.

Like Swift, Burke, a "second son" of a different sort, also conflated national and parental origins in his life and in his writing. In one striking incident he equated colonial origins with subordination to paternal domination when he introduced himself to an Indian expatriate as "a runaway son from a father, as you are" (Kramnick 54). Like Swift, Burke was separated from his parents for a substantial portion of his childhood. From the age of six to eleven, he lived with his maternal uncle's family in Ballyduff, where he attended a hedge school.[12] Conor Cruise O'Brien speculates that Burke's extended habitation with geographically distant relatives was intended discreetly to provide "the basics of a Catholic education" (20).

Born to a father who conformed religiously to evade sectarian laws, and ensnared in a perpetually vexed relationship to his Irish Catholic heritage, Burke was, like Swift, the product of Anglo-Irish colonial dynamics. But he radically differed from Swift in his family's relative economic security, his dual religious and cultural roots and identities, and his relatively intimate and charged relationship to his parents. For although he came of age amid a diffuse and extended family of affiliation, Burke's middle-class parents acted as a boundaried nucleus within a larger field of family relations. Within the close emotional quarters of his nuclearizing family, Burke exhibited what Isaac Kramnick has described as severe Oedipal anxieties owing to his father's explosive, controlling temperament. According to Kramnick, Burke's conflicted relationship to his father and, by extension, to superior males — a stance that was complicated by his probable bisexuality[13] — entrapped him in a simultaneously adulatory and rebellious relationship to male authority figures and the British state throughout his life.[14]

In Swift's writing, the sacrificial relationship between the imperial fathers and their colonial children — figured as monstrous generation in the service of a cannibalistic social order — is graphic and unadorned. Edmund Burke, the colonial product of a hybridized Irish Protestant middle class rather than the displaced offspring of an eroding English bourgeoisie, domesticated Swift's autophagous intergenerationality and instated it at the center of his political theory. As with Swift, children constitute crucial political capital in Burke's figurative intergenerational compacts, on which I focus in this section. In Burke's writing, however, an obsessive focus on institutions largely occludes the children whose labor and loyalty are at stake. Typically, Burke's representations of the stable, dignified institutional transmission of political loyalty, constitutional values, national identity, property, and privilege invoke pre-Oedipal longings for fulfillment through passive subordination to powers beyond the self. Periodically, however, this representational pattern oscillates, exposing a devil's bargain lurking beneath the surface of Burke's seductive rhetoric.

Central to Burke's political philosophy, as Terry Eagleton has pointed out, is a preoccupation with the key political problem that plagued the social stratum in which he came of age: the construction of political legitimacy through the passing on, over time, of a confirming narrative anchored securely in the past (*Heathcliff* 42). Burke's mature political philosophy is obsessively concerned with the need to make political bonds flesh, to forge "obligations written in the heart" (36). Fundamental to this central Burkean project of transmitting values and loyalties inextricably wed to sentiment are, unquestionably, the heterosexual dyad and the nuclear family. Burke was, however, a highly ambivalent inductee into the social forms that resided at the center of his political philosophy. Although he tacitly relied on them to accomplish the functions that were central to his political thought — the preservation of property, bloodlines, and traditional values — he repeatedly evinced personal suspicion of romance and marriage.

Burke's first published work, *A Vindication of Natural Society* (1756), reflects his ambivalent position relative to the British state.[15] In *A Vindication,* Burke allowed himself the liberty to write publicly only at the expense of disguising his identity, in order to articulate ideas he purportedly disbelieved. Two dominant, opposed drives seem to animate *A Vindication:* fear, which led the young Burke to disguise his identity and distort his ideas, and assertiveness, which compelled Burke, even though ambivalent, to speak rather than stay silent. These central motivations affirm Kramnick's rendition of Burke as a fearful "runaway son," sporadically renegotiating his own beliefs to win the protection and love of aristocratic father substitutes. They also reenact the structuring schema that Tom Furniss discovers at the heart of Burke's "sublime experience": "an escape from [a] fatal stasis" provoked by overwhelming fear, "through strenuous [affirmative] action" (25). Within Furniss's model, this ambivalence reflects Burke's middle-class position and the contradictory imperatives of a waning system of aristocratic patronage (calling for an attitude of passive obeisance), together with an as yet uncertain market economy that promised to reward vitality and initiative.[16]

Although Burke distanced himself from the ideas expressed in *A Vindication* from the outset (he first published it under the name of the late Lord Bolingbroke and included a preface in the second edition disclosing the book's "ironic intent" [Kramnick 89]), the essay nonetheless works out a founding opposition between the family and society that continued to structure Burke's thought throughout his career. In this purported send-up of free thinking, the family—ultimately to become the legitimating template for all social relations in Burke's oeuvre—is schematically opposed to society so that it can be reincorporated into society on specific terms.

Burke's political philosophy is governed by the anxiety to obscure a national "primal scene": "those acts of forcible expropriation from which all of our current titles and estates descend" (Eagleton, *Heathcliff* 43). In this early work, however, Burke shields himself with irony in order to violate his subsequent prohibition against inquiries into origins, briefly unveiling the *axis mundi,* or core precept, through which the Burkean social contract would bind the family horizontally to the national order and vertically to posterity.

The patriarchal nuclear family was to become Burke's central, authorizing paradigm for a civil society secured through a shared reverence for inherited traditions. As Bolingbroke, Burke establishes a central, constitutive dichotomy between the "natural" nuclear family and its "unnatural" extension: society. Following the line of inquiry standard to social contract theorists, Burke's fictional freethinker returns to humans in "the state of nature" and finds that "the mutual desires of the sexes uniting their bodies and affections, and the children which are the results of these intercourses, introduced first the notion of society, and taught its conveniences" (1: 11). Numerous contemporary theorists have exposed the sleight of hand by which scientists and theoreticians may unwittingly project accustomed social forms onto the natural world, confirming, as here, heterosexuality and the nuclear family as God's and nature's ordained models.[17] This passage imaginatively severs communal bonds of "species being" through its retroactive imposition of the emergent nuclear family into human prehistory. Its isolated, primal family, which Burke terms "natural society," is opposed to "political society," a social formation made up of "the union of many families into one body politic" (11). It is through the conjuncture of the family to the body politic, Burke-as-Bolingbroke contends, "that we [come to] owe an implicit reverence to all the institutions of our ancestors" (11–12).

This passage, which significantly foreshadows the family's position in Burke's mature political philosophy, figuratively reenacts the work of industrial capitalism, pulling society apart into naturalized nuclear families and putting it back together as an Oedipal state formation in which the psychic relations of the nuclear family romance are written large. Burke thus inverts the process by which the emergence of the capitalist nation state re-formed human community in its own image—the patriarchal, hierarchical, isolated heterosexual family unit—by contending that society was formed in imitation of the (a priori) nuclear family.[18]

Having exorcised a spate of unbankable freethinking ideas that would continue to haunt his unpublished writings throughout his career, Burke emerged from a period of *Giovanni's Room*-like seclusion with his intimate companion Will Burke; married Jane Nugent, a Catholic woman; and established a new ménage composed of Jane, himself, and

Will (Kramnick 79). He lived with both Jane and Will throughout most of his remaining life. Burke's enviably inclusive domestic arrangements, his Irish origins, his family's crypto-Catholicism, Jane's Catholicism, and his own suppressed heterodoxy made him personally vulnerable to public criticism, ridicule, and political attack. The rhetorical patterns through which his conservative political philosophy was articulated reflect an acute awareness of this vulnerability, as well as the dominant discourse of the age, as Furniss would have it. Burke's ambivalent sexuality, for instance, ironically coexists with a penchant for spectacular binary representations of gender,[19] and his unconventional living arrangements, with his rhetorical preoccupation with the patriarchal family. In his philosophy, Burke identifies an Irish, Catholic, sexually ambivalent self with a suppressed, "natural" self that must be placed in protective (or securely private) custody.

This conviction gives rise to the fundamental Burkean paradox expressed in *Reflections on the Revolution in France:* in the name of liberty, "the inclinations of men should frequently be thwarted, their will controlled, and their passions brought into subjection." This exercising of systematic checks upon rebellious internal impulses "can only be done *by a power out of themselves,* and not, in the exercise of its function, subject to that will and to those passions which it is its office to bridle and subdue" (Burke's emphasis 2: 333). In a wry paraphrase of Burke's position on America, Terry Eagleton has crystallized Burke's characteristic promulgation of mitigated freedoms achieved through corporate submission to an externalized state apparatus: "What they ought to have done was to allow the colonies to associate the very idea of their own freedom with the sovereignty that holds them down" (*Heathcliff* 38). The characteristic shape of this paradoxical freedom achieved through submission, as Kramnick suggests, would have been conditioned by Burke's own subjectivity, which leveraged private space for an Irish, Catholic bisexual ménage through the strict maintenance of a British, Protestant, masculinist, and heterosexual public identity.

It is important to emphasize, however, that the relation between Burke's public and private personas was not, for him, contradictory or hypocritical. Rather, like many Anglo-Irish writers who succeeded him, Burke loved the exterior that secured his life's interior.[20] The complex interrelationship between Burke's public and private personas is demonstrated by his astonishing openness in connecting himself to the very national, religious, and sexual minorities that a "closeted" Irishman, Catholic, and homosexual would inevitably have shunned. His marriage appears (against a backdrop of poems, letters, and journal entries in which Burke laments the necessity of marriage and confesses his insensibility to women's charms) to have been a marriage of convenience, and yet he chose a Catholic wife and incorporated her father, a doctor who had seen him through a nervous breakdown, into their household. He took public stands against colonial oppression in India and Ireland, and he cherished his friendship with the eighteenth century's most celebrated romantic friends, the Ladies of Llangollen. Most extraordinary is Burke's passionate defense before the House of Commons of William Smith and Theodosius Reed, who were attacked by a mob and brutally pilloried for "sodomitical practices." One of the men was killed by officers of justice who, in Burke's words, "forced his head through the hole, [so that] the poor wretch hung rather than walked as the pillory turned around" when he (being short) "could not reach the hole made for the admission of the head" (cited in O'Donnell, Appendix, 1).

Burke's best-known articulation of the contract that results from the civic alienation of desire and the reaffixation of the libido to the state occurs in *Reflections on the Revolution in France* (1790). Burke frames his central argument for a historical compact between the living and the dead with a particularly flamboyant application of the conventions of "travel literature" (Deane, *Strange Country* 4), describing revolutionary France as a cannibalistic society in which children hack their father to pieces and then place him in "the kettle of magicians," hoping to "renovate [his] life" (Burke 1: 368). It is in the light of this allegorical scenario that Burke elaborates his most famous views on the conservative social contract:

Society is, indeed, a contract. Subordinate contracts for objects of mere occasional interest may be dissolved at pleasure; but the state ought not to be considered as nothing better than a partnership agreement in a trade of pepper and coffee, calico or tobacco, or some other such low concern, to be taken up for a little temporary interest, and to be dissolved by the fancy of the parties. (368)

The petty and easily rescindable contracts of mercantile exchange in colonial contexts, which operate in this passage as the crass, material Other against which Burke's sanitized, transcendental state is defined, reflect (by preemptively denying) the interpenetration of economics and governance at the heart of the imperialist state.

Shortly thereafter, Burke claims the dead, the living, and the unborn as coparticipants in the transhistorical social contract that he structurally opposes to the forces of capital: "As the ends of such a partnership cannot be obtained in many generations, it becomes a partnership not only between those who are living, but between those who are living, those who are dead, and those who are to be born" (368). The energies of the living to which Burke lays claim in this passage are, however, precisely those appropriated by the crass forces of capital in the (denied) processes of imperial state formation that propel unwilling bodies across oceans in pursuit of pepper and coffee, calico or tobacco, and a few other "low concerns" (slaves) too trivial to mention in such a lofty framework. This passage encloses subjectivity within an inescapable tautology, morally hemming it in with unspecified but absolute obligations to the dead and unborn and placing historical agency and responsibilities for law and custom where they will be safe: beyond the reach of the living.

Burke's ambivalence concerning the autophagous system that he championed, in which the agency of the living is, under threat of an apocalyptic and unsalvageable rupture, consumed by the dead, resurfaced poignantly in a published letter to his son, Richard (1793). In this famous, unfinished letter, Burke again lays out his convictions concerning the advantages of a social order based on inherited prescription. Within such a social order, children, in recognition of the efforts of their ancestors in accumulating property, titles, and rights on their behalf, return the favor through their absolute allegiance to this ancestral order. In the course of the letter, Burke insists that his son is the beneficiary of all his efforts. In describing the nature of intergenerational obligations, he intones, "All titles terminate in prescription; in which (differently from Time in the fabulous instances) the son devours the father, and the last prescription eats up the former" (McCormack, *From Burke* 45). In this passage, Burke invokes the figure of Time as a father devouring his children, only to dismiss it. This image resembles that of Swift's children nailed in barrels, which is also invoked only to be dismissed, except that here Burke seeks to exorcise (rather than make explicit) images of a diabolical compact that his references to inheritance appear to have conjured unbidden. Burke's rhetoric in this passage encodes a private moment of hesitation about the autophagous social contract he championed. In the letter, Burke insists that the imbrication of family and state through inheritance represents a sacrifice by parents on behalf of their children, rather than an autophagous social contract through which a society (via a traditional system of inherited wealth and power) devours its own offspring.

Richard Burke died of tuberculosis in the year following the letter's publication, just ten days after his election to Parliament. In the wake of his son's death, Burke drastically reconsidered his position on the obligations of children to their parents. In private letters, he grieved that out of his "desire to immortalize his own achievements" he had caused his son's premature death. Burke concluded that by burdening his son with responsibility for his disordered finances and requiring him to campaign, despite his delicate health, for a safe seat in a rotten borough, he had "thr[own] him away by every species of neglect, and mismanagement" (Kramnick 175). In his eulogy for his son, Burke reflects that parents "are but too apt to think more of what the children owe to them than what they owe to their children." In what amounts to an implicit recantation of his political life's work, he concedes sadly that parents "are made for their children, and not their children for them" (Kramnick 57).

Castle Rackrent
The Rise and Fall of the Big House Family

Like Swift and Burke, Maria Edgeworth, the leading Anglo-Irish writer of the early nineteenth century, grew to maturity against a shifting tableau of relatives and parent surrogates. Her childhood, spent in two countries in the care of various caretakers, represents, like Burke's, a sort of mediating form between the disembodied and purely juridical family romance of Swift's childhood and the Oedipal family cell that would, as Mary Jean Corbett argues, emerge in Anglo-Ireland in part through Edgeworth's own propagandistic deployment of Burke's familial and gender norms. The Cromwellian immigrants who produced Swift and Burke's "New Anglicized" Old English parents represent two significant strands within a permeable and diffuse settler colonial middle class prior to the invention of a more cohesive "Protestant Ascendancy" at the end of the eighteenth century (McCormack, *From Burke* 69). Edgeworth's family, however, represents a new phase in the life of the settler colony. Edgeworth and her father stand out as watershed figures in Anglo-Irish culture primarily owing to their dogged commitment to making Ireland the center of their creative and intellectual lives. This new dedication to Ireland on the part of an emergent Anglo-Irish intelligentsia gave rise to two firm commitments in Edgeworth's writing: to rationalize and Anglicize Ireland, and to invent within literature a plausible Irish identity and history for the Anglo-Irish.

Edgeworth was, in these fundamental aims, a product of her time and culture, as well as her class. During this period, stirred by Burkean notions of the sublime, Anglo-Irish antiquarianists were fictionally re-creating the Irish past in droves. While Edgeworth's oeuvre has frequently been set in opposition to the antiquarianist project, it is in certain respects simply a more successful version thereof. In antiquarianism, the ferocious, ongoing impulse that began with the Plantation of Ulster in the sixteenth century to remap, rename, and reconstitute Irish land and culture as a geographical and cultural extension of England spawned its own contradictions. Fascinated with an idealized Celtic past, which it invokes, in Eagleton's words, to symbolically "und[o] past crimes in the name of a politically refurbished present" (*Heathcliff* 180), antiquarianism is preoccupied with the lineage of ideas, cultural practices, and the transmission of property and typified by a detached, quasi-anthropological interest in extinct or dying cultural practices. In certain ways the counterpart of British and Continental gothicism, antiquarianism represents both a forerunner of cultural nationalism and the seedbed of Anglo-Irish gothicism. It is in Edgeworth's first novel, *Castle Rackrent* (1800), that antiquarianism's aspirations to, as Eagleton has it, create a livable present by rewriting the Irish past conjoin with an ironically realist sensibility to create an allegorical nation-as-family that has continued to shape gothic representation in Ireland through two intervening centuries.

Expressing overtly sentiments that many other critics endorse implicitly, Seamus Deane has chivalrously expressed his anxiety that Edgeworth be "rescued from the bondage of too close an association" with her most famous antiquarianist contemporary, Lady Morgan (*Short History* 93). As Deane's account in *A Short History of Irish Literature* makes clear, however, Edgeworth's novels emerged out of the same milieu as did the writings of Lady Morgan, and they reflect or respond to many of antiquarianism's guiding preoccupations. Moreover, Edgeworth's close epistolary friendship with the greatest of the Celtic antiquarians—Sir Walter Scott—and the remarkable structural parallels between her 1809 novel *Ennui* and Morgan's paradigmatic Anglo-Irish antiquarian romance, *The Wild Irish Girl* (1806), suggest covert affiliations between her rationalist antisentimentalism and the romanticism of her antiquarian counterparts. These affiliations and their generic and historical significance are especially evident in *Castle Rackrent.* Through its acerbic realist deformations of specific antiquarian conventions, Edgeworth's first novel pushes the antiquarian toward the gothic, establishing new and enduring conventions for Anglo-Irish writing in its depiction of the fall of a Big House family, a social unit that, from the standpoint of literary convention, has been plummeting ever since.

As Julian Moynahan has noted, in *Castle Rackrent* Edgeworth establishes "some features that will guide, if not absolutely determine, the development of Anglo-Irish writing after her" (39). These features were created through Edgeworth's introduction of previously suppressed aspects of Irish quotidian life into a conventional frame in a manner that bitingly undermines or reverses its import. Politically, Edgeworth's innovative mixing of modes has concomitantly mixed implications. Through an ironic introduction of "real life" (Gonda 212) into antiquarianism, Edgeworth paved the way for the emergence of a hegemonic, naturalized Anglo-Irish identity within Irish society. In so doing, however, she simultaneously established conventions that guided the development of the critical strand of Anglo-Irish writing that I call gothic realism.

Castle Rackrent's constitution of a present purged of past transgressions, its preoccupation with the intergenerational transmission of property, and its frame narrator's detached, philosophical interest in the manners and mores of times past are consistent with antiquarian conventions. Formally, however, the novel notably complicates antiquarianism's conventional framing of an ancient, unchanging Celtic culture with the words of an authenticating Anglo-Irish or English interlocutor. Instead, in rendering four generations of an Anglo-Irish family through the words of the family's Irish servant, Edgeworth reverses a central, constitutive aspect of antiquarian formal relations.

Edgeworth's use of irony, generated in her reversal of the antiquarian novel's conventional power relations, created the possibility of an Anglo-Irish strand of literary realism that was not only intimate and detailed but also allegorical. Thus Edgeworth's ostensible reversal of antiquarian subject/object relations is—as Teresa Michals suggests— far from straightforward in its ramifications. The novel's substitution of Anglo-Irish customs and life histories for native Irish customs and life histories, along with symmetrical substitution of an Irish informant of the working class for a bourgeois Anglo-Irish or English presenter, founded a lineage of critical representations of Big House families that recurs throughout the history of Anglo-Irish women's writing. We cannot, however, be satisfied with celebrating the novel's reversal of the conventional antiquarian reduction of the Irish to the raw material of "native informants." It is also important to acknowledge that in temporarily destabilizing reified Irish/Anglo-Irish identities, Edgeworth performed a valuable ideological service on behalf of the consolidating Anglo-Irish Ascendancy. In situating the Anglo-Irish in the narrative position conventionally held by the native Irish, Edgeworth supplies a primal Anglo-Irish family as the atavistic forerunners of the contemporary Protestant Ascendancy, a group that was in the process of reimagining itself during this period. By appropriating the native's historically rooted status for the Anglo-Irish, this displacement furthers the ends of settler colonialism by, in effect, narratively reenacting the dispossession of the native Irish.

This textual insertion of the Anglo-Irish in place of the Celt is particularly notable in the novel's substitution of the Anglo-Irish Big

House in place of the conventional antiquarian round tower or romantic ruin. In *England's Ruins: Poetic Purpose and the National Landscape,*
Anne Janowitz argues that images of ruins and castles in eighteenth-
century British literature offer access to but simultaneously enact a
breach with the past. In *Castle Rackrent,* the Big House stands, as Ian
Watt observes of the castle in *The Castle of Otranto,* as "a symbol of the
continuing life of its founder" ("Time" 163), but through its family's
moral discreditation and economic decline, it also establishes an absolute, purifying breach with the past. The novel's Burkean incorporation
of architecture and familial intergenerationality as symbols of political
and cultural continuity suggests that Edgeworth was already experi-
menting with Burke's trope of the patriarchal family as a figurative and
literal resolution to social disarray, a trope that, as Corbett has shown,
Edgeworth fully embraced in *The Absentee.* Like Burke, however, the
young Edgeworth found herself obliged to perform a sort of writerly
exorcism in preparation for her later work shoring up the Anglo-Irish
social order. And like Burke, who masqueraded as Bolingbroke to pub-
lish his first work of political philosophy, Edgeworth performed this
early exorcism through the mouth of an alter ego of a different class and
group: the Rackrent's servant, Thady Quirk.

In *Castle Rackrent,* Edgeworth takes as her central, Burkean tropes
the family and an ancient house as figures for an ironic national/political
allegory. Like Burke, she effaces the central issues of children and procreation, depicting the Anglo-Irish family as a self-regenerating (and
indeed a self-generating) institution. In other ways, however, Edgeworth represents familial generationality as a process of attrition rather
than accumulation. The Rackrent family system *does,* like "Time in the
fabulous instances," consume its offspring via a process of intergenerational corrosion.

Edgeworth's misgivings concerning the family as a vehicle for social
stability may have exceeded Burke's own because Burke was generally able to suppress the guilty and lawless provenance of the traditions and aristocracy he venerated through tropes of continuity that
acceded an air of changeless immortality to the English state.[21] Edgeworth, however, required a decisive means of distancing the fledg-
ling Anglo-Irish hegemony from its less historically effaceable origins.

While her later novels, particularly *Ennui,* representationally blur past and present through depictions of a hybrid aristocracy of the Irish spirit that the Anglo-Irish (paradoxically) embody, in *Castle Rackrent* Edgeworth found it necessary to establish a radical temporal breach between the Anglo-Irish present and past.

The novel situates the Rackrent family in a remote Irish past in part through the early narrative slippage by which the O'Shaughlins—"related to the Kings of Ireland" (8–9)—are bloodlessly transposed "by Act of Parliament" into Rackrents (9). Thady's impenetrable account of this transposition, which takes place through a complex structure of inheritance between "cousins-german," depicts the Rackrents as only nominally displacing an earlier, native Irish line from which the family continues to derive its legitimacy.

Similarly, the rupture that divides past and present in *Castle Rackrent* collapses two historical moments—one past, one future—into one absolute symbolic, temporal division. Like other critics, Seamus Deane has found historical significance in the narrative's setting "in the years before . . . parliamentary independence in 1782" (*Short History* 92). If the text's constitutive temporal divide is 1782, however, Edgeworth's narrator superimposes the anticipated Act of Union on that founding cleavage, situating it as both a reaffirmation and a fulfillment of the original aims of independence.

This doubly reinforced rupture is both emphatic and simultaneously unstable, blurring the very temporal boundaries it seeks to reinforce. In the novel's preface, the anonymous narrator assures the reader that its characters typify "a certain class of the gentry of Ireland some years ago" and that "the race of Rackrents has long since been extinct in Ireland" (4). But in the preface's final paragraph, the narrator unexpectedly makes recourse to the Act of Union to once again, this time anticipatorily, relegate these characters to the Irish past. This parting gesture betrays considerable uneasiness concerning the status of the bodies over which the narrator has so insistently pronounced last rites: "When Ireland loses her identity by an union with Great Britain, she will look back with a smile of good-humoured complacency on the Sir Kits and Sir Condy's of her former existence" (5). This novel's preface thus enacts a burial, positing the ensuing narrative as a sort of graveside eulogy. But this burial may, according to the narrator's own hedging logic, be premature. The preface's final paragraph, moreover, makes Irish *identity* synonymous with the eighteenth-century Anglo-Irish family of alliance that the novel depicts; it foresees the Act of Union as ensuring the final, irreversible eradication of that identity. In this schema, the eradication of Irish cultural identity through military conquest and subsequent dispossession at the hands of the English and Anglo-Irish is figuratively reversed: it is the Anglo-Irish, rather than the Irish, who are effaced through a process of English acculturation, and it is through the (happy) eradication of Anglo-Irish identity that Ireland is freed of the burden of a disagreeable past.

This strategy of consigning the Rackrents firmly (and repeatedly) to an archaic past frees Edgeworth to embellish the family as a bleak, extended metaphor for Irish politics and economics while disclaiming her allegory's contemporary significance. The impenetrable mysteries of the ever shifting but never changing Rackrent line, which, like money within capitalism, seems to multiply without propagating, stand opposed to the immutable but continually evolving Thady. The body of the *Castle Rackrent* narrative opens with Thady's description of his own symbolic transformation over the years from *"honest Thady"* to *"old Thady"* to *"poor Thady,"* a transformation that parallels the Rackrent family's descent from the legally and contractually obsessed Sir Murtagh — the first Rackrent to preside within Thady's own memory — to the family's established position as an "old" Anglo-Irish family, which Murtagh's inheritor, Sir Kit, manipulates to seduce the daughters of the local gentry (while his wife is safely locked away in an upper room), to the family's poverty and ultimate ruin shortly before the death of Sir Condy. Thady thus reflects the family's status in a manner that befits his elaborate expressions of loyalty: "As I have lived, so will I die, true and loyal to the family" (8).

Yet Thady also invokes, through his loving description of his mantle — a piece of clothing that culturally distinguishes him from Jason, his gentlemanly, assimilated son — the image of the seventeenth-century Irish woodkern. Whereas the novel veils the Rackrents' origins in the mists of Irish history and the ineffable machinations of Parliament, native Irish origins are put on display through the figure of Thady and his cultural affiliations to a recent Irish past. The emergence of an Irish middle class that was estranged, like Edmund Burke's father, from its own social origins is recalled in Thady's remark that "to look at me, you would hardly think 'poor Thady' was the father of attorney Quirk" (8).

The novel's ironic interpolations of the woeful financial state of some Anglo-Irish families with the shabby state of the descendants of the ancient Celt figure the shadowy symmetrical losses imposed by colonial relations. The founding loss of dignity and agency that accompanies the colonizer's participation within a colonial society manifests in the novel's opening pages in the seizure of Sir Patrick's corpse as collateral for his unpaid debts. This event in the posthumous biography of a rack-renting landlord introduces a pattern of decreation that resembles patterns of autophagy I have explored throughout this chapter. In response to the seizure of his predecessor's corpse, Sir Murtagh first suppresses a threatened "rescue" of the corpse by the mob, then self-righteously withholds payment from Patrick's creditors, in effect laying claim to previously committed funds through the symbolic manipulation of his progenitor's death (11–12). The seizure of Sir Patrick's corpse, along with exploitation by the incoming Rackrent heir to justify retaining as much inherited capital as possible, depicts the family as an inert system that reproduces itself and consolidates its wealth through death.

This theme of familial antiproduction recurs throughout the novel, in which contractualized marriages and a rigidly politicized marital economy blight sexual and affectional relations between husbands and wives from the outset, and children never ensue. *Castle Rackrent* pursues a narrative logic that effaces coupling and procreation in a manner that emphasizes the Rackrent family's progressive economic and social dissolution. Wives are largely invisible, seen as economic or legal ciphers rather than personalities, and when they "add" to the family, they do so through the extraction of surplus value from the tenantry and direct infusions of capital, rather than childbirth. Sir Murtagh's wife engorges the family's coffers with her skillful rack-renting techniques, while Sir Kit marries a Jewish woman in Bath when his overseer cannot squeeze any additional revenues from his tenants, confining her in the house's upper recesses for seven years in an attempt to force her to give him her jewels. Not one of the four generations of Rackrent heirs reproduce, and none, apart from Sir Condy (seen retrospectively as a child in sketchy descriptions by Thady) appear as children. Rackrent heirs spring full-grown from distant family "lines" in the novel, autonomous and devoid of bodily origins, as the family itself appears to have been called into being through a magical act of parliamentary naming.

The final emptying out of the Rackrent family is foreshadowed in Edgeworth's representations of the empty house, abandoned after Sir Condy goes to take his place in Dublin as a member of parliament (61). This evocation of the empty Big House in the process of being reclaimed by nature, with its doors ajar, its windows broken, and rain pouring in through the roof, is familiar to us from Yeats's oeuvre, and it also prefigures the image of the Big House in flames that recurs in twentieth-century fiction. As in Yeats's play *Purgatory,* Edgeworth's image of an evacuated manor house sets the scene for a culminating devil's bargain that concludes a series of sexual and political compromises.

Although considerable attention has been given to marital closure as an allegory for imperial relations in eighteenth- and nineteenth-century British novels, less attention has been given to the devil's com-pact, a second category of symbolic social contract that recurs through-out the early nineteenth century as the gothic, colonial counterpart to the imperial marital contract. In *Castle Rackrent,* a series of promises or vows made by Sir Condy binds him to actions he consciously de-plores, beginning with the fateful flip of a coin with which he decides between Judy McQuirk, his native Irish lover, and Isabella Moneygawl, an Anglo-Irish heiress who is demanding that he elope with her to Scot-land. The coin toss reflects an internal struggle between love and pride: Isabella's father has locked her up and ordered her to forget Sir Condy, thus affronting Condy's class pride. Condy's gamble resolves in favor of Isabella, much to his dismay, thereby rendering Sir Condy the victim of his own, self-imposed contract. During Condy's brief parliamentary career, his hopes are again dashed when "against his conscience [he] very honorably" supports the government in return for "a place that was promised him," on which the government reneges (61).

In these secular "devil's bargains" Sir Condy's worse angels over-whelm his better ones in expectations of venal gratifications that in any case fail to materialize. The pattern whereby Sir Condy's inner drives take on an external life, returning to act on him as alien and hostile forces, is quintessentially gothic. In *Castle Rackrent,* the specific "bargains" that delineate Condy's fall are of two particular types that were to become recurring tropes of Anglo-Irish gothic realism; one involves his sexuality, and the other, his political conscience. Condy's status as a man no longer under his own control—as, in effect, a man already dead —is figured most eloquently in Thady's own comparison of Condy, "head and shoulders in debt" but like many of his class "liv[ing] the fast and the better for [being ruined]," to "the ducks in the kitchen yard just after their heads are cut off by the cook, running round and round faster than when alive" (58). In Sir Condy's marriage and his career as a Dublin MP, he acts against his libido and his conscience at the behest of the social order that, in effect, owns him, insofar as his position within it authorizes him to spend long after his resources are gone.

Condy's self-inflicted marriage to Isabella allegorizes both the fundamental dilemma of the colonizer, entrapped within an unbreachable contract of his own making, and the colonial system of mandatory heterosexuality which Swift depicts as devouring and which Burke describes as the cleansing means by which state authority's illicit origins must be legitimated. Through his marriage to Isabella, whose prodigious spending is connected to her loveless marriage (she spends to assuage her loneliness, and Condy lets her spend to appease his guilt), Condy is ultimately forced to seek an annual income. Given his privileged class and ethnicity, coupled with his lack of wits or marketable skills, his sole career option, as Edgeworth humorously suggests, is as an MP. Thus Condy's marriage forces him directly into the service of the colonial government, which exploits the copious indebtedness that his privileged position permits by bribing him to vote for policies that violate his conscience, then betraying him by withholding payment for these "services."

This pattern finds its completion in the "devil's bargain" whereby Thady's son, Jason, strips the debt-ridden, alcoholic Sir Condy of his house and lands. Jason, the novel's only (and mysteriously motherless) child, represents a recurrence of Anglo-Irish anxieties concerning Irish reproduction. Thady's line thus ultimately "wins" the colonial war of reproduction. The narrative pattern his victory initiates, whereby a native Irish tenant or employee exploits the moral weaknesses of a Big House heir to regain possession of the land of which his or her ancestors were dispossessed, recurs in later texts that I will discuss in the course of this book. In this case, Jason's dispossession of Sir Condy enacts the completion of a devil's bargain. The Rackrents, a conceptual invention of Parliament, have lived on the backs of their peasants and the fat of the land far beyond the peasants' and land's ability to produce. They have continually renegotiated marital contracts, inheritances, rents, and their status relative to the government in order to prolong the state of living death in which they have subsisted from the start. As Jason tells Condy when confronting him with the painful and long-denied reality of his indebtedness, "The balance has been running on too long" (74). The social and material splendors with which the Rackrents have been surrounded evaporate as in a fairy tale, and Sir Condy, the most sympathetic Rackrent and the only one who appears to have had a childhood, is consumed by the autophagous system he has inherited. Having looked forward throughout his life to a grand funeral, Condy dies, unmourned by anyone but Thady.

By deforming antiquarian conventions through the introduction of ironic elements carefully chosen for their disruptive, disturbing energies, Edgeworth draws together some of the fantastic and grotesque allegorical elements of Swift, the socially normative metaphoricity of Burke, and aspects of literary realism. The result is a strand of gothic realism that derives its vitality from native Irish customs and oral traditions, political and historical allegory, and the affective life of the Anglo-Irish family as it responded to internal and external pressures within the Anglo-Irish family romance.

Reproduction and the Politics of Colonial Domination

In the settler colony, reproduction becomes, in effect, warfare by other means. In seventeenth-century Dublin, for instance, Protestant commonsense associations of fecundity and visibility with political power gave rise to acute waves of anxiety concerning Catholic numbers and visibility. In the section of his 1981 book, *Dublin,* entitled "Dissent,

Rebellion, and the Commonwealth: 1603–1662," Somerville-Large describes in considerable detail the various relations that existed in Dublin between Protestants, Catholics, and Quakers, who were also persecuted during his period. Throughout this period, as various episodes of anti-Catholicism that Somerville-Large recounts make clear, there was a dialectical interrelationship between institutional anti-Catholicism and the vigilance of Protestant immigrants concerning Catholic visibility, volubility, and numbers. Significantly, the chapter ends with a nonsectarian atrocity, an episode in 1659 in which Dublin's colonial authorities ordered beadles and constables "to imprison all beggars, idle women and maidens sellinge apples and oranges, and all regraters, all idle boys . . . others trafficked in eggs, hens and various commodities', who were then enclosed in a large cage in the Cornmarket for examination and punishment—in many cases deportation to the West Indian plantations" (132). Such acts of mass repression must have helped to institutionalize virulent anti-Catholic prejudice among the Anglo-Irish, who would have learned from such shockingly cruel events to forge safety for themselves via bonds of institutional identification with the capricious powers that oversaw colonial life through increasingly ritualized and fervent expressions of Protestant Loyalism and anti-Catholicism.

An intensive focus on demographics during this period reflects the interests of a nascent settler colonial order dependent on the production of children to camouflage itself as a natural and undifferentiated feature of the Irish landscape. Within such a system, especially in its earliest phases, when alliances and hence cultural identities are at their most unstable, settler children, on whom their elders rely for their own psychological and material security, need to learn things without being told and without asking. Under such circumstances children must learn, and learn profoundly, not to question, not to seek coherence. Such children are, therefore, epistemically disempowered in a fashion that parallels but also exceeds the fundamental ways in which all children are disempowered within the patriarchal nuclear family.

Within a Manichean colonial system, children of the colonizer represent passive extensions of the life of the settler colony and English capital, while children of the colonized represent extensions of the system of social death. In these texts, however, a blurring of Irish and Anglo-

Irish identity occurs. In Swift's representations of an economy that eats children, Burke's representation of a transgenerational contract that maintains order and transmits property through the invisible reproduction of children, and Edgeworth's depictions of a Big House family that intergenerationally devours itself, the colonizer and the colonized are, ironically, figured in identical or reversible terms. In the chapters that follow, these parallels continue to play out. Irish and Anglo-Irish identities in various ways symptomatically blur and collapse, so that both Irish and Anglo-Irish children are depicted as appropriated, unconscious bodies spoken by a demonic god of colonial history that, over time, consumes colonizer and colonized alike.

Chapter 4

"A Very Strange Agony"

Parables of Sexual Subject Formation in

Melmoth the Wanderer, Carmilla, and *Dracula*

For it was ever, as it is now, the singular destiny of Ireland to nourish within her own bosom her bitterest enemies, who, with a species of political vampyrism destroyed that source from whence their nutriment flowed.
— Lady Morgan, *Patriotic Sketches of Ireland*

A hybrid mixture of Anglo-Irish antiquarianism and English anti-Catholic gothicism, the nineteenth-century Anglo-Irish paranoid gothic supplies my paradigmatic gothic family romance. As I argued in the introduction, the function of the gothic family romance is to reincorporate denied feelings, perceptions, and experiences within a story that simultaneously rationalizes them and categorically denies their relationship to the family. The logic of the "classic" family romance identified by Freud runs, The duke *must* be my father because he is rich, handsome, and powerful. The logic of the gothic family romance runs in the opposite direction: The man that enters my sister's bedroom at night *cannot* be my father, because that man is Transylvanian, homosexual, and a vampire." Read as an exercise in self-protective projection, the nineteenth-century Anglo-Irish gothic is decipherable as much through its denials as through its assertions.

As a narrative means by which disavowed affect and perceptions concerning Anglo-Irish family life may be "told" without *telling*, the paranoid gothic incorporates and simultaneously disclaims the autophagous dynamics of settler colonial reproduction that are so clearly

connected to English colonialism in "A Modest Proposal," to governance and inheritance in Burke, and to the Anglo-Irish family in *Castle
Rackrent*. Because the conventions of the gothic are accepted as fantasy,
however, details of subject formation within the Anglo-Irish family can
be expressed within this generic vocabulary more explicitly than they
could have been in earlier Anglo-Irish writing.

Throughout the nineteenth century, in response to "the progressive decline of ascendancy hegemony" (Lloyd 133), representations of
the contradictory position of the Anglo-Irish family became increasingly dissociated from Anglo-Irish consensus reality and the conscious
minds of individual writers. Conventions that had once overtly satirized the Anglo-Irish position became charged with unconscious meaning as the position of the Anglo-Irish grew increasingly tenuous and
(hence) unspeakable.[1] Whereas in 1807 Lady Morgan was overtly figuring British governance in Ireland as "a species of political vampyrism"
committed by England against Irish and Anglo-Irish alike, by 1820
Charles Maturin's *Melmoth the Wanderer* was situating vampirism, cannibalism, and parasitism nearly everywhere *but* Ireland and projecting
blame for the resulting carnage onto the Catholic Church.

Crucially at issue in *Melmoth the Wanderer,* "Carmilla," and *Dracula,*
the best-known works of Anglo-Irish gothic literature, are themes already familiar from eighteenth-century Anglo-Irish literature, where
they appeared as overtly political metaphors: sterile or self-consuming
systems, devil's bargains, and the sacrifice of children. In the nineteenth
century, however, a rupture opened between the Anglo-Irish conception of political and social reality and the increasingly fantastic world of
Anglo-Irish gothic literature. As I hope is already apparent, however, I
contend that it was not the *literature* which became more out of touch
with reality. In fact, the Anglo-Irish gothic grew increasingly explicit in
its depiction of Anglo-Irish subject formation. This is particularly true
of the ways these texts depict patterns of exploitation and abuse within
families—arguably inevitable in an economy that predicates profit on
the isolation of the family and on the manipulation of children—as
organizing channels of affective and subjective "production" throughout a larger society and across time.

In these narratives, a mysterious entity associated with the primal scene of colonial appropriation invisibly shapes the lives of gothic protagonists. Typically this force remains latent until protagonists reach sexual maturity, at which point it strikes from without, as an alien yet uncannily familiar presence that takes up residence within literal or symbolic families. In these texts, the onset of sexual maturity precipitates an escalating series of diabolical assaults. David Punter reads the impending marriage that coincides with the onset of Dracula's machinations as emphasizing the cohesive nature of the bourgeois family, "seen around the moment of maximum bonding, on the eve of marriage" (2:18). That the onset of persecution coincides with the attainment of maturity across all these texts, however, suggests less a bourgeois opposition between the security of nuclear families and the isolation of vampires than an unconscious commentary on sexual maturation among the Anglo-Irish. A wide array of coming-of-age narratives in *Melmoth* (especially those of John Melmoth the younger, Monçada, and Isidora); Carmilla's first ball, where she is seduced into a new life as a vampire; Jonathan Harker's new marriage; and Lucy Westenra's impending marriage — all herald the onset of supernatural assaults.

In each text, moreover, such assaults precipitate competition among representatives of an array of institutions (such as priests, psychiatrists, and doctors) to account for behavior or beliefs that are, by the norms of the social order, uncanny and therefore require specialized explanations and procedures. Institutional competition in these narratives takes the form of discursive maneuvers that serve to establish new legal, medical, and religious subject positions. This textual production of new subject positions provides a crucial clue to the paranoid gothic's roots in historical projection. For while the gothic depends for its effects on the assertion of a static, immutable, and Manichean cosmology, the continual eruption at its center of historically situated struggles for institutional power calls our attention to the historical mutability of power that gothic's representational precepts deny. Most significant for my project, the horror of supernatural and institutional assaults in each of these texts is heightened through their affiliation with images of child sacrifice.

As Christopher Craft observes, the gothic incites readerly pleasure through its depictions of quasi-sexual transgressions, only to pass itself off at the last moment as a cautionary tale through its self-righteous expulsion of the monstrous (72). Maturin, Le Fanu, and Stoker ultimately side with the heteronormative forces that violently reorder the pandemonium their demonic protagonists unleash. Their final, triumphal reassertions of heteronormativity do not, however, vitiate their value as articulate if unconscious readings of the processes and costs of sexual subject formation within the Anglo-Irish settler colony.

As Ann Cvetkovich has argued, in *Capital* Marx makes the appropriation of surplus value visible by using sensational and gothic figurations to express the means by which "the life that exists in the worker's body is transferred to the production process . . . [so that] the symbiotic relation between the worker and the other raw materials required to produce commodities, the flesh, blood, nerves, and muscles of the worker give life to the system of production but leave the body itself dead with fatigue and sensory deprivation" (183). In these three central productions of the Anglo-Irish paranoid gothic, strikingly similar narrative patterns make visible the relationship between sexuality, reproduction, and colonial hegemony in Ireland. In this chapter I explore the experience of sexual maturation within the Anglo-Irish family as it emerges in these most voluble accounts of children sacrificed to diabolic intergenerational compacts.

These texts have in common, in Le Fanu's terms, certain "remarkable resemblances," some of which I have already mentioned. They project distinctly Anglo-Irish social and political anxieties onto remote regions of the European Catholic periphery. Most significant, the texts share a depiction of a primordial, ancestral crime that recurs generationally in the form of a demonic, transhistorical protagonist. John Melmoth's 1646 portrait; Carmilla's ancestral portrait, which *lives* more vitally than does Carmilla; and Dracula's account of his history, in which "it is impossible to tell if what is at stake is Dracula's personal longevity or his total identification with his line" (Punter 2:17) — all supply Burkean figures of an intergenerational familial compact in which the vitality of the living is sacrificed to the aims and requirements of the dead.

"I Am Staked against a Community, a Priesthood, a Nation"
Male and Female Subject Formation in *Melmoth the Wanderer*

In *Melmoth the Wanderer,* the opening scene depicts John Melmoth the younger's journey from Trinity College through County Wicklow to attend upon his dying uncle, John Melmoth the elder. "Old Melmoth," an emblematic mass of settler colonial pathologies, dies "as he ha[s] lived, in a kind of avaricious delirium" (19), believing himself alone and penniless amid a throng of people whom he distrusts and a sea of hoarded wealth. When John Melmoth arrives, his uncle bids him enter a secret closet to view a portrait he has kept hidden there. The portrait dates from 1646, the period immediately preceding Oliver Cromwell's instatement as governor of Ireland in 1649. Melmoth's uncle tells his nephew that he is dying of fright, because, he proclaims, the portrait's "original is still alive" (18).

Following his uncle's death, Melmoth asks an aged healer, Biddy Brannigan, to tell him "the odd story that . . . was in the family." In response to his request, her figure grows "frightfully dilated, like that of Virgil's Alecto, who exchanges in a moment the appearance of a feeble old woman for that of a menacing fury" (24). The connection between this figurative renewal of Biddy Brannigan's powers and Melmoth the elder's death enacts a Manichean relationship between the interests of the native Irish and those of the Anglo-Irish. Crucially, however, despite the evident cleavage that divides the native Irish from the Anglo-Irish, Biddy Brannigan is the only one who can tell Melmoth the story of his family's history. Her immersion in the Irish oral tradition renders her largely impervious to hegemonic revisions of history. She thus retains access to historical narratives that are repressed within (but intimately concern) the Anglo-Irish domestic sphere.

The healer's privileged position relative to the Melmoth family's internally repressed history dramatizes an epistemological breach between the Anglo-Irish domestic sphere and its surroundings maintained through the repression of origins within that sphere. The intergenerational repression of "family secrets" via the (partial and incoherent) narratives that legitimate familial and national retention of property and social privilege in a colonial setting cyclically renews a distinction between the epistemology of the colonizer and that of the colonized. In *Melmoth,* however, the mechanisms for such a renewal are distintegrating because, as we learn, a devil's pact established at the time of Cromwell is coming to an end.

As in Poe's "The Fall of the House of Usher," the scandal of the Melmoth line can die only with the line itself. The family's diabolical progenitor, Melmoth the Wanderer, is marked by his extreme longevity and his reappearance at the deaths of family patriarchs as embodying the family's immutable form, in opposition to which Melmoth the younger represents only its generational contents. The novel's narrative trajectory—which terminates in Melmoth the Wanderer's expiration—thus suggests that Melmoth the younger will not reproduce, that the family line will die along with its founder. In this sense the frame narrative of *Melmoth the Wanderer,* as well as its most prominent inner story, that of Monçada, could be read as offering a vision of a costly and barely survivable escape from an elaborate system of familial and economic control that is, over time, breaking down.

In the novel's notoriously labyrinthine interior narratives, a series of children are sacrificed by their parents in the name of a variety of religious ideologies. East Indians are portrayed as sacrificing their children to various deities by flinging them in the path of a hurtling idol or leaving them at the altar of a goddess to starve (293–94). One set of Catholic parents sacrifices its son to the Catholic Church, whose representatives offer eternal forgiveness in return for his forced admission into a monastery; another attempts to sacrifice a daughter to a loveless marriage, thereby precipitating a chain of events leading to her death in the dungeons of the Spanish Inquisition. In a Protestant family, a son comes close to death when he sells gallons of his own blood to pay for food for his family, and his sister comes to the brink of prostitution after the family is cheated of an inheritance by the Catholic Church (420–23). In these and other episodes in the narrative, youths are hounded by a series of social institutions, nearly always with the connivance of their parents. Moreover, these persecutions take specific forms that I identified in Chapter 1 as those which, during the early modern period, underwrote the growth of capitalism, the production of new gendered and sexual subject positions in England, and the intensification of English imperialism in Ireland.

As Chris Baldick observes, the novel's convoluted "stories-within-stories" (x) repeatedly return to the inheritance theme of the frame narrative in which they are couched. It is "family wealth," Baldick points out, "which repeatedly brings disaster to the novel's leading characters." All the novel's central characters are "in their various ways imprisoned by their own mercenary relatives, in an arrangement which marries the inheritance plot of realist fiction to the confinement plot of the gothic novel" (xviii). In my readings of the narratives of two characters — Monçada and Isidora — I will trace out the particular relevance of wealth, inheritance, and the accompanying policing of epistemology for the sexual subject formation of men and women within the Anglo-Irish settler colonial order.

Like Pierre Rivière in Foucault's edited collection *I, Pierre Rivière,* Maturin's protagonists are often treated as bones of contention among competing institutional discourses. Representatives of an array of institutions (all of which are simultaneously depicted as extensions of the Catholic Church) vie for the opportunity to extend their institutional power through their ability to account for the subject's particular social aberration. Typically, the maturation of the protagonist, whether male or female, is causally related in the narrative to these institutional persecutions, so that the process of sexual maturation is itself revealed to be, as Norma Alarcón has observed, ideologically "implicated through and through" (222). The question of sexual maturity is situated at the heart of the matter, as though the acquisition of secondary sexual characteristics itself, for both male and female protagonists, inexorably provokes institutional bids to control and define their identities.

In Monçada's story, such processes of institutional persecution illustrate the autophagous nature of family bonds within a colonial social order in which capitalism and compulsory heterosexuality are interdependent. In this narrative, a young Spaniard is pressured by representatives of the Catholic Church to renounce "the world" (that is, his sexuality) as a means of compensating for his mother's sexual "crime" of having conceived him before marriage. This crime is also linked to his mother's class position, because her working-class origins had precluded her marriage to Monçada's father and driven the young couple to resort to extramarital intercourse in the first place. Monçada's parents' "sin," a response to religious and economic constraints that prohibited their erotic and emotional gratification within a system rigged to produce such transgressions, generated a child earmarked from birth for a sacrificial position within that system: the illegitimate child. Monçada's mother is offered the opportunity to redeem herself through her child, whose forced admittance into a monastery is represented to her as the only means by which she may respectably retain the goods and status that her crime has (through her marriage) gained her.

The marriage's founding transgression, as the priest who pushes Monçada's parents to extort a monastic vow from him suggests, can be kept a *private* matter only through the enforced sacrifice of its offspring, through which the original transgression can be used to extend the church's ranks and strengthen its bonds with a high-ranking family. In atonement for his mother's sin, Monçada is situated outside "the world" and prohibited from claiming a coherent sexual identity. In compensation for her "illegitimate" class transformation, he is placed outside the class structure and forbidden the status, power, and privilege that his illicit conception secured for her.

Significantly, the inverse complementarity that relates Monçada's fate to his parents' and subsequently to his own sexuality strikingly resembles the logic by which Jonathan Swift situated his life relative to his parents' reproductive powers and by which Burke related his son's death to his own ambition. Figuratively, Monçada's story reenacts the sexual subject formation of the Anglo-Irish boy. By birth he inherits an intergenerational sin—a crime connected with a culpable act of reproduction—through which his parents were enriched. He is made responsible for both morally absolving and socially hiding this transgression by surrendering his own sexuality to perpetuate the religious and national system that has benefited his parents. As Monçada reflects during a lengthy period of confinement in a monastery that allegorizes both the child's struggles against interpellation and the role of homophobia in coercing ideological uniformity, he is by birth "staked against a community, a priesthood, a nation" (179).

While eighteenth-century English gothic novels also frequently demonized Catholicism, it is noteworthy that *Melmoth the Wanderer*, a late addition to the gothic canon and a nadir in the gothic anti-Catholic tradition, was written by a Church of Ireland curate in a country in which Catholic/Protestant power relations were virtually the reverse of those the novel depicts. Baldick writes: "To attack Catholicism was not for Maturin, as it was for Lewis in his prurient Gothic novel *The Monk* (1796), an antiquarian fancy-dress frolic. It was a very serious duty of his vocation, to which he was earnestly committed" (xiii). In keeping, then, not only with the conventions of eighteenth-century English gothic but with his own religious convictions as well, Maturin repeatedly traces responsibility for the malicious treatment of his protagonists to Catholicism's corrosive impact on families, communities, and nations.

As Julian Moynahan has observed, however, Maturin's family history may have paradoxically supplied the "basis for covert identification between Irish Huguenot Protestants and Irish Catholics. Both traditions showed a similar pattern of persecution, confiscation, and flight abroad in approximately the same era of the 17th-century wars of religion" (46). Evidence for a suppressed and guilty identification with the Catholic Other appears, for instance, in Maturin's sympathetic portrayal of Monçada, who undergoes persecutions at the hands of the Catholic Church similar to those which he might have undergone, had he been Irish, under the Penal Laws. More speculatively, evidence for such a covert identification may also be found in same-sex couplings, in which a fearful unconscious identification with the Catholic Other appears transposed into depictions of a prohibited attraction to one's likeness. Same-sex romances that are ultimately revealed (sometimes to the surprise of the lovers) as heterosexual represent a comic variation on the sexual threats that dramatize the Catholic Church's demonic alterity. Both elicit feelings of anxiety, confusion, fear, and repulsion that would have been familiar to the author not from his wealth of experience in Catholic monasteries but from the mundane experiences of Anglo-Irish domestic life.

Baldick discerns a distinctive interaction between gothic conventions and the horror that is, in the novel, most closely associated with domestic relationships. The novel evinces a "curious dialectic," he notes, whereby "the monotonous becomes intense, while intensity becomes monotonous." Maturin appears, Baldick concludes, to seek "the sources of Gothic horror in a realm usually assumed to be very remote from it: that of domestic realism" (xviii). Central to this transposition of intensity into monotony and vice versa is a textual focus on protagonists' somatic feelings of horror in response to bodily and spiritual violations. Such violations and the "monotonously intense" sensations that accompany them are, as Eve Kosofsky Sedgwick has remarked, commonly associated with "the unspeakable," a conventional gothic trope that she persuasively connects with homosexuality (*Between Men* 94).

Central among the novel's monotonously repetitive violations is Melmoth's unspeakable proposition, which is (Sedgwick's delightful intimations notwithstanding) that some sufficiently desperate individual barter his or her soul to the devil in return for a 150-year life span, thereby releasing Melmoth from his own devil's bargain. Melmoth makes this proposal unsuccessfully several times in the course of the novel. His quest for a mortal willing to accept his offer, moreover, continually leads him to characters who are, like Monçada, threatened by an array of secular devil's bargains. Throughout the novel characters suffer from unspeakable but decisively sublunary horrors that accompany instances of institutional intrusion through which their subjectivity is markedly reconstituted. As we have already learned from Sedgwick, the unspeakable events that gothic protagonists register subjectively, but that gothic novelists cannot or will not objectively describe, refer to sexual practices—homosexuality, male rape, and incest—that "run counter to the official version" (90). My own readings of such episodes, however, seek to locate such acts within the Anglo-Irish sociosymbolic order and to specify the cultural meanings with which they are invested.

At the intersection between Maturin's gothic fantasy and the processes of male subject formation that it persistently reenacts are homophobia and the fear of bodily violation. The centrality of homophobia to Anglo-Irish subject formation is dramatized in Monçada's struggle within the monastery, in which processes of domestic interpellation are made nightmarishly visible. The complex relationship between subjectivity and real or projected physical violation is mapped out when Monçada first sets out to establish the coerced nature of his monastic vows. After secretly conveying his testimony to a lawyer, he is filled "with an *indefinite* fear" (138; Maturin's emphasis). The "indefinite" fear that suffuses Monçada is epistemic in nature; he is engaged in a high-stakes struggle to assert his own subjective reality within an order that negates it. When he is confronted by his Superior with a copy of his testimony, Monçada's analysis of the conflict between them focuses on the mutually negating quality of their modes of understanding. He reflects, for instance, that the Superior's claim that monastic life is "the only life that can promise tranquillity here, or ensure salvation hereafter" is "uttered by a man confused by the most frantic passion" and thus constitutes its "own refutation" (139). Through a similar strategy of reversal, Monçada asserts to the Superior that although his own violation of monastic decorum (in contacting a lawyer) represents a regrettable act of violence against the system, it is "not reprehensible" because "those who forced me into a convent are guilty of the violence which is falsely ascribed to me" (139).

Like a parent within the nuclear family, the Superior is free to disavow and suppress the circulation of any "knowledge" concerning his own emotions and motivations, including, under normal circumstances, any knowledge or suppositions his inferiors might obtain through noticing obvious contradictions between his espoused beliefs and his behavior or affect. Monçada's observations challenge the Superior's assertions by remarking on readily available evidence of which the Superior claims to have no knowledge. Monçada thus represents a bearer of knowledge that is, within the parameters of the system, incoherent, unknowable. His fidelity to an unspeakable truth that he refuses to disavow eventually provokes systematic attempts to drive him, or at least cause him to appear, mentally ill.

The monastic system constitutes Monçada as the agent of an unspeakable crime. Before his interment in a dungeon, Monçada begs the four monks who are his tireless persecutors, "Of what am I guilty?" and then, "Why am I not told of my offence?" The (otherwise ominously silent) monks respond in unison, "in a voice that seemed to issue from the bottom of a sepulchre, 'Your crime is ——,' " but the Superior cuts them off, signaling them to be silent. Monçada responds to this gothic gap by agonizing with redoubled horror over what signifier might be inserted into it.[2] He especially seems to fear one unspeakable charge when he reflects that "I did not know of what crime they might be disposed to accuse me," adding that he had "heard the crimes of convents were sometimes *unutterably* atrocious" (emphasis added). He wishes, now that the "unspeakable" has, in effect, come up in connection with possible charges that might be leveled against him, that "a *distinct* charge . . . be preferred against [him]" (emphasis added). He is as anxious now, he asserts, for a "distinct" charge as he had been to evade such a charge "a few moments before" (135).

Within this passage, the emergence of "the unspeakable" into Monçada's thoughts reverses his wishes, so that now he is most afraid lest he be charged with something vague, longing only for a clearly defined accusation. As I will show, this renegotiation reflects homophobia's power as a discourse that is always available as the ultimate institutional threat, like the possibility of being accused as a witch was, a century earlier, an ever present threat for subjects who dissented too vigorously or stubbornly from established social norms. The effect of Monçada's unspoken realization that he could be accused of homosexual crimes marks a moment at which he rapidly and wholeheartedly internalizes the will of a larger social system — a moment of interpellation. Monçada's relationship to institutional power is reconfigured at the first thought of "unspeakable" vices. Whereas he has previously sought in every way to oppose the institution and to refute all charges against him, he now wishes for the trial that he had previously dreaded and reasons from within the monastic symbolic order rather than from outside it.

In this scene, the "homosexual panic" of which Sedgwick writes appears as a highly instrumental ideology, exercising powerful institutional leverage capable of radically reordering male subjectivity, especially in extremis. I would add to Sedgwick's arguments that homophobia also subsequently exerts — as events will suggest — a second, more localized, and more devastating impact on the formation of male subjectivity, which can frequently be discovered in operation in the materials that I examine in this book. Homophobia sees pleasurable homosexual contact as an unspeakable horror, and in so doing, it holds violent homosexual contact, especially anal rape, to be a privileged, unspeakable, and even *uncodable* category of damage, one that is maintained as an explosively charged form of punishment that symbolically enacts the death of the subject.

In the episode that follows the Superior's discovery that Monçada has smuggled an account of his confinement to a lawyer, Monçada assumes that he is to be murdered when the Superior and his henchmen come bearing cords and a sackcloth. He "confesses" to feeling "disappointed" when he is stripped of his habit, covered with the sackcloth and bound with the cords, rather than strangled with the cords and stuffed into the sack as he had anticipated, since in these preparations "something worse than death appeared threatened" (143). This foreshadowed "thing worse than death" materializes on the day when Monçada's case is finally to be heard. It takes the form of an event that is left "unspoken" and is passed over much more briefly and with less emotional elaboration than are Monçada's other sufferings.

The hour of trial approached. For the honour of human nature, — from the dread of violating decency, — from the dread of apparently violating truth, — I will not attempt to relate the means they had recourse to the morning of the Bishop's visitation, to qualify me to perform the part of a possessed, insane, and blasphemous wretch. The four monks I have before mentioned, were the principal executioners, (I must call them so). — Under pretence that there was no part of my person which was not under the influence of the demon,   *   *

*   *   *   *

This was not enough. I was deluged almost to suffocation with aspersions of holy water. Then followed, &c.   *   *   *

*   *   *   *

This passage, which terminates in semantic devastation, appears to encode the "death" foreseen in Monçada's earlier fears of a superlative and unspeakable injury. The passage characterizes the monks' action as an "execution" that "dishonour[s]" human "nature," violates "decency," and is of a type that is routinely dismissed as unbelievable. Monçada's assertion that the monks acted "under pretence that there was no part

of [his] person . . . not under the influence of the demon" implies that
he has been sexually violated and probably gang-raped.[3]

This "unspeakable" episode, which is either suppressed by Monçada
himself or obliterated in the manuscript, rhetorically parallels certain
effaced accounts of traumatic experiences in eighteenth-century English and Irish literature, ranging from Clarissa's rape to Gulliver's oral
violation by a monkey.[4] It also parallels experiences reported by Nationalist prisoners in Ireland from the nineteenth century to the present.[5]
In Maturin's novel, as in *Clarissa, Gulliver's Travels,* the accounts of
Nationalist prisoners, and texts that I focus on in the following chapters, instances of abuse, especially rape and incest, appear only in trace,
surrounded with a cloud of more detailed descriptions of less unspeakable, but suggestive, events. This pattern resembles what Carol Barringer has found in her research on incest survivors' rhetorical strategies,
in which patterns of escape and evasion were repeatedly used to suppress memories of actual rape even in the midst of appalling episodes
otherwise told "in precise, inescapable detail" (11).

In Monçada's account of sexual assault, and those of Nationalist
prisoners, I would argue, a specific script is enacted whose central, defining moment is represented by anal rape. Male-on-male sexual assault
represents a particularly violent enactment of social death; it constitutes an overwhelming and at the same time unspeakable injury that
establishes the dominance of an order over a subject or, in some semi-
public contexts such as prisons, over an entire group. Its power within
the symbolic order is ensured through homophobia, which constitutes
homosexual contact as *peccatum illude horribile non nominandum inter
christanos,* a crime too horrible to speak. Homophobia obliterates all
distinctions between chosen and involuntary homosexual acts, which
are lumped together as uniformly shameful. Homophobic horror and
denial therefore drain homosexual rape of rape's conventional significatory position as the devastating counterpart of chosen lovemaking.
Male rape victims are, like incest victims, frozen in the untenable position of having sustained an injury that, owing to taboo symbolic con-
tent, shatters and discredits them as signifying agents, setting them
at odds with a symbolic order predicated on their continuing silence.
Given the homophobic constitution of anal rape as a violation of more

than just the body and the collateral construction of masculinity as "that which is *not* penetrated,"[6] the male victim of sexual assault, like the incest survivor, becomes the bearer of a forbidden traumatic experience that threatens, if spoken or perhaps even recalled, to shatter the symbolic order on which he must rely if he is to be restored to a sense of wholeness and agency.

Sexual assault in *Melmoth the Wanderer* represents the culmination of a series of institutional assaults against Maturin's protagonists, centering around bids on the part of competing institutions to define them under increasingly extreme rubrics. It is temporarily unclear, for instance, whether Monçada is most likely to be sentenced as a criminal, exorcised as a demoniac, incarcerated for a madman, or burned as a heretic. All these possible forms of institutional reprisal are mobilized in response to Monçada's insistence on a simple truth: that his monastic vows were extracted under duress. Although several institutions compete for discursive control over Monçada, all are in harmony concerning a single point: there can be no admission that Monçada's oath was coerced, even though the fact that he is willing to risk his life to take it back should suffice as proof it was. That this series of escalations culminates in sexual assault is particularly telling: the assault is a means of manipulating and controlling Monçada at a moment when overt coercion might entail exposure. It is also notable that rape constitutes the culmination of escalating attempts at control through homosexual panic. Monçada's rape paradoxically manifests the ultimate, arbitrary power of the system and demarcates the absolute limits of that power. With this episode, Monçada's epistemology is permanently altered, as was Clarissa's after her assault by Lovelace. Like Clarissa, he enters a temporary state of insanity that corresponds to Taussig's "space of death," a realm of horror that is concomitantly a domain of illumination (*Shamanism* 4). Through a superlative act of oppression Monçada is liberated from his fear of death and thereby freed to withdraw his energies from a system that can no longer compel his cooperation through misinformation, intimidation, and force.

Isidora, a female protagonist whose betrayal by her family in the name of the church parallels Monçada's, undergoes a similar transformation within her family; unlike Monçada, however, she cannot survive the transformation process. Like Clarissa, her only means of escape from a devouring family is by abandoning the gendered body that culturally justifies and incites her violation. Just as Monçada's incarceration by his family and the Church reenacts early modern processes of subject formation through the appropriation of his sexuality, the policing of his epistemology, and his production as a heterosexual male through institutional processes of sexual terrorization, Isidora's story symbolically parallels the historical events that reconfigured female subjectivity in early modern England. For instance, calling attention to the origins of bourgeois marriage in early modern juridical repression, Isidora compares her impending enforced marriage to a stranger, contracted by her father, to death at the stake or the scaffold (372). In her attempt to escape an arranged marriage, Isidora secretly marries Melmoth in a virtual black mass and dies, starved and tortured (but before she can be tried for the death of her infant daughter), in the prisons of the Inquisition.

Isidora is first found to be "insane" (336) and later heretical when she challenges the definitional power of a family in which she is constrained and dominated by "those whom [she] cannot trust or love." Isidora (generously) describes her mother as "severe" and her brother as "violent" (342). Her father, a Marxian caricature of capitalist voraciousness tarted up with a veneer of Catholic dogma, engages in unconsciously erotic fantasies concerning this long-estranged daughter, who has been separated from the family since infancy and raised by nature on a deserted island. He delightedly reduces her to a series of erotic synecdoches, as "natural ringlets that would not obey their new mistress, art — and that slender, undulating shape — [that] would soon be folded in [his] arms" (382).

Along with the inmates of monasteries, Isidora's father, Francisco di Aliaga, numbers among the novel's broadest caricatures. He is represented as a businessman so absorbed in the getting and exchanging of capital and commodities that when his adult daughter is miraculously restored to the family after an absence of nearly two decades, he does not reply to his wife's letter bearing the extraordinary news for a year, explaining that he was "hindered by concerns of business" (369). Di Aliaga's lust for commerce is halfheartedly subordinated to his Catholicism through the attribution of his defects to his devout reduction of others, including his daughter, to "soul[s] and . . . subject[s]" to be recovered for heaven (369).

If the central devil's bargain that Monçada seeks to evade is the negation of his sexuality through enforced monastic life, sexual terrorism, and rape, the parallel pattern in Isidora's case is confinement within the family, an arranged marriage, and ultimately death. Symbolic incest, figured in her father's fantasies and, by extension, in his demand to control her sexuality and to deploy it according to his own promptings through marriage, is the central symbolic contract that Isidora struggles to evade. Isidora escapes her "claustrophilic" family by secretly marrying Melmoth. Yet just as Clarissa may, within Richardson's cosmology, be sexually violated but remain spiritually pure, by the laws of Maturin's cosmos Isidora may marry Melmoth in an abandoned and desecrated church with a deceased monk in attendance, have sexual intercourse with and become impregnated by Melmoth, bear his child, and die yearning for him without imperiling her soul, for she refuses his formal (unspeakable) request to the last.

Monçada's and Isidora's stories exemplify the series of confrontations between conflicting epistemologies that the novel repeatedly stages. These conflicts foreground the central role of historical representation and occlusion in the establishment and maintenance of the nuclear family, property rights, and state authority. Each protagonist winds up the loser in one of the novel's series of parallel epistemological struggles, and each is cast into a space of "unspeakable horror" (48), a gap within the dominant symbolic order out of which no experience can credibly be articulated. Both protagonists, however, ultimately escape the systems in which they are ensnared, in a pattern that corresponds to Abdul JanMohamed's schematization of the means by which social death may undo itself.

In "Rehistoricizing Wright: The Psychopolitical Function of Death in *Uncle Tom's Children*," JanMohamed traces Richard Wright's exploration of the relationship of African Americans to death in Jim Crow society. He reads Wright's stories sequentially, finding the culmination of a process of growing resistance to social death in an episode in which the bond between the Jim Crow system and the subject, Taylor, is traumatically ruptured by a superlative act of oppression that leaves nothing left to lose and hence nothing to fear (223). For Monçada, this supreme injury takes the form of anal rape, an experience through which he loses the fear of sexual violation (including the fear of being defined as homosexual) that previously controlled him. He is thus enabled to flee to Protestant Europe and ultimately to Ireland, which this trajectory situates as the heart of a pure and rational Protestant Order. But Isidora's case illustrates the potential difference that gender can make in this pattern. For Monçada, Maturin can envision the possibility of ultimate liberation from a system that appropriates male sexuality, and thus controls male subjectivity, through a religious and homophobic reign of terror. For Isidora, however, a geographical escape from parallel conditions—short of a return to the edenic, unpopulated island where she grew to maturity—is impossible. Isidora is the object of an extended system of incestuous violation; her father's blind insistence on controlling her sexuality confronts her with the sexualized threat of her own negation. Caught between an emotionally encroaching family and a system of compulsory heterosexual exchange that mandates her sexual violation, she is enabled to cheat (and retroactively indict) her tormenters through her mercifully untimely demise.

Maturin's asymmetrical paralleling of male and female social death calls attention to the relatively more localized and contingent appropriation of male sexuality within the nuclear family. The little boy (provided he is willing to sacrifice a broad range of perceptual and sexual possibilities) can expect to grow into a position of authority and relative autonomy within the family. But the little girl, because she constitutes the means by which the family system is reproduced, is more deeply embedded within that system. She remains perpetually suspended between the family of origin and its mirror image, an adult heterosexual dyad that constitutes simultaneously the only acceptable escape and the perpetuation of the very system that subjects her to social death. In the texts I examine, all too frequently death is, for this girl child, the only alternative to involuntary collusion with the forces that appropriate her life energies to extend into the future a system of social and literal death.

"Your Forms Wound Me"
Subject Formation in "Carmilla"

Sheridan Le Fanu's novella "Carmilla" is a largely first-person account of the protagonist's seduction, first as a child and then as a young woman, by the vampire that gives the book its title. The narrative depicts the process of sexual maturation within a culturally and socially isolated domestic sphere as one of progressive enslavement to a historically determinate object choice. As in the other texts I consider in this chapter, the homoeroticism of "Carmilla" rationalizes affective horror associated with sexual maturation at the same time that it foregrounds a forbidden attraction to sameness characteristic of the Anglo-Irish child's ambivalent national/cultural identification. Additionally, "Carmilla's" emphasis on the transgressiveness of homosexual desire serves as a screen for the routine sexual violation of children within the heteronormative family.

Carmilla enters Laura's life as an unexpected guest at her family's isolated estate in Styria, a province of southeast Austria, after the coach in which she is traveling overturns near their castle. Laura's girlhood in Styria closely resembles the enclosed and isolated childhood of an Anglo-Irish girl. Her family resembles an Anglo-Irish family in its internal dynamics, its ambivalent relationship to the culture that surrounds it, and its economic raison d'être. Although Laura's "father is English, and [she] bear[s] an English name," she has never seen England, which she nonetheless refers to as "home." Economics plays an evident role in her family's isolated, liminal life in a land (significantly, a province rather than a country) where they live owing to economic necessity, since, as she explains, "a small income . . . goes a great way" in that part of the world (72).

Laura's description of her life at nineteen (she is recalling these experiences at twenty-seven) emphasizes her family's seclusion, its constriction, and its disconnection from the surrounding countryside. The nearest inhabited village lies seven miles away, while a deserted village lies within three miles, its relatively greater proximity further calling attention to the emptiness of the landscape. Laura's mother, "a Styrian

lady," died in Laura's infancy. "I and my father," Laura reports, with in-
decipherable emotion, "constituted the family at the schloss" (73). The
family's cultural disconnection from its surroundings is emphasized
not only through the death of the only Styrian in the family but also
through the many western European languages that Laura speaks with
her father; her governess, Madame Perrodon, of Berne; and her tutor,
Mademoiselle De Lafontaine (73). Laura's situation, in its geographic
isolation, the constriction of her family unit, and its cultural insularity,
represents a reductio ad absurdum of the Anglo-Irish settler colonial
family. The story that unfolds there offers a paradigm of female sexual
development within the Anglo-Irish settler colonial order.

The story of Carmilla's arrival is connected with what Laura calls
"the first occurrence in my existence, which produced a terrible impression upon my mind, which, in fact, never has been effaced" (74). When
Laura was six years old, she was awakened to find herself alone. She
recalls that she was not frightened, for she was *"studiously kept in ignorance* of ghost stories, of fairy tales, and of all such lore," a reflection that
recalls the constitutive role of ignorance in the Anglo-Irish child's identity formation and also stresses the family's role in isolating the child
from the oral culture of the surrounding society. Laura reports that she
was "vexed and insulted at finding [herself], as [she] conceived, neglected," and she "began to whimper, preparatory to a hearty bout of
roaring" (74; emphasis added). Laura's vexation and wounded pride are
reminiscent of the feelings that Freud attributes to the girl child upon
her discovery of her physiological "inferiority" within a sex/gender system that privileges the male. As Gayle Rubin sums it up, the little girl
may choose from "three alternate routes through the Oedipal catastro-
phe[: she] may . . . repress sexuality altogether . . . [or] protest, cling
to her narcissism and desire, and become either "masculine" or homosexual . . . [or] she may accept the situation, sign the social contract,
and attain 'normality' " (96). Laura's "whimper, preparatory to a hearty
bout of roaring," suggests that her initial reaction, at least, is protest.
As she prepares to register her vexation with her caretakers, however,
she sees "a solemn, but very pretty face looking at [her] from the side
of the bed" (74). In this "first occurrence in [Laura's] existence," the
initial connection by an orphaned girl of the absence of her mother's

surrogate with her own physiology, which she is just beginning to see as inadequate, is interrupted by the arrival of a beautiful mother/lover, who "caresse[s her] with her hands, [lies] down beside [her] on the bed, and dr[aws her] towards her, smiling" (74). As Rubin has pointed out, "If the pre-Oedipal lesbian were not confronted by the heterosexuality of the mother, she might draw different conclusions about the status of her genitals" (91). This scene rescripts the Oedipal crisis along the lines that Rubin suggests, but with a disturbingly incestuous twist, as here the little girl becomes the direct object of a mother figure's eroticized caresses. Laura, however, feels "delightfully soothed" and falls asleep again, only to wake to "a sensation as if two needles ran into my breast very deep at the same moment" (74). When she yells, her assailant "started back, with her eyes fixed on me, and then slipped down upon the floor, and, as I thought, hid herself under the bed" (74).

This scene mixes a clinically accurate representation of the onset of the female Oedipal crisis accompanied by a compensatory fantasy of a common sort by which the little girl reassures herself that she *can* attract and sustain nurturing from an idealized mother/lover, with a scene of childhood sexual violation that is, in the vocabulary of the gothic family romance, enacted by a lesbian vampire who bites the child's breast and escapes by crawling under her bed. This passage encodes the Anglo-Irish child's profound ambivalence toward parental nurturance, which is simultaneously gratifying and necessary and which she nonetheless experiences as covertly exploitative and injurious. It also graphically invokes the affective experience of physical or emotional incest.[7] The passage precisely renders the child's profound desire for nurturance and her deep yearning for the tenderness and love of a parent figure. By juxtaposing the bliss that parental nurturance evokes with the horror of an incomprehensible violation, "Carmilla" identifies the Anglo-Irish girl's attempts to define herself in a family that undermines her ability to situate herself with the loss of coherence that accompanies incest.

Laura never forgets this event, which produces an impression that "stand[s] out vivid as the isolated pictures of the phantasmagoria surrounded by darkness" (76). But she reaches the age of nineteen without additional incident, although her repeated emphasis on her family's isolation and her stricken reaction on hearing that a visit from a young woman her age has been canceled suggest that she is at best lonely and at worst trapped. When Carmilla reenters Laura's life through a coaching accident near the schloss, Carmilla at first appears "lifeless" (80). When she is found to be alive but too ill to continue on the vital errand on which her mother must continue, both Laura and her father are eager to secure Carmilla as a houseguest.

One significant glimpse into Carmilla's symbolic identity emerges in this scene through the figure of an additional passenger in the coach who is seen only by Mademoiselle De Lafontaine, who is "something of a mystic" (78). She describes "a hideous black woman, with a sort of coloured turban on her head, who was gazing all the time from the carriage window, nodding and grinning derisively towards the ladies, with gleaming eyes and large white eye-balls, and her teeth set as if in fury" (83). The woman's blackness, grin, eyeballs, and menacing teeth suggest a grotesque racial caricature, while her "coloured turban" marks both her and Carmilla's colonial origins. This barely glimpsed figure encodes the novella's otherwise repressed anxiety concerning colonial relations and ethnic and cultural difference within Ireland. Le Fanu juxtaposes Carmilla's seemingly perfect adherence to western European standards of beauty and charm against a figure that dramatizes all that Carmilla's pleasing appearance masks. The aged, dark-skinned, and rageful crone who is, like the details that betray ethnic and religious difference in Ireland, visible only to the trained eye, emblematizes the Styrian Carmilla's largely invisible ethnic difference.

Later in the narrative, Carmilla's invisible differences more overtly parallel those that divide the Irish from the Anglo-Irish. When Laura sings along with a hymn that hurts Carmilla's ears, Carmilla bursts out angrily, "How can you tell that your religion and mine are the same"? In words that describe precisely the effect of Anglo-Irish religion and culture on native Irish culture, Carmilla tells Laura, "Your forms wound me" (92). For the most part, however, Le Fanu, like Maturin, determinedly projects Irish colonial tensions elsewhere. The demonic black woman in the coach invokes the dark-skinned East Indian female rather than a recognizably Irish figure, embodying the moral and geopolitical alterity at the root of the creation and circulation of creatures such as Carmilla.

Another glimpse of a submerged, demonic system is afforded when Carmilla's mother transmits to Laura's father the "solemn injunction" (88) to secrecy that governs Carmilla's stay. Having drawn him aside, Carmilla's mother changes dramatically: she speaks "with a fixed and stern countenance, not at all like that with which she had hitherto spoken," and Laura is "filled with wonder that [her] father [does] not seem to perceive the change" (81). This evident collusion with Carmilla and her party indicates that Laura's father has been hypnotized by Carmilla's mother. Figuratively, however, this collaboration with a supernatural force bent on devouring his daughter bespeaks a particular unconscious collusion between parents and the forces of imperial domination. Such unconscious pacts appear repeatedly in Anglo-Irish texts; in their most extreme form, they lead caretakers to hound children to their destruction in the service of intergenerational structures of control within and beyond the Anglo-Irish family.

Central to my understanding of Carmilla's identity is Laura's discovery, in a newly cleaned picture of her mother's ancestor Mircalla, Countess Karnstein, of an exact likeness of Carmilla dating from 1698, the period that marks the beginning of the first anti-Catholic penal laws (Foster, *Modern Ireland* 154). Le Fanu emphasizes the painting's "startling" lifelike qualities. Just as Carmilla, at first glance, appeared lifeless, the painting "seemed to live," thereby ominously revealing the ongoing presence of a purportedly vanished past. On seeing it, Laura exclaims, "Carmilla, dear, here is an absolute miracle. Here you are, living, smiling, ready to speak, in this picture. Isn't it beautiful, papa? And see, even the mole on her throat." Once again, Laura's father colludes with Carmilla. He laughs, agreeing that "it is a wonderful likeness," but looks away and to Laura's surprise "seem[s] but little struck by it" (97). The portrait explicitly figures incest, a theme that I have thus far only inferred from the emotional and symbolic contents of Laura's childhood memory, since, as Tammis Elise Thomas points out, Mircalla Karnstein is Laura's relative. Significantly, Bertha Rheinfeldt, Carmilla's last victim, is also related to the Karnsteins through her maternal line. Thus Carmilla, while seemingly an external invader, is actually an insider masquerading as an outsider. The portrait, or what it implies — that Carmilla embodies the family's self-perpetuation through the intergenerational sacrifice of its daughters—reiterates and also elaborates on the Burkean intergenerational compact. Through intergenerational bonds of familial violation and compulsion, Carmilla, a figure for the ongoing transmission of ancestral crimes, reproduces her vampiric subjectivity through sexual subject formation, "according to an ascertained and ghostly law" (Le Fanu 136).[8]

Shortly after Carmilla's arrival, once she is ensconced in a room in the castle, Laura makes haste to make her introductions and is staggered to realize that Carmilla's is "the very face which had visited me in my childhood at night, which remained so fixed in my memory, and on which I had for so many years so often ruminated with horror" (85). Thus, as Laura reaches maturity, she experiences the return of a particular entity that in her childhood made "a terrible impression . . . [on her that] never has been effaced" (74). The precise nature of this entity, while hinted at in the depiction of the initial assault and in the scene of the overturned carriage, is further explicated as the narrative unfolds.

While Carmilla's visits in Laura's earliest childhood brought horror, her presence in adolescence precipitates exquisite pleasure. As Thomas has aptly paraphrased, "during the daylight hours, Carmilla and Laura kiss, hold hands, and gaze into each other's eyes; during the evening hours Carmilla enters Laura's bedroom and penetrates Laura's breast with her teeth" (6). The relationship between Laura and Carmilla's daytime and nighttime activities parallels the relationship between Laura's childhood encounter with Carmilla, which induced horror, and her adult encounter with her, which induces passion. Thus the narrative logic of the novella suggests that what was originally internalized as horror resurfaces in the adult as desire. In addition to metaphorizing the production of adult heteronormativity in the Anglo-Irish settler colony, however, Carmilla's relationship to Laura is also shot through with anxiety concerning the Anglo-Irish child's national identity. As we have seen, for instance, in *Castle Rackrent,* the projective capacities of the gothic family romance allow for figurations of colonialism that, like the Rackrents, simultaneously embody both the colonized and the colonizer. Although Carmilla is clearly a figure for the intergenerational mechanisms of psychic and biological reproduction that perpetuate the Anglo-Irish colonial project, as a Styrian, she also embodies ethnic alterity.

As I have argued, the Anglo-Irish child's internalization of a sexual and gendered identity that upholds the contradictory imperatives of the Anglo-Irish social order gives rise to paranoia concerning a racial division that is simultaneously invisible and absolute. The lesbian nature of Laura's bond to Carmilla provides a screen that allows Le Fanu to express the unpleasant affect associated with both the sexual and national Oedipal wounds through which Anglo-Irish identity is constituted. The novella's lesbian theme defamiliarizes (and thus gothicizes) the queasy admixture of emotions that was, by the nineteenth century, widely accepted as the wholesome norm in cases of heterosexual love. It also dramatizes the anxiety that questions of adult romantic and erotic attachment arouse when negotiated in relation to a national identity so tenuously situated as to be perpetually on the verge of collapse into its Other. Laura reflects, for instance, that in response to Carmilla "I experienced a strange tumultuous excitement that was pleasurable, ever and anon, mingled with a vague sense of fear and disgust. . . . I was conscious of a love growing into adoration, and also of abhorrence. This I know is paradox, but I can make no other attempt to explain the feeling" (90). The theme of lesbian love would have greatly exacerbated the nineteenth-century reader's uneasiness with Laura and Carmilla's affair. The homophobic discomfort that the text evinces enables Le Fanu to foreground the "very strange agony" (99) that accompanies the production of Anglo-Irish heteronormativity and to inscribe within a lesbian love affair connections between childhood sexual encroachment and adult identity formation and object choice within the Anglo-Irish family.

The text seeks its resolution in Carmilla's ritualized killing, which takes place in the passive voice without any clear agent but under the authorizing gaze of "two medical men, one officially present, the other on the part of the promoter of the inquiry" (134). If a clue to the vampire's projective origins within the culture and the psyche of the author may be found in its hardy resistance to death, Carmilla's death suggests a particularly powerful and repressed bond with her creator, Le Fanu, who must stake her through the heart, decapitate, and ultimately burn her under the eyes of a watchful triumvirate of patriarchal authorities. Her destruction is directed by an itinerant aristocrat who appears unexpectedly just after Carmilla, exposed as a vampire by General Spielsdorf, has fended off the general's hatchet-wielding assault and fled (131). Baron Vordenburg—a gaunt, tall, strange-looking man who dresses all in black (132) and first enters the narrative through a doorway through which Carmilla has only just exited—is himself a distinctly vampiric figure (134).

Surrounding Carmilla's death are a number of elaborate institutional and ceremonial rituals, including a medical examination of Laura in which the connections between social institutions and father/daughter incest are hinted at when the doctor in attendance gravely instructs Laura's father to "lowe[r her] dress" to expose the marks of the vampire on her breast (111). Through Carmilla's death and the reimposition of patriarchal authority, heteronormativity is ostensibly reestablished, although, as Thomas has argued, Carmilla's mother remains at large and Laura, who has subsequently died, may have become a vampire herself (24). The submerged question of incestuous enmeshment and its historical determinants is never resolved, however. Indeed, within the framework of my reading, the novella's open-endedness in regard to the "increase and multipl[ication]" of vampires calls attention to the ongoing colonial appropriation of children's sexuality, as well as its cyclical reemergence in adult heteronormativity (136).

Unquestionably, the text's coding of childhood sexual imperilment and self-destructive adult object choices as homosexuality reflects a common displacement of anxieties surrounding mundane forms of sexual transgression within the domestic sphere onto demonized sexual outsiders. Indeed, General Spielsdorf's intention of "reliev[ing] our earth of certain monsters, and enabl[ing] honest people to sleep in their beds without being assailed by murderers" (116) distinctly resembles the demonizing rhetoric with which various sexual scapegoats, from homosexuals to sex offenders, are still pursued in a contemporary social order which continues to insist that the freedom to sleep in our beds free from assault is a matter of relieving our earth of external, readily identifiable monsters.[9]

Dracula
"The Center of a Hideous Circle of Corruption"

In *Dracula,* traces of patterns evinced in *Melmoth the Wanderer* and *Carmilla* remain most in evidence in the novel's Transylvanian frame narrative. It is within the frame narrative that the novel's most explicit sacrifice of a child accompanies its clearest expression of homosexual passion. At Castle Dracula, Dracula's unreserved expressions of desire for Jonathan Harker accompany the text's most horrific and explicit image of pedophagy, in which Dracula throws a moving, whimpering bag at the feet of his three wives in a transaction that explicitly exchanges a child's life for Harker's. When Dracula comes upon his wives eagerly encircling the enthralled Harker, he drives them away, informing them decisively, "This man belongs to me!" In a "soft whisper," gazing attentively at Harker's face, he accedes, "Yes, I too can love" (53). This scene reenacts the profoundly conflictual feelings of desire and fear that sexual subject formation precipitates within the nuclear family, especially in the isolated, contradictorily positioned settler colonial family. Dracula's role as dominant patriarch who contains devouring maternal desire but who himself, through his boundless sexual agency, poses a potentially more grave threat to the child, reproduces Dorothy Dinnerstein's account of the societal impact of mother-monopolized childrearing (33). According to Dinnerstein, the confinement of women to the roles of bearing and rearing children, from which they have been obliged to seek whatever gratifications they may, gives rise to intense gynophobia among their emotionally and physically overrun offspring. This, in turn, gives rise to a system of patriarchal authority in which Western society has vested tremendous powers in a magical attempt to protect itself from the violations and intrusions inflicted by mothers in early childhood (171–75). Certainly, Dracula's displacement of his wives—at the explicit price of the child he gives them to devour—re-enacts the classical Freudian substitution of the child for the phallus on which Dinnerstein elaborates, only with more explicit results: the audible wailing of the child Dracula throws to his wives introduces the reader to the autophagous logic at the heart of vampiric reproduction, as the female vampires close in on the infant intent on draining rather than transmitting life energy.

In addition to staging the emotional trade-off at the heart of the patriarchal family, this episode also allegorizes the implications of a transnational system based on such autophagous families. As Stephen Arata points out, Dracula has hunted the peasant child he exchanges for Harker's life while wearing Harker's clothes, thereby calling attention to the equivalence between the actions of the British state that Harker embodies and Dracula's own predatory activities. This equivalency is, however, even more complex than Arata acknowledges. Like "A Modest Proposal," *Dracula* reveals not only the imperial state's symbolic cannibalism but its autophagy as well: Dracula preys on poor children of his own nation, a pattern that Lucy Westenra extends into the West as the "bloofer lady" (185), whose nocturnal predations on working-class children signal the arrival of vampirism in England.

As Franco Moretti has persuasively argued, *Dracula* evinces a subtextual horror of capitalist reconfigurations of the social contract (83–87). In Moretti's reading, however, Marxian and Freudian readings of the text must be undertaken separately, whereas I argue that the novel's horror of capitalist appropriation is expressed through figures that fall squarely within Freud's domain: those pertaining to sexual subject formation and family relations. Like *Melmoth the Wanderer* and *Carmilla*, *Dracula* identifies capitalist interpellation with sexuality and family relations. The characteristic paranoid gothic fear of interpellation is expressed in *Dracula* as fear of homosexuality (Schaffer), to which I will return, and as fear of women's sexuality (Howes 108–10). Lucy Westenra is, of course, the novel's central figure for the terrors inherent in women's sexuality, even as she is simultaneously, as the "bloofer lady," a figure for new forms of capitalist appropriation.

Lucy first enters the narrative via a sequence of letters describing three proposals of marriage she has received in a single day. Feeling deeply moved by the two men she has turned down, she expostulates to Mina Harker, her confidant, "Why can't they let a girl marry three men, or as many as want her, and save all this trouble?" Lucy's genesis from nineteen-year-old belle of the London marriage market to a "foul Thing" to be hunted down and destroyed (225) begins, it should be noted, with the three marriage proposals — an emphatic coming-of-age scenario — and her expressed desire to run afoul of the British system of domestic reproduction. Matters escalate when, in response to Lucy's sleepwalking during their sojourn in Whitby, Mina begins to lock the door of their room every night. Mina undertakes this act of domestic containment at the suggestion of Lucy's mother, who first resorted to this measure to restrain Lucy's father (76).

Lucy's life trajectory represents in many respects the culmination of a by now familiar pattern. In several of the texts I have considered, a female protagonist breaches stringent restrictions governing female sexuality, is increasingly confined within the domestic sphere, and finds herself, as the result of her resistance to that confinement, cast into a world of alterity. The specific nature of these protagonists' crimes against heteronormativity and their resulting fates differ, however. Clarissa rejects sexual union with anyone but a man she can respect; her death explicitly indicts the commodification of bourgeois women within a mercantilizing economy. Isidora, while similarly seeking to evade a match she finds repugnant, actively asserts her sexuality by marrying the diabolical Melmoth and bearing his child; her death, while tragic, is cast as a welcome release from an untenable network of interlocking worldly and supernatural pressures. Laura, bereft of nearly all social contact, falls prey to the wiles of a (purely supernatural) lesbian vampire; in this case, it is Carmilla rather than Laura who is destroyed in a sadistic scene narratively punishing the women's transgression, while Laura slips through the narrative mesh, potentially going on to spawn her own vampiric lineage. In Lucy, the polarized figures of Laura and Carmilla (or Clarissa and Mrs. Sinclair) are fused in one innocent but sexually transgressive woman whose unregulated sexuality leads her into a world of vampiric reproduction and whose much explicated postmortem rape/stake scene is depicted as simultaneously punitive and a heroic rescue undertaken by a collective of courtly lovers.

Lucy's brief career as the bloofer lady, hunting English children and tearing their necks to feed on their blood, constitutes the world of the vampire, like Mrs. Sinclair's brothel in *Clarissa*, the Catholic Church in *Melmoth the Wanderer*, and the realm of lesbian desire in *Carmilla*, as the autophagous underside of the rational world, in which all ordinary rules of decency are reversed. As the belle of the marriage market, Lucy was valued as a potential producer and nurturer of children. Following her death, Lucy enacts the norms of motherhood in reverse, hunting working-class children rather than giving birth to her own bourgeois brood, and thus shaping children's subjectivity through a process of covert depletion rather than charming supplementation. In effectively uniting the virgin and the vampire in Lucy—in suggesting that the innocent victim and the diabolical predator are aspects of a single subjectivity—Stoker calls attention to the shadow side of the bourgeois woman. Stoker's figuration of Lucy suggests that the woman whose unconscious desires are the most potentially lethal is she who most ardently conforms to her ascribed role of beneficent subservience. Lucy's transformation suggests that the more guilelessly such a woman consciously seeks to please men and fulfill her prescribed role as domestic nurturer, the more fully she will unconsciously live out her role within and contribute to a familial and national economy that runs by feeding on its own offspring. Through this depiction of a shadow system of enforced sexual reproduction and predatory mothering, Stoker highlights the role of the bourgeois woman in covertly expanding Dracula's autophagous empire through the process of vampiric reproduction.

In a monologue delivered to Jonathan Harker while at Castle Dracula, Dracula relates a geopolitical history of the vampiric economy that makes explicit the role of the family in its emergence and diffusion. Dracula's own family history is the history of imperialism, the fight "for lordship" over the people "of Europe, ay, and of Asia and Africa too" (30). In a tale which recalls the military roots of European nationalism and which evokes the colonial subjugation of Ireland, Dracula recalls a primal scene in which a figure who represents at once a remote ancestor and Dracula himself, "had to come alone from the bloody field where his troops were being slaughtered, since he knew that he alone could ultimately triumph! They said he thought only of himself. Bah! what good are peasants without a leader?" (30–31). Dracula's revulsion at the thought of "peasants without a leader" immediately precedes his lament that blood, with which feudal lords once drenched the fields, is now "too precious a thing to waste" (31). In this passage, Dracula's activities as a paterfamilias, overseeing production and consumption within his own and foreign families, replace his earlier, overtly political struggles to establish national and racial domination on the battlefield. Dracula's career evidently underwent a drastic shift, from mass-scale imperialist wars to a diffuse system through which he, like capitalist production, covertly drains living subjects of their life's essence, gradually subordinating them to his will and depleting their lives. Dracula's midlife career change corresponds to the shift from repression to indoctrination that accompanied the transition in western Europe from feudalism to capitalism, and to the shift in Ireland from overt colonial domination to colonial/familial occupation signaled by the Act of Union in 1801.[10] Dracula's transition encodes the means by which leadership within modernity reconfigured itself hegemonically, building on power differentials brought into being through mass-scale repression. Domestic "leaders," whether of countries and corporations or their own domestic "castles," came to extract power, profit, and pleasure more discreetly, through invisible but irresistible channels first established in the state-sponsored repression of early modernity.[11]

As is often the case in readings of vampire texts, mine ultimately turns on an allegorical interpretation of the vampire's bite. As I read the above passage, the vampire's bite represents the means by which imperial repression transformed itself into a system for siphoning off life through a web of intrafamilial affective, ideological, and material bonds. Such an intricate pattern of inexorable reproduction is reiterated but ascribed to homosexual or vampiric rather than heterosexual reproduction, in both *Dracula* and perhaps its most significant source, the proceedings of Oscar Wilde's trial. In her article " 'A Wilde Desire Took Me': The Homoerotic History of *Dracula*," Talia Schaffer points to the striking similarity between Jonathan Harker's fears "that Dracula might 'create a new and ever widening circle of semi-demons to batten on the helpless' " and the "widely reported comment" by Wilde's judge, Justice Wills, calling Wilde "the center of a hideous circle of corruption" (400). Both depictions exhibit the logic of the gothic family romance: each ventilates the horror that attends the appropriation of bodies within the capitalist nuclear family and the associated reproduction of capitalist subjectivity indirectly, through expressions of homosexual panic.

Like the nuclear family's processes of self-perpetuation, Dracula's bite, which figures a mode of reproduction that is projectively associated with homosexuality, renders invisible the reproduction of capitalist and imperialist social relations. The historical moment of transformation which the bite reenacts corresponds to the shift from primitive accumulation to the "invisible" appropriation of surplus value that marks the emergence of capitalism. It also corresponds to a shift in emphasis away from spectacularly public modes of juridical discipline, toward a domestic sphere that invisibly accommodates children's minds and bodies, via compulsory heterosexuality, to an economic and national order that Dracula refers to repeatedly as an empire.

The vampire's bite also, however, encodes an additional level of social occlusion specific to the Anglo-Irish family. As I have argued, the Anglo-Irish settler colonialist family was the key social institution by which displaced middle-class British subjects, unable to establish sexually and socially authorizing family structures within Britain, could set themselves up as respectably British *outside* Britain in British colonial possessions and territories. As a self-replicating and seemingly private structure, the Anglo-Irish nuclear family, in turn, authorized British settler colonialism in Ireland through the systematic repression of that system's material origins. The geographically displaced replication of the British nuclear family secured the British state's imperial holdings by recasting political and economic appropriation as the private, domestic arrangements of individuals. Within this oscillatingly British and Irish, public and private family structure, children were the vehicles through which appropriated Irish lands were transformed into Anglo-Irish estates, and the principal means by which British imperialism transformed Ireland into a political and economic extension of England.

The system of vampiric reproduction that both Le Fanu and Stoker depict turns on an invisible network of connections that drain the individual subject even as they invisibly build a transnational web of power relations. Within the Anglo-Irish settler colony, compulsory heterosexuality, like the bite of the vampire, serves to build an empire through "invisible" or private acts within British families that just happen to be located in Ireland. Children become the conduits through which Irish resources are channeled back to the imperial metropolis, while constituting the living bonds that secure their parents' ties to Britain, thereby validating their parents' right to political and economic privilege in Ireland. Within the settler colonial family, the child constitutes the commodity par excellence. It is through the production of children as tangible proof of the colonizer's indigenous status, and through the exploitation of the child's innocence—the child's ability to absorb and accept as absolute fact an internally contradictory narrative—that British settler colonialism took root in Ireland and came to organize, dominate, and profit from the social order within which it was implanted. The Anglo-Irish paranoid gothic, in turn, functioned within Anglo-Irish culture as a crypt for historical material that continued to "haunt" a "new order" into which it could not be incorporated.

Individualism and the Devil's Compact

The rarified domestic sphere that good citizens such as General Spielsdorf and Stoker's Van Helsing are concerned to protect from demonic "outsiders" is the product of Reformation-era ideologies and economic and legal transformations that established the individual as the sole viable economic unit and hence the only site of agency. Anglo-Irish invocations of the Reformation in gothic literature and public discourse repeat this pattern of individuation and isolation through the promotion of fears pertaining to penetration and contamination by alien collectivities. The fearful association of Catholicism with black magic and depraved practices has led a number of Anglo-Irish writers from Maturin to Yeats and contemporary unionist propagandists to envision the Catholic rank and file as requiring an external (Protestant) power structure for protection from a transcendental evil that will otherwise enter the Catholic community via its own priestly class. This vision of a benign, secular Protestant authority that intervenes to protect vulnerable Catholics from a combination of spiritual corruption and physical dissolution is promoted in *Melmoth the Wanderer,* when the Catholic Monçada ultimately flees, of all places, to Ireland to save himself from the Inquisition's omnipresent malice; in Yeats's early play *The Countess Cathleen,* in which an Anglo-Irish woman trades her soul for gold to feed the materially and spiritually underprivileged Irish masses and re-claim their souls from the devils to which they have bartered them; and in Ulster unionist propaganda from 1969 to the present, which sporadi-cally espouses the opinion that most Catholics in the North are decent folk, deceived or intimidated into complicity with terrorism through the joint offices of the Irish Republican Army (IRA) and the Catho-lic Church. These "good" Catholics, this line of argument proceeds, are quietly depending on Protestant hegemony to restore "decency" to their homes and neighborhoods.

In the nineteenth-century paranoid gothic, the relationship of indi-vidualism to autophagous family and social dynamics is already ob-servable symptomatically in figurations of the (often sexual) sacrifice of children to transgenerational compacts. The role of homosexuality, which frequently emerges in such figurations, is to capture the trans-gressive feel of affective and erotic relations within the Anglo-Irish family while disavowing the family's relevance to such scenarios. Gothic scenes of child sacrifice in these texts dramatize the contradiction in-herent in a model of individual autonomy predicated on a system of private landownership that is brought into being only through a covert system of intergenerational transmission.

Throughout the Anglo-Irish gothic tradition, culminating in the work of Yeats, whatever protective, communal magic the Catholic Church in Ireland continued to tolerate[12] was countered with an indi-vidualistic approach to magic and power that constituted the collec-tive as the site of corruption.[13] In the Anglo-Irish paranoid gothic, the isolated pursuit of pure, individualistic agency is depicted sympa-thetically, even when that pursuit leads protagonists into negotiations with malevolent transcendental forces, as it does Maturin's Melmoth, Le Fanu's Baron Vordenburg, and Yeats's Countess Cathleen.[14] Such negotiations are frequently redeemed when they enable the protago-nist, counterpoised against shadowy demonic collectivities, to act as an individuated force for the good despite the suspect provenance of his or her power. Within the moral universe of these narratives, power is spiritually "pure" only when it is untainted by the corrupting forces of community.

In the gothic narratives discussed in this chapter, the emergence of bourgeois individualism, compulsory heterosexuality, and a binary sex/gender system in Ireland are reenacted in recurring struggles over the deployment of children's sexuality and in the divergent fates of their male and female characters. Children's position as private property and the traumatic shaping of children's epistemologies via toxic religious ideologies reiterate early modern interactions between Reformation-era religious terror, the rise of capitalism, and the constriction of the family.

Image patterns within these texts reflect the subjective history of British colonialism in Ireland. Yet the narratives also depict the processes by which social institutions (most centrally, the family) generationally reproduce modern, individualist subjectivity. In the following chapter, I will explore the systemic position that the subject takes up in order to function as such an autonomous individual. As I will argue, the emergence of Anglo-Irish gothic realism in, for instance, *The Picture of Dorian Gray* heralds a more explicit thematization of the paradox inherent in such a model of individual autonomy.

Throughout the evolution of gothicism in Ireland, however, the trope of child sacrifice specifies the position of Anglo-Irish children relative to the British state, pointing to the specialized role of the family within the settler colony. There in particular, to return to the words of Lady Morgan in this chapter's epigraph, the homely processes of private, familial "nourish[ment] within [Ireland's] own bosom" continued discreetly to compel the Anglo-Irish to "destro[y] that source from whence their nutriment flowed."

Chapter 5
Irish Gothic Realism and the Great War
The Devil's Bargain and the Demon Lover

There is a vast store of mythology in both Western and South American cultures concerning the man who sets himself apart from the community to sell his soul to the devil for wealth that is not only useless but the harbinger of despair, destruction, and death. — Michael Taussig, *The Devil and Commodity Fetishism in South America*

What appears to [the German soldier male] — however alien he may feel it to be — as the *defining quality* of his humanity is in fact the most social aspect of his being: the state of his drives as produced by patriarchal capitalism of the nineteenth and twentieth centuries. . . . The soldier male is forced to turn the periphery of his body into a cage for the beast within. In doing so, he deprives it of its function as a surface for social contact. — Klaus Theweleit, *Male Fantasies,* vol. 2

The work of Maturin, Le Fanu, and Stoker established an Anglo-Irish gothic literary tradition that has been highly influential in twentieth-century Irish literature. It is in Oscar Wilde's *The Picture of Dorian Gray,* however, that we find the beginnings of the self-consciously critical Irish gothicism that lends vitality to much of the best Irish writing of this century. In gothic realism during this period, a familiar narrative pattern is redeployed: as in *Melmoth the Wanderer, Carmilla,* and *Dracula,* the isolated individual who traffics with extracommunal forces is destined to be consumed by them. Beginning with *The Picture of Dorian Gray,* however, this narrative's conventional alien, demonic forces are redefined within a realist framework, and the social forces that deliver the subject into negotiations with such entities are themselves made visible. As one critic has pointed out, *The Picture of Dorian Gray* is an excellent illustration of William S. Burroughs's maxim that capitalism at its most effective does not aim to sell the product to the consumer but to sell the consumer to the product.[1] The anticapitalist ethos that comes to the fore in these later gothic productions deliberately reverses, as Marx frequently delights in doing, our conventional expectations concerning what is being consumed and what is doing the consuming.[2]

Narratives that enact versions of the Burkean social contract proliferated in Ireland throughout the twentieth century, emerging, for instance, in a rural Ulster narrative pattern explicated by Henry Glassie in *Passing the Time in Ballymenone: Culture and History of an Ulster Community.* Writing from within the community's symbolic system, Glassie locates meaningful cultural oppositions in the figures of the saint and the witch. According to Glassie, the saint, who also appears as both priest and as outlaw/rebel, is identified with community and primitive communism and with holy communion, the giving of wine which is itself sacred and which extends sympathetic sanctity to all acts of giving. The figure of the witch, which also appears as a landlord and a lawyer, is associated with isolation, greed, surplus value, exploitation of one's neighbors, idleness, community discord, and legally enforced pacts with the devil. Such diabolical pacts will, as the stories about them demonstrate, eventually devour the foolish farmer who attempts to barter his communally constituted soul in return for the opportunity to exploit his neighbors for financial gain (548).

The power of Glassie's analysis lies in its minute, meditative, and obsessive focus on the worldview of a narrowly defined border community in southern Ulster; it is undoubtedly for this reason that his valuable work in Irish narrative has been so little assimilated into the field of Irish literature. Nonetheless, Glassie offers an evocative point of departure for a culturally and historically specific understanding of changes in twentieth-century Irish gothicism in relation to the larger European gothic canon.

If gothic conventions as they appear within twentieth-century Irish narrative are to be fully understood, they must be conceived of as the material record of the struggles, frustrations, goals, and apprehensions of a specific historical and cultural moment (and its corresponding symbolic universe), as well as partially stable cultural artifacts with autonomous histories and specific intertextual and aesthetic relationships that are not necessarily formed in response to a specific historical moment. In citing a specific convention an author may be in dialogue with a prior moment or may (as is especially common in Irish narrative) be citing a prior moment as the precedent for a certain theoretical analysis or course of action within the present. The figures of the saint, the witch, and the devil's bargain function within the specific representational system of folk narratives in Ballymenone and simultaneously circulate within a national and international system of intertextually constituted conventions. The historical residue that attaches to representational patterns through which various ideologies have at one time been mediated, what Stuart Hall has called "historical lines of tendention" (Grossberg 57), connect the saint, the witch, and the devil's bargain as they appear in the folklore of Ballymenone with previous conventional uses of these figures and with both the recent and the ancient history of literal saints and witches, in Ireland and elsewhere. Were we to set aside the intertextual background of these conventions, we would be left with an artificially random and arbitrary set of figures, stripped of their native significatory powers. Yet Irish gothic tropes such as the devil's bargain clearly represent a crucial means by which Irish authors of both Anglo-Irish and native Irish descent have attempted to make sense of and also resist their specific conditions in modern Ireland.

For instance, the gothic figuration of the devil's bargain as it appears in *The Picture of Dorian Gray* and the Ballymenone narratives can be understood as, among other things, an alternative to the Manichean construction of the Irish by their English colonizers as "feminine."[3] As I have argued, the paranoid Irish gothic used gothic conventions to negotiate gender construction, identity, and the anxiety-provoking issues of "sameness" and "difference." In later Anglo-Irish narratives, such as *The Picture of Dorian Gray,* Yeats's "The Rose of Shadow," Bowen's "The Demon Lover," and other texts I discuss in subsequent chapters, these issues are also negotiated, but to differing ends.

A shift in the central focus of the Irish Protestant gothic tradition seems to have been connected to a disabling awareness of the British gaze. As Anglo-Irish society felt itself to be transforming and becoming unlike itself within an increasingly unsympathetic English gaze, it desperately groped for an acceptable sexual/national identity through the mediating mechanism of gothic projection. A critical strand of gothicism that encoded the problematic position of the Anglo-Irish relative to the English gradually overshadowed earlier gothic impulses. Gothic expressions of guilty fear either of retaliation by or absorption into the dispossessed native Irish grew increasingly muted as these possibilities loomed larger on the immediate political horizon. As British policies toward Ireland threatened to reduce the Anglo-Irish to the status of "Irish" either literally, through the granting of Irish autonomy, or figuratively, through the demonizing and generalizing representations of "the Irish" that began to emerge in England from the 1860s, gothic representation seems no longer to have been adequate to contain Anglo-Irish fears of impending persecution. The transitional Anglo-Irish gothicism that emerged in the work of Yeats, Synge, and Lady Gregory in Ireland and in the work of Oscar Wilde in England instead encodes anxieties pertaining to historical repetition. These more critical, self-conscious gothic productions typically acknowledge the historical culpability of the settler colonial system. Often they express an anxious wish to break out of a series of violent generational spirals that are increasingly situated as emanating from within the very structures through which the Anglo-Irish family has sought to protect and perpetuate itself. Gothic tropes in these later texts also frequently parody or counter perceived British characterizations of the Irish (including the Anglo-Irish) as irrational, depraved, and grotesque.

The automatic impulse to situate Anglo-Irish gothic literature within a stable, British-defined textual and social universe may be productively decentered, however, if we also read Anglo-Irish gothic conventions in light of Ballymenone's saint/witch dichotomy. For my purposes here, this dichotomy will demarcate a potentially oppositional alternative to the gendered master/peasant binary that came to inflect much of Irish literary representation over the course of British colonialism. This alternative saint/witch dichotomy resembles the well-known "corrido hero/ranger" opposition identified by Américo Paredes in the lyrics of Mexican American border ballads.[4] Like the saint/witch dichotomy, the corrido hero/ranger opposition serves to neutralize a dominant group's

Manichean construction of the Others whose culture and land it is in the process of plundering. In Texas, the ranger/bandit dichotomy inscribed Mexican Americans as criminal by definition. Similarly, English depictions of Irishness have, in effect, criminalized (or pathologized) Irish identity. British essentialist constructions of the Irish as inebriates, liars, dreamers, malingerers, bombers, and terrorists are decentered or obliquely opposed (rather than refuted or projected back) in an oral tradition that lines up outlaws, priests, revolutionaries, and saints as the forces that make community coherence possible, while representing the lawyer, the landlord, and the witch as in league with the forces of satanic individualism. Within this system of representation, the familiar gothic conventions have clearly undergone historically and culturally determinate changes; figures corresponding to the romantic, isolated Melmoth, Carmilla, and Dracula, all explicitly asocial figures, are reframed within Irish folklore as figures for the colonial system itself or for the effects of that system.

The Elizabethan "Great Chain of Being" (of which Catholicism was constituted, in the original gothic novels, as the demonic shadow) has been reorganized in the narrative conventions identified by Glassie and in the narratives on which I focus in this chapter. Within these narratives, colonialism, monarchy, and capitalism are constituted as the shadow-underside of an otherwise orderly and comprehensible world. These modifications of the quasi-conventional figure of the witch and of the highly conventional "devil's pact" do not present a counterargument to British Manichean representations of the Irish. Rather, they are irrelevant to the terms of debate set by the British. The conventions of the saint and the witch ignore essentialist constructions of race in favor of specific acts or patterns of thought and action that they show to be allied with the sacred or the demonic. Sacred patterns of giving lead to increased community solidarity, whereas demonic patterns that create hierarchy and hence exploitation within the community destroy community solidarity and dehumanize those who set themselves apart from human community by appropriating labor as surplus value through rents, fees, or wage labor.

A locally responsive analysis of Irish manifestations of the gothic, then, would suggest that the "devil's bargain," which in England entails the taking into oneself of an essential evil through volitional negotiations with a transcendent and eternal demonic force, in Ireland takes the form of a structural, local, and relational condition that is symptomatic of rather than fundamental to a state of alienation from one's communally constituted "humanity." While I will retain an awareness of the larger Continental gothic tradition out of which emerge the specific narratives I examine, it will be this specific, relational conception of the gothic on which I will predominantly rely in the readings that follow.

"Something That Would Breed Horrors and Yet Would Never Die"
The Picture of Dorian Gray

As Ed Cohen argues in his essay "Writing Gone Wilde: Homoerotic Desire in the Closet of Representation," *The Picture of Dorian Gray*'s central, complex trope of a subject irreparably split into "the image of his body and his body itself" (81) is the product of cultural representation. During the painting of Dorian Gray's portrait, the painter Basil Hallward and the aesthete Lord Henry Wotton reorient Dorian pictorially and verbally, "in relation both to his own identity and to his social context" (80). The finished portrait, a composite emblem of the two older men's desire (since as Basil paints, Lord Henry's monologue elicits on Dorian's face the striking "look . . . never seen before" [Wilde 158] that sparks the painting into life), shows Dorian to himself in a new and exciting erotic context. Dorian's sudden, acute awareness of his body as the object of male sexual desire causes him to "internalize an identity that excites his body only to make it vulnerable to the passage of time" (Cohen 80). Prompted by the sudden, radical sexual awakening that the painting elicits, Dorian makes his spontaneous fatal wish, that he might exchange his soul in order that "it were I who was to be always young, and the picture that was to grow old" (168). Dorian's speech act linguistically enacts a separation of his body from his soul, so that, as Cohen argues, "the 'I' of the speaking character is projected against the visual image of the 'I,'" and "his body is evacuated and thereby removed from the flow of time" (81).

Cohen elucidates some of the most striking implications of Wilde's representational and narrative strategies by exploring *The Picture of Dorian Gray* as an exemplary site at which to initiate a broader exploration of the representational strategies used by some Victorian men as a means to articulate alternative masculine sexual practices and identities. These practices and identities, Cohen reminds us, were at risk at a historical moment when "the discursive production of . . . the 'true' bourgeois male" was consolidating itself through the discursive production (and exemplary persecution) of "the homosexual" as its defining antithesis (69). The novel's representation of a radical and irreparable breach between bodily desire and representation, however, has implications and intertextual connections that extend in directions other than those Cohen explores. Eve Kosofsky Sedgwick, for instance, briefly gestures in these alternate directions in her characterization of the schism between person and persona that typified Wilde's own mode of existence, which she associates with representational complexities connected to Wilde's national as well as sexual subject position. According to Sedgwick's analysis:

Wilde's alienizing physical heritage of unboundable bulk from his Irish nationalist mother, of a louche swarthiness from his Celticizing father, underlined with every self-foregrounding gesture of his person and *persona* the fragility, unlikelihood and strangeness — at the same time, the transformative reperceptualizing power — of the new "*homo-*" homosexual imagining of male-male desire. By the same pressure, it dramatized the uncouth nonequivalence of an English national body with a British with an Irish, as domestic grounds from which to launch a stable understanding of national/imperial relations. (*Epistemology* 176)

A rupture parallel to that which Sedgwick identifies in Wilde's self-construction, between persona and person or the socially and representationally produced subject and the body, is conventionally encoded in a number of Irish and Anglo-Irish narratives that resemble *The Picture of Dorian Gray* in their general outline. Although an exploration of Wilde's representational strategies as characteristic of a larger Anglo-Irish corpus might seem to lead away from or even to contest the fine work that has been done by queer theorists such as Cohen and

Sedgwick, my intention in widening the cultural context within which Wilde's narrative structures may be read is to add another dimension to our understanding of these structures. I am specifically interested in the problems of masculine self-representation that Cohen, Sedgwick, and others have explored as these were shaped, in England and in Ireland, at later points in the twentieth century by international and imperial relations.

The late-Victorian changes in masculine self-representation that, as Cohen argues, *The Picture of Dorian Gray* encodes and contributes to came to crisis in the early years of the twentieth century, on the battle-fields of the First World War. The open homoeroticism that character-izes much of the poetry and many of the memoirs and accounts of this war (Fussell 270–309) represents an extension of the publicly homo-erotic discourses identified by Cohen and others as characteristic of the fin de siècle period. Beginning in the late nineteenth century, as Cohen argues, a British male *heterosexual* subject position was consolidated through the systematic elaboration of a *homosexual* identity. The re-lationship of Anglo-Irish men to these developments was, I contend, especially fraught. Throughout the consolidation of what Sedgwick has called "the modern dispensation" (*Epistemology* 131), Anglo-Irish men, with their ambivalent relationship to British national identity, seem to have supplied an especially salient source of representational raw ma-terial, thus constituting an important site for the negotiation of particu-larly delicate matters pertaining to gender, sexuality, and nationality.

During the Victorian period, the Anglo-Irish Wilde was publicly scapegoated so as to produce an infamous emblem of a more broadly constituted, juridical homosexual identity (associated, from the outset, with aristocracy and with the arts). As Cohen argues, the emergence of a commercial, bourgeois British masculine heterosexuality was enabled through the public construction, via Wilde, of an aristocratic, artistic (and, I would add, ambiguously foreign) homosexual identity that was set up as British masculinity's antithesis. During the First World War, the (Anglo-Irish) Irish nationalist Roger Casement was semipublicly discredited through the circulation of the retyped transcripts of his per-sonal journal, in which he detailed his homosexual activities during his tenure as a British diplomat in South America.[5] Casement's subsequent execution was deemed tolerable by Britain's elite owing to the repulsion generated among them by privately circulated excerpts from his journal. Like Wilde's trial, Casement's highly publicized trial and his postmortem public exposure as a homosexual made a lasting contribution to the symbolic construction of both homosexuality and heterosexuality in England. His execution — publicly as an Irish nationalist, a German collaborator, and a British traitor and privately as a homosexual — reinflected Wildean aristocratic aestheticism and otherworldliness by explicitly connecting these prior "known" qualities of the homosexual with treason, collaboration, and anticolonial resistance. Casement's subsequent demonization as a sexual and (hence) national deviant served to modify earlier British constructions of the homosexual (and thereby the heterosexual); deviations from national and heterosexual norms were articulated, through the figure of Casement, within a closed circuit, with each reflecting and discrediting the other. This convenient wartime modification of the British symbolic order infused Victorian constructions of the heterosexual businessman with patriotic loyalty, thereby heightening national claims on business and industry during a time of national crisis. Casement's oscillating Anglo-Irish subject position, its ambivalence intensified through a simultaneous emphasis on his former diplomatic career and his later, fervent identification with Irish nationalism, enabled such a modification because it allowed British authorities to construct him, contradictorily, as both a cautionary *example* for British men and as the antithesis of British manhood. Casement was represented simultaneously as British and therefore a traitor and a sexual monster (as opposed to a rebel with appropriately barbarous customs), and as a national Other, as Irish, and therefore deserving of public discreditation and death.

Following World War I, as Paul Fussell notes, the homoerotic discourses that had been so instrumental in consolidating bourgeois heterosexual masculinity through the early twentieth century grew increasingly muted (306–7). During the war, the mutually constitutive interrelationship between heterosexual and homosexual masculinities reached its apogee; homoerotic bonds between officers and men and among the ranks were, if Fussell is correct, nearly ubiquitous, although generally not preclusive of heterosexual attachments. By the end of the war, however, the heterosexual term had, surprisingly, all but eclipsed the homosexual term on which it had, until recently, relied for its own definition, rendering it, for a period, virtually invisible.

Given the significant renegotiations of masculinity relative to nationality and sexuality that took place in Britain during the First World War, as well as the ambivalent and sometimes vulnerable position of Anglo-Irish men relative to these changes, it is perhaps not surprising that this war has emerged as a particularly urgent locus for contemporary Irish literary interrogations of heterosexual masculinity's "modern dispensation." In current-day Irish literature thematizing the experience of Anglo-Irish men in World War I, homoeroticism represents, in addition to "itself," a metaphor for all human love, eroticism, and bonding. The basis for the symbolic connection between the literal fact of homosexual love and a broader constellation of human connections that homosexual love, in these texts, persistently figures may be found in the historical position of Anglo-Irish men, whose ambiguous national identity has, at times, constituted them as the ideal national/sexual scapegoats against which an increasingly rigid bourgeois, British heterosexual masculinity was defined. An especially significant trope that emerges in some of these narratives fulfills itself, as do *The Picture of Dorian Gray* and the Ballymenone narratives, in the fatal reintegration of sundered elements of the self. The cyclical patterns of dispossession encoded in both Irish representations of postcolonial social relations and Anglo-Irish representations of national and sexual subjectivity recur in these contemporary depictions of World War I in ways which suggest possible connections between these various spirals of dispossession and which also elucidate the role of the Anglo-Irish settler colonial system in perpetuating them within Ireland.

Gothicism and the Great War

In *The Great War and Modern Memory,* Fussell suggests that spatial and temporal separation—which Sedgwick has identified as a central gothic convention (*Coherence* 12–13)—is crucial to the narrative assimilation of that war into modern British literature and consciousness

(90). Fussell emphasizes irony, characterized by its "doubled," mutually "separated" narrative elements, as the dominant mode through which memories of war that would otherwise blur into undifferentiated carnage take narrative shape in memoirs, accounts, and literary renderings of the Great War. He calls attention to World War I literature's obsession with "contrast," "antithesis," and "binary vision" (105), concluding that, for Siegfried Sassoon, whose oeuvre he finds thematically typical (90), "'the line' divides everything and *always* will" (105; emphasis added). He opens his discussion of "the theater of war" with the section "Being Beside Oneself," in which he discusses the internal schism precipitated by the theatricality of war. He indicates that both spatial and temporal dichotomies are crucial in narrative accounts of World War I and offers numerous examples of dichotomized, mutually exclusive depictions of time and space, in which "before" and "after" the war form a temporal axis of separation (90) and "the Boche line" (105) forms a spatial axis.

If we read Fussell's overview of narrative accounts of the Great War through Sedgwick's account of the gothic, the liminal space between "before" and "after," that is, the war itself, and the liminal space No Man's Land, dividing the opposing sides, constitute what Sedgwick terms "the breach," the site of "the worst violence, the most potent magic, and the most paralyzing instances of the uncanny" (*Coherence* 13). In Sedgwick's model, the breach between mutually exclusive binaries generates paralysis. In particular, the breach represents the site out of which proceeds a particularly complicated form of "paralysis": the repetition compulsion, which perpetually conceives of itself as breaking free from an intolerable stasis only to reenact the precise pattern of behavior through which this stasis is perpetually restored.

The specifically gothic character of the rumors that "developed into [the] fully fleshed narrative fictions" (Fussell 121) recounted by Fussell offers excellent evidence for a gothic relationship between horror and liminality that begins to take shape in Great War narratives, even during the war. The "ghostly German officer-spy who [according to numerous accounts] appear[ed] in the British trenches just before an attack" (121), for instance, is liminal in a number of ways: he is neither quite obviously one of the British nor obviously "the enemy," he is neither clearly dead nor quite reassuringly alive, and he is a "German" who appears on the wrong side of "the Boche line." The ghostly German seems related to both the "magical" and the "uncanny" in that "no one sees him come or go," and his cyclical reappearances at various unexpected places and moments represent a "mystery" that is "never solved." Narratively, he foreshadows the violence Sedgwick associates in her analysis with the "breach" (122).

Sedgwick's spatial, linguistic, and psychological descriptions of gothic conventions, in dialogue with Fussell's suggestive readings of World War I narratives, forms the basis for my understanding of gothic conventions in Irish literary depictions of the Great War. In the analysis that follows, I explore the relationship between sexuality (especially homoeroticism), liminality, division, and repetition in twentieth-century Irish literary gothicism across a small but heterogenous selection of texts. I hope that my analysis will suggest ways in which a broad-ranging, comparative, historically specific approach to these literary conventions may help us both to understand historical representation in the Irish literary tradition and to elucidate some of the powerful feelings with which imperial relations, masculinity, and war have been invested in modern Irish literary memory.

The Anglo-Irish Demon Lover Trope

She . . . felt that unnatural promise drive down between her and the rest of all human kind. . . . She could not have plighted a more sinister troth.
— Elizabeth Bowen, "The Demon Lover"

William Butler Yeats and Elizabeth Bowen, two of the best-known authors of the Anglo-Irish Protestant Ascendancy, have both written short stories in which the folkloric "demon lover" trope is wedded to a gothic sensibility that, like *The Picture of Dorian Gray,* expresses what Sedgwick has described as the gothic's central preoccupation: "the [violent] lengths there are to go to reintegrate . . . sundered elements" (*Coherence* 13). In Yeats's suppressed short story "The Rose of Shadow," Michael Creed, the demonic master of a coasting smack, is "killed, with a blow from a boat hook," by Peter Herne, the brother of Oona, his most recent "conquest." A year later he returns to claim his beloved and destroy her family (228). In Bowen's celebrated short story

"The Demon Lover," a woman makes a promise during the First World War to a "faceless" lover, who returns to claim her during the Second. Deeply woven into the narrative structure of these stories is a repetitive logic turning on the issue of an unbreachable but intolerable separation that is intensely conditioned by Irish history.

Many of the most critically read Irish texts—Joyce's "The Dead"; the cycles within cycles of *Finnegan's Wake;* Beckett's obsessively repetitive drama; and the pastoral, folkloric repetitions of Yeats's early poetry and the more sinister cyclings of his later meditations on history—exhibit both an obsession with and a terror of the seemingly intractable repetitions that Irish history and Irish literature appear to have inscribed into each other.[6] The narrative structure of Yeats's short story suggests precisely such a horror in its depiction of an act of violence (Peter Herne's killing of Michael Creed) that sows the seeds for a later, more monstrous cataclysm. The primal, folkloric logic of "The Rose of Shadow" seems to work at cross-purposes with conventional Anglo-American interpretations of the Christian resurrection narrative by linking the "renewal" figured in the reunited lovers to the simultaneous destruction of the Herne family. Yeats's ending presents us with an ambiguous "rebirth" achievable only at the expense of a great deal of unambiguous death and devastation; both rebirth and devastation are linked causally to a previous triggering act of violence. The specialized understanding of the resurrection observable in Yeats's short story is additionally visible in a number of literary depictions of the Easter Uprising: Terry Eagleton's *Saints and Scholars* has James Connolly repeatedly stressing that the Uprising's "failure" has sown the seeds for a later (repetitive) "success"; in "Easter 1916" Yeats emphasizes a "terrible beauty" that is born out of violence and in its assertion that "all is changed, changed utterly," foresees, as does he in other poems on the same topic, "The Rose Tree" and "Sixteen Dead Men," a later, greater cataclysm; and Iris Murdoch, in her account of the Uprising in *The Red and the Green*, depicts Easter as figuring an epistemic and repetitive violence: "that *is* the point; we arrive at the grave to find it empty" (161).

Bowen's short story displays a similar narrative logic. As in "The Rose of Shadow," "The Demon Lover" links the gothic reunion of divided lovers with historically repetitive violence. The relationship between the gothic reunion of a self with some incomprehensible, unspeakable thing from which it has been divided (Mrs. Drover with her faceless lover) and the horror of mass violence (European civilization in the context of World War II) is less tightly constructed in "The Demon Lover." Yet it is historically significant that both Mrs. Drover and the European nations made promises (or treaties) in World War I the implications of which they did not, at the time, foresee; in both cases the "coming due" of these promises arrives in the form of an unanticipated and appalling reunion in which the past, figuratively, devours the present.

Bowen's short story, although set in England, displays a narrative logic that exhibits patterns of repetition and historical recurrence that are characteristic of Anglo-Irish narrative structure.[7] In it, an isolated woman who is claimed by a supernaturally returning lover is depicted as a sleepwalker, as overtaken by a sort of stasis or paralysis. Mrs. Drover moves in an "unfamiliar queerness." She finds a mysterious letter left at her shut-up London house, which she experiences as permeated by a "whole air of being a cracked cup from which memory, with its reassuring power, had just evaporated or leaked away." This curious evaporation of memory, the force by which history is shaped and kept under control, "made a crisis — and at just this crisis the letter-writer had, knowledgeably, struck" (664). Bowen constructs the house as a liminal space no longer imbued with the present or properly in contact with the stabilizing past. In this moment of "crisis," both stasis and action seem dangerous to her protagonist; either might lead to paralysis, to a situation in which she would find herself caught in the very arms whose embrace she seeks to evade. As it happens, in the perfect compromise between action and stasis (an active decision to take a cab allows for her passive removal from the house), Mrs. Drover places herself directly into the possession of "Mr. Driver," and the past and present merge into a frozen and horrendous tableau that represents the final ascendancy of a historically predetermined stasis. Yeats's Oona, although she *seeks* a reunion with her murdered lover, is even more definitively overtaken by a deep, visionary thrall from which she questions her mother about whether the dead "wander near to us" ("Rose" 229). She awaits her lover's return with "all the submission which had been in the heart of woman from the first day" (231); once again the apocalyptic consummation of the demon lover scenario is shown to represent the fulfillment of a historically (and, in Yeats's analysis, theologically) determinate paralysis.

The pattern expressed in the short stories of Yeats and Bowen is a paradigm for an aversion to repetition that also expresses itself as a horror of liminality, historical paralysis, and the transgression of categorical boundaries. This paradigm also appears in two contemporary Irish texts. Both Frank McGuinness's 1986 play *Observe the Sons of Ulster Marching toward the Somme* and Jennifer Johnston's 1974 novel *How Many Miles to Babylon?* express variations on the "demon lover" theme. But Johnston and McGuinness complicate the paradigmatic narrative tension between a "horror of isolation" and a "horror of union" by adding an overt awareness of the "horror of sameness" that derives from a specific moment in Anglo-Irish history at which a cultural double bind entrapped young Anglo-Irish men into a destructive devil's bargain, the repercussions of which are still being felt in contemporary Ireland.

Homoeroticism, the Great War, and the Imperial Demon Lover

First, the Ulster Division at the Somme
Going over the top with 'Fuck the Pope!'
'No surrender!': a boy about to die,
Screaming 'Give 'em one for the Shankill!'
'Wilder than Gurkhas' were my father's words
of admiration and bewilderment.
Next comes the London Scottish padre
Resettling kilts with his swagger stick,
With a stylish back-hand and a prayer.
Over a landscape of dead buttocks
My father followed him for fifty years.
At last a belated casualty,
He said—lead traces flaring till they hurt—
'I am dying for King and Country, slowly.'
— Michael Longley, "Wounds"

I got out to create, not destroy. But the gods wouldn't allow that. I could not create. . . . [W]hen I saw my hands working they were not mine but the hands of my ancestors, interfering. . . . I could not create. I could only preserve. Preserve my flesh and blood, what I'd seen, what I'd learned. . . . I was contaminated. I smashed my sculpture and I rejected any woman who would continue my breed. I destroyed one to make certain. And I would destroy my own life. I would take up arms at the call of my Protestant fathers. I would kill in their name and I would die in their name. To win their respect would be my sole act of revenge. — Frank McGuinness, *Observe the Sons of Ulster*

In Michael Longley's poem "Wounds," Frank McGuinness's *Observe the Sons of Ulster Marching toward the Somme,* and Jennifer Johnston's *How Many Miles to Babylon?* the experience of Anglo-Irish Protestants in the Great War is associated with the trope of "the living dead" and with a sometimes grotesquely articulated homoeroticism. The narrative logic of each of these texts appears to have been conditioned by both the devil's bargain and the demon lover thematics.

In Irish texts that thematize World War I, the demon lover trope finds expression through an older or isolated self who confronts a younger, socially constituted self who, seeking power, sexual gratification, or community membership, made a bargain that has now come due. We can detect this pattern, for instance, in Yeats's poems in memory of Lady Gregory's son, Major Robert Gregory. In "An Irish Airman Foresees His Death," Yeats envisions Robert Gregory as trading "the years to come" for an ecstatic, yet ominously Coleridgean "life in death" (328). Yet, in the originally suppressed "Reprisals" (791), the spirit of Gregory returns to the Irish countryside to see the havoc wreaked there by the Black and Tans, British soldiers on whose side he had fought. In "An Irish Airman," Yeats envisions Gregory as bartering his life gladly; Gregory's status in "Reprisals" as a member of the "cheated dead" derives from the blatant British betrayal of his misplaced loyalty. Choosing to fight those he did not hate in order to guard those he did not love, Robert Gregory was betrayed because he gave his service to an imperial power that, in recompense, made war on his people.

In Yeats's poems, we can sense a devil's pact whereby Gregory barters his *Irishness,* his status as a "species being," as Marx calls it in *The Economic and Philosophical Manuscripts* (*Early Writings* 126), in return for power, coded in one of its more palatable forms in "An Irish Airman" as "abandon" and identified with isolation, individualism, and the rejection of community. At the same time, we can also recognize a "demon lover" thematic of the specific sort I have outlined. Robert Gregory returns, in effect, to confront his communally constituted self that is now, in the bodies of "his tenants" (recalled in "An Irish Airman" as "my countrymen Kiltartan's poor"), being rent apart by "half-drunk or whole-mad soldiery." In this sense, the demon lover and the devil's bargain thematics merge, so that what are ordinarily understood to be separate, if related, narrative patterns cannot in this case be readily broken back into their constituent parts.

In Frank McGuinness's *Observe the Sons of Ulster,* a play written over sixty years after the war, we find this pattern accentuated. McGuinness foregrounds "difference" and "sameness." His central character, Pyper, his name a dialogical sign for Pan (god of sexual abandon) and for the military musician, has signed up, unlike his comrades, because he felt himself to be "too different" rather than because he yearns for conformity. While his comrades have enlisted to fight alongside the English to "have life and have it more abundantly," through a mystical participation with the colonialist power structure, Pyper clearly wishes to die. Ironically, both Pyper and his comrades find fates "different" from those they sought. Pyper, an aristocratic homosexual who seeks to "kill" his difference along with the biological life of his illicit body and its illegal and unrepresentable desires, is forced to live on, suffering his way into a demonic conformity. In the play's culminating moment, he is transformed from a delightful homosexual fool figure with a penchant for morbid puns into a living corpse, ravaged by the gods of nationalist history and chauvinist religion. His comrades, on the other hand, who had hoped to live out expanded lives through an active merging with the imperial will, become "different men" (76) through the alchemy of death. The Arnoldian feminization of the Irish by the British here impels a set of Irish Protestant youths, anxious to prove their national allegiance and hence their masculinity, into the deadly (but unquestionably masculine) role of British foot soldier.

Only Pyper, a homosexual and so an irremediably "feminized" man, recognizes (and continually brings up, to his comrades' discomfort) the gravity of their situation. Pyper's significatory strategies decenter discourse, upsetting the expectations of those around him. His verbal seduction of David Craig, for instance, unsettles David's secure grasp of binary gender divisions by playing on and conflating Christian tropes of sin, temptation, and carnality, associated with Eve, and sacrifice, death, and spiritual redemption, associated with Christ. In their first encounter, Pyper offers David "a piece of apple," thereby reenacting Eve's purported sexual temptation of Adam. David deflects Pyper's "sinful" offer through a stereotypical, commonsense Protestant strategy, protesting that he "[has] work to do" (14). The sexual carnality associated with Eve merges in this dialogue into the sacrificial, redemptive love of Christ when Pyper asks David, "Did you not join up to die for me?" (15). This theme of a Christlike homoerotic sacrifice is repeated throughout the play in ways that call attention not only to the homoerotic underpinnings of Christian agape but also to how this homoerotic agape is deployed in the context of imperial militarism as a way to seduce young men into "dying for each other" (16), as David Craig agrees philosophically that they might.

As a homosexual man, Pyper has no representable position of authority within discursive norms equating masculinity and heterosexuality with autonomy and authority, so he specializes in discursive anarchy. David cautiously begins to flirt with Pyper after admitting, in response to Pyper's erotically charged question, "Are you *rare*, David?" that he is when he wants to be (16). When Pyper solicits his "experienced" opinion on the differing attractions of men and women, David bursts out in frustration, "Why ask me? Do you expect me to know?" Pyper secures the bisexual subject position that David has just implicitly admitted to (by acknowledging that he doesn't distinguish between the beauty of men or women) by observing, "I think you are a rare boy, David. When you want to be, as you say" (32).

Just as McGuinness's protagonist alternately effaces and exploits external difference, particularly gender difference, to achieve his ends, McGuinness also exploits for its dramatic possibilities the "difference within" that Fussell contends is inevitably experienced by conscriptees, who "know they are only temporarily playing their ill-learned parts" (191). One of the play's especially gothic scenes takes place immediately before the final charge, when Pyper and Roulston, a former Protestant minister, attempt to locate, in time and in space, "the breach" out of which conflict emerges. In their exchange it is clear that they are locked into a system in which their energies are being appropriated against their own interests, but against which there is no way to fight back:

Pyper: There's no fight back?
Roulston: There's just the fight.
Pyper: The good fight?
Roulston: The everlasting fight.
Pyper: Inside us?
Roulston: And outside us. (79)

As Pyper and Roulston conclude, the conflict in which they are engaged is liminally located; like ideology, it is ineffable, it appears transhistorical and immutable, and it is situated both within and outside oneself simultaneously.

The ongoing generational transmission of destruction that is ironically designated by Pyper as "the good fight" manifests, for Pyper and his comrades, as "tak[ing] up arms at the call of [their] Protestant fathers." This destructive process claimed Pyper in spite of himself, for it precluded his "creating" anything new and destined him only to "preserve" himself and, through himself, a system that negates both his life and his death by requiring him to "kill in [the Protestant fathers'] name and . . . die in their name" (57). In France, where he initially fled to escape "Carson's dance" (the blood pact through which Edward Carson bound all adult Protestant men to fight to the death to maintain Protestant hegemony and a British identity for Ulster; 56), Pyper recalls that his life was preserved, once he discovered that his hands could only extend the work of his ancestors, because he had at last made (or acknowledged) "a covenant" (18).[8] The "good fight" to which Pyper's covenant binds him emerges out of the breach that the original Ulster plantation created both "inside," within the Protestant psyche, and "outside," between Protestants and the Catholics, against which several of the characters in the play obsessively define themselves. The unshakable sense of religious "rightness" that from the first characterized and underwrote Ulster Protestants' alienation from their compatriots is cyclically redeployable not as a means to *create,* as Pyper's inability to escape and begin again as a French sculptor emphasizes, but as an astonishingly effective means to *preserve* the Protestant settler colonialist order through the symbolic or literal destruction of religiously constituted Others.

Anxiety concerning sameness and difference is played out in the gift of an Orange sash that Anderson, one of the play's two Protestant extremists, makes to Pyper. This scene is reminiscent of Fussell's ghostly German spy narrative in which the appearance of a mysterious liminal figure who has "something wrong with his uniform" signals the onset of mass slaughter (121). Anderson tells Pyper, "We've noticed something missing from your uniform" (77). As in the ghostly spy narrative, a deviation in uniform presages massive violence. In this narrative, however, Pyper's *acceptance* of conformity with his apparently heterosexual comrades (who actually describe a homoerotic continuum) in effect *denies* or effaces the liminality that is the only space in which he can effectively maintain an identity; here, it is the evaporation of liminality in Pyper's acceptance of a securely Protestant identity that signals the onset of violence.[9]

The aged Pyper has previously appeared only in the play's opening monologue, a Beckettian segment in which he addresses a demonic god of history who orders him to recite accounts of the war to be recycled as fuel for the current unionist struggle in Northern Ireland to retain a "British" identity. This ravaged, history-assailed elder Pyper reappears as the play's eight young characters are entering battle, chanting "Ulster. Ulster. Ulster" in preparation for the charge over the top at the Somme.

The chant ceases and the men freeze. Young Pyper, returning, as it were, from the mists of the past, recites with the aged Pyper a litany to which elder Pyper responds, invariably, "Ulster."

Younger Pyper: The temple of the Lord is ransacked.
Elder Pyper: Ulster.
    (Pyper reaches towards himself.)

Younger Pyper: Dance in this deserted temple of the Lord.
Elder Pyper: Dance.
  (Darkness.) (80)

In this final scene, the shell of narrative falls away, and Elder and Younger Pyper, purified signs for a historical past and present, respectively, reach for each other, collapsing history in a moment of chilling recognition. The "dark God" of blood sacrifice in the name of Ulster unites the past and present in a demonic embrace.

The embrace, a mysterious "dance" within a deserted and ransacked temple, and the apocalyptic merging of a violent past with an equally violent present at the behest of a demonic god, signal the presence of the demon lover motif. The desire that impels the aged Pyper finally to embrace and glorify the Somme is his yearning for his lost lover, David Craig, who died in that battle. The play's culminating depiction of a forbidden embrace between two men who are in fact *the same* man foregrounds the sense in which prohibitions against gay and lesbian love are also, literally and metonymically, prohibitions against self-knowledge and the possibility of a coherent self. As I will show, both McGuinness's play and Jennifer Johnston's novel *How Many Miles to Babylon?* use gothic forms of representation to suggest that where either sexual or national self-knowledge is forbidden by fiat, desire will inexorably return in ghastly, distorted, and destructive forms.

In *How Many Miles to Babylon?* a similar crisis between "difference" and "sameness" is depicted in the life of Alexander, the paralyzed and isolated only son of a Dublin-area Big House. Johnston, along with other Protestant women writing in the Republic, has been critically marginalized as a "Big House" writer, as though that space, when occupied by a female, by definition cannot produce literature worthy of any serious critic's political or literary attention or analysis.[10] *How Many Miles to Babylon?* nevertheless stands as a clear-eyed and searing indictment of both colonialism and gender construction in Ireland.

The narrative is framed by the figure of Alexander, alone, writing because, since he is "an officer and a gentleman," "they have given [him his] notebooks, pen, ink and paper." He asserts his isolation and paralysis from the outset, as a sort of manifesto. Like Yeats's Gregory, he is "committed to no cause, [he loves] no living person. . . . There is no place for speculation or hope, or even dreams . . . [he has] not communicated with either [his] father or [his] mother" (1). He begins the review of his life that he undertakes while awaiting execution with the terse statement, "As a child I was alone" (3).

Alexander is parented by an English-identified, isolated mother and an Irish-identified, community-minded father. His mother is associated with the demonic and isolating properties of British imperialism: she systematically isolates her son from every sentient being in his environment, including his father, in the name of bringing him up "English." Johnston's attribution of this pro-English, isolationist mania to a Big House mother instead of, as we might expect, to a father reverses gendered power roles: the mother identifies with the empowered and dominating English, whereas the father identifies with the downtrodden and disenfranchised Irish. Through her appropriation of an a priori colonialist discourse, Alec's mother gains substantial *gendered* power through a sort of devil's bargain. She isolates herself and her son in return for the subject position "head of household." The text suggests that she requires this absolute power in the household in order to veto any possibility of sex between herself and her husband, whom she married in desperation when her English lover abandoned her during pregnancy. She appropriates his English subject position to symbolically castrate her Irish-identified husband, and we come to see her point: society dictated that she marry or descend into a life of prostitution or some other liminal female space in which rape (economically or physically coerced sex) would be inevitable.

In marrying a man whom she can stave off, Alec's mother fends off a violation which is always imminent, always, under patriarchal law, "her fate," but which is always deferred. Alec's mother is able to seize just enough power to legislate her own bodily desires, or at least to prevent their direct (and socially mandated) violation. Her continual acts of deferral, however, culminate in her effectively orphaning Alexander by telling him that his father is not his biological father. She discursively *enforces* Alec's status as English, thereby compelling him to enact the final blood sacrifice that her devil's bargain demands: he must fight and die for England. In this "demon lover" narrative, the mother protects, at enormous cost to herself and her family, the abandoning British lover who represents a bodily desire which she refuses to split off from herself and which symbolically returns to claim and devour its own offspring.

Alexander's sole hope emerges when he befriends and loves Jerry, a working-class, Irish Catholic stable hand. Jerry, as he matures, is becoming increasingly conscious of the nationalist struggle, and Alexander's love for him represents the possibility that Alec will break out of his "privileged" English isolation and live out the community-minded wish of his father, who tells him: "I would like to know that you will always do what is best for the land. Not for you or for her or the strange dreams that may come into your head. Here, the land must come first. You understand. It is the country's heart. It was taken from the people. We . . . I must be clear. . . . We took it from the people. I would like to feel that it will, when the moment comes, be handed back in good order" (42–43). To this he pathetically adds, "We are not totally bad." What Alexander does not know is that his life and his body are not his own; any communal bonds that his father and Jerry might bring into his life are severed, as if on cue, by an imperialist war that his mother requires him to join. His life is to be hers and England's. Alexander finds himself prevented from acting on his unrepresentable (and therefore unspeakable) desire for a working-class, Irish Catholic man. He is isolated and ultimately consumed by a system that categorically forbids the sorts of intimacy between men across class and national groupings that his love for Jerry represents. Difference and sameness, in the last instance, determine the trajectory of Alexander's life, but a preexisting system of geopolitical representation determines who shall be "different" and who "the same." Alexander's personal preferences, his ties of affection and love, exert no force, nor do those of any other individual player within the global game of representation set in motion by imperialist economic priorities that isolate and fragment communities into individual "selves" who may then do business, sign contracts, give or sell their land or labor, or die in defense of geographically remote property and profits.

Alec's continued attempts to touch, nurture, defend, speak with, or spend time with Jerry are perceived by the British military order as aberrant not because of the ways in which Alec and Jerry are the same (it seems likely that a passion for a man of his class would not have met with similar forms of scrutiny and punishment) but because of the ways in which they are different. Alec is expected to act as an officer; his open interest in and friendship with a common Irish foot soldier seems to elicit in his commanders a horror of miscegenation, reminding them of Alec's own "difference" from them — his feared and mistrusted "Irishness." Alec is irresistibly drawn toward Jerry, and his repeated approaches lead to increasingly worse consequences, principally for Jerry. His final choice to "defend" Jerry is the last available to him: he chooses to shoot Jerry from behind rather than allow him to be hung, thus cheating the British of their prey and taking on himself the death that the British power structure had, one way or another, intended for Jerry's class and subject position, not Alec's.

Observe the Sons of Ulster and *How Many Miles to Babylon?* like *The Picture of Dorian Gray,* metaphorize the hopelessness of an eroticism that can express itself only through a series of self-alienating and ultimately self-defeating maneuvers, through the trope of "the living dead." In McGuinness's play, David Craig observes: "Whoever comes back alive, if any of us do, will have died as well. He'll never be the same" (74). The parallel between the living dead and the soldiers at the Somme (predestined corpses who do not yet know that they are dead) points to the sense in which imperial power relations alienate human "species being," that intersubjective space in which human beings bond through their species needs, which include both the biological need to prolong and preserve life and social needs for communality, shared gratification, bodily pleasure, touch, acceptance, and mirroring. These legitimate needs are prised apart from the individual when they are set in conflict (through, for instance, gender inequality) or through a second set of representational "needs" that are *made* crucial to the subject's psychic and often physical sense of safety (prove yourself heterosexual and therefore a loyal British subject or you will be denigrated, shamed, and attacked). The living dead which McGuinness depicts and which Alec, Jerry, and Bennett toast on their illicit trip into the French countryside (where they seek to make contact with *community,* a symbolic search that will cost two of them their lives) represent both the ways in which we all are "spoken" by history and the position of all men and women whose personal and erotic loyalties are outlawed. The living dead trope refers most literally to the bodies of men in battle, who are, in a sense, only deferred corpses, even if they actually survive, as David Craig points out. The figure of the living dead, implicit in both the Irish devil's bargain and the demon lover narrative, provides in these texts an overdetermined, paradigmatic figure for the position of the Anglo-Irish soldier in the First World War. These soldiers fought and died in defense of a nation that regarded their country with contempt, a nation that initially fragmented and then continually undermined the renewal of self-identified and nonsectarian community in Ireland.

In these two texts, as in *The Picture of Dorian Gray,* self-love and love of others "like" oneself are inseparably bound up. The enforced failure of love, or the distorted forms that love must take when it can be expressed only through a narrow spectrum of officially sanctioned channels, foreordains a repetition compulsion that cannot be altered because the underlying motives that drive the repetition are denied or proscribed and the emergence of these motives into action is policed into the single, narrow code through which they may be expressed.

The denial of same-sex love in itself produces such compulsive repetitions, as Dorian Gray reflects after he first hides the altered painting from Basil Hallward, the one man who might have extricated him from the field of fascinated compulsion within which his schismatic relationship to the thing in his attic enmeshes him. After decisively rejecting Basil, Dorian sees, with sudden clarity, that it was not his youthful beauty that Basil had loved. He recognizes for the first time that Basil's love "was not the mere physical admiration of beauty that is born of the senses, and that dies when the senses tire," but that it had been "such love as Michelangelo had known, and Montaigne, and Winkelmann, and Shakespeare himself" (Wilde 273). Thus he recognizes the homosexual nature of Basil's love at the same time that he recognizes that it is not an objectifying but a humane and humanizing love. "But it was too late now" (273). Dorian realizes that his interpretation of Basil's love as a form of acquisitive commodification (which, given the aristocratic circles he moves in, represents the only form of love he knows) was, as Cohen argues, a *mis*reading; ultimately, Dorian seals his fate by killing Basil, the displaced desire for whom has entrapped him within a sterile double bind of destructive, narcissistic conquests. In *The Picture of Dorian Gray, Observe the Sons of Ulster,* and *How Many Miles to Babylon?* the death of the loved one represents the end of creative possibilities for an alternative future. From the moment of his rejection of Basil onward, as Dorian reflects, "the past could always be annihilated. Regret, denial or forgetfulness could do that. But the future was inevitable" (273–74).

The repression of spontaneous love for "one's own kind" is thematized in these texts through the figure of forbidden homoeroticism, which represents both itself, a central fulcrum point on which pressure may be exerted as a means to manipulate not only homosexual but also more or less heterosexual men (see Sedgwick, *Between Men*), and, symbolically, all the forms of love, including self-love, which are outlawed under an imperial order that mandates dutiful sacrifice in the name of individuals, nations, and values that may be personally repugnant. These complex narrative representations of thwarted and misdirected love figure ways in which Anglo-Irish Protestants have perceived themselves as "different" from their native Irish compatriots, therefore rejecting those with whom they actually share a common cause in favor of the British, who were actually "different" but to whom they believed themselves to be similar. The groupings of sameness and difference in these two texts suggest that in refusing (through legislation or social convention) to allow for love between those who are "the same" (that is, in outlawing homosexual love), we ensure that history itself will continue to be "the same" rather than different, as repressed male needs for passionate and tender bonding with other men, regardless of individual sexual orientation, continue to be readily supplied only in the context of athletic, military, national, or corporate collectivities.

In both McGuinness's and Johnston's texts, European gothic conventions enter into dialogue with Irish history through the introduction of male lovers who allegorize divided halves of a self that has lost access to significant portions of its history, body, and psyche. Both texts figure the reunion of male lovers apocalyptically, as realizable only via what Sedgwick has described as "violence or magic of a singularly threatening kind" (*Coherence* 13). Both texts figure Irish geographic, psychological, and historical alienation as the product of a wrongly prohibited union. In them, Ireland's colonialist past is depicted as having left Irish subjects, both in the six and in the twenty-six counties, "split off," self-alienated, anxious regarding national, religious, and sexual sameness and difference, and ambivalent about whether the present is the same or different from the past.

Continued interest in the First World War among contemporary Irish writers indicates that the appropriation of Anglo-Irish loyalties in that war remains a live issue today in both the Republic and the North. Moreover, the recurrent image of the living dead in conjunction with literary depictions of World War I suggests that the "blood compact" of the Somme (itself a reaffirmation of the Battle of the Boyne) continues to divide Irish community against itself. The "cheated [Anglo-Irish] dead" of World War I, like Oscar Wilde, "bayonetted through and through from both sides, by the vectors of [sexual disclosures] at once compulsory and forbidden" (Sedgwick, *Epistemology* 70), live on in the fragmented discourses of a lacerated land in which national, historical, and sexual self-knowledge remain unrepresentable and where the northern Protestant majority continues to favor an abstract and isolating communion with a distant, masculinized power over the formation of local, inclusive community based on common regional experience and shared community interests.

Chapter 6
Somebody Else's Troubles

Post-treaty Retrenchment and the (Burning)

Big House Novel

A doll in the doll-maker's house
Looks at the cradle and bawls:
"That is an insult to us."
But the oldest of the dolls,
Who had seen, being kept for show,
Generations of his sort,
Out-screams the whole shelf: "Although
There's not a man can report
Evil of this place,
The man and the woman bring
Hither to our disgrace,
A noisy and filthy thing."
— W. B. Yeats, "The Dolls"

In return for nothing, the [Anglo-Irish] young are compelled to adopt a
time-honoured set of manners and attitudes, to be "sealed" and "finished",
so that the social forms may survive the death of their contents.
— Declan Kiberd, *Inventing Ireland*

In the passage by Declan Kiberd that I have taken as my second epigraph, the "sealed," "finished" bodies through which "social forms"
outlive their human contents resemble Yeats's intergenerationally immutable dolls, who denounce a newborn baby as "a noisy and filthy
thing." The dolls, who are "disgrace[d]" by the primal scene the baby

presents — the messy original on which their unfeeling, sanitized bodies are modeled — are opposed in the poem to the vulnerable, unregulated bodily life of the pre-Oedipal infant. They may also be, in the context of this reading, productively opposed to the "open," "exposed" body of the burned-down Big House.[1] Not all Anglo-Irish children, however, grew up to play the same role in the maintenance of "time-honoured manners and attitudes." If all Big House children were "effectively told to embalm themselves alive, perform approved routines, and deny all feeling," only the female half were reduced to this living death, in Kiberd's words, "in return for nothing" (370).

Ascendancy women, as Anna Parnell lamented, suffered from "the custom of the upper classes . . . 'giving all, or nearly all, to the sons and little or nothing to the daughters.' " Their allowances were "at the mercy of family fortunes — if these declined, then one of the first economies was to cut off these stipends." Entrapped in positions of perpetual economic dependency, these women were, in Parnell's words, "little less the victims of the landlords than the tenants themselves" (cited in Ward 7). This crucial difference in the material position of males and females within the Anglo-Irish social order supplies the basis for their asymmetrical representations of the destruction of the Anglo-Irish domestic sphere during the Easter 1916 Uprising and the Anglo-Irish War, or the Troubles (1919–21). In this chapter I read Yeats's *Purgatory* as a family romance that denies male desire for a liberating (but disloyal) return to pre-Oedipal (and hence preideological) origins by projecting such traitorous desires onto a demonized female sexuality. Yet in similar accounts by women, attractions to forbidden ideological and sexual possibilities hover much closer to the threshold of consciousness.

Gendered Troubles in Post-treaty Ireland

Anglo-Irish women's depictions of the Irish anticolonial struggle represent an anticolonialist tradition that has been obscured within Irish literary studies. Of the novels I discuss in this chapter, Iris Murdoch's *The Red and the Green* — set during the Easter Uprising — best exemplifies the pattern by which Anglo-Irish women's writing has been marginalized within the Irish canon. Unlike male Anglo-Irish writers from Swift to Beckett who spent much of their lives outside Ireland, Murdoch—an Anglo-Irish woman with an international reputation as a British author—has not been treated as a national icon worthy of critical reclamation. Instead, like the writing of earlier Anglo-Irish women such as Lady Morgan, who many critics evidently *wish* had left the country, Murdoch's writing is treated as a pollutant against which the Irish canon must be protected. For instance, in a short article published in *Eire/Ireland* in 1983, R. B. Kershner dismisses Murdoch's Irishness as "at best dubious" (144). "Like an entire class of writers since the 17th century," Kershner contends, Murdoch was born into "a well-established Anglo-Irish family, educated in England, and thereafter returned to the country of her birth only for vacations" (144). Without adding to or reflecting on this life trajectory, which he evidently feels speaks for itself, Kershner goes on to explain away *The Red and the Green* as "the requisite Irish novel" that such nationally dubious writers are evidently compelled to write. He then debates whether the novel is, in fact, Irish—in which case it would be a " 'sport' thrown out as a sop to sentiment and vague Yeatsian responsibility"—or whether it is "central to Murdoch's canon," in which case, as other critics cited agree, it is not "importantly Irish" (144). By positing a binary opposition between Murdoch's oeuvre and Irish writing, Kershner and other critics have excluded from discussions of Irish literature a novel that affords a rich and critical depiction of Anglo-Irish subjectivity during the crucial, formative period leading up to the Anglo-Irish War and the signing of the Anglo-Irish Treaty.

In this chapter I situate *The Red and the Green* and three Anglo-Irish women's novelistic depictions of the Troubles relative to Yeats's "burning Big House" play, *Purgatory,* to explore a tradition that has been banished from the official records of the Irish literary canon because of its affinities to a heterogenous pre-treaty nationalism. Although Murdoch's case is a specialized one, the dynamics underwriting *The Red and the Green*'s marginalization are widespread. A more general and covert subordination of Anglo-Irish women's writing has taken place through critical manipulations of the subgeneric "Big House novel." One example of how this category for analysis has been deployed to devalue and simultaneously bypass an intrinsically significant corpus of literature occurs in *Celtic Revivals,* in which Seamus Deane hastily invokes a sketchily defined Big House tradition to initiate a discussion of Yeats's mythic distortions of Irish history. In linking Yeats's sensibility to an ongoing Big House tradition, Deane identifies a significant intertextual connection informing modern Irish fiction that could provide the basis for a more broadly constituted Irish canon. But in the context of Deane's argument, Big House fiction is invoked only to take the brunt of his critique, whereas Yeats's writing receives the benefit of closely reasoned critical analysis and is simultaneously buffered from accountability for its representations of a refined traditional "culture besieged by barbarity." Culpability for Yeats's aristocratic enthusiasms is instead transferred to "twentieth-century Irish fiction which draws heavily on Yeats's poetry," such as "Elizabeth Bowen's *The Last September,* Aidan Higgins's *Langrishe, Go Down,* Thomas Kilroy's *The Big Chapel,* John Banville's *Birchwood* and Jennifer Johnston's *How Many Miles to Babylon?"* (31–32). Although the "Big House" writers whose work Deane dismisses en masse as "an anachronism" are not all female, a familiar strategy of gendered scapegoating is inherent in Deane's admonishment of a largely female, subgeneric form for the excesses of Yeats, a male high modernist (32).

The term "Big House novel" has served in this way simultaneously to invoke and to dismiss a range of writers from Somerville and Ross through Jennifer Johnston whose work has seldom been seriously discussed in relation to the Irish canon. Rather than inaugurating serious critical analysis, this term can operate as a shorthand invocation of unspecified but presumed political, intellectual, and aesthetic deficiencies, much as Hawthorne's "damned mob of scribbling women" served as a designation sufficient to constitute its referent's dismissal.[2] Paradoxically, such dismissals, often made with more than a hint of nationalist scorn, have silenced a chorus of anticolonial critiques that could, if recovered, enrich and complicate our appreciation of Irish nationalism's breadth and variety in the years leading up to the signing of the Anglo-Irish Treaty in 1921.

The exclusion from post-treaty literary and historical discussions of the perspectives of women with the social vantage point, leisure, and education from which most persuasively to critique the Anglo-Irish colonial system corresponds to Éibhear Walshe's account of postcolonial Ireland's "denial of difference." As Walshe suggests, the progressive denial of "difference, with its incipient threat of dissidence," gained force after the signing of the treaty, "as the post-colonial struggle to escape the influence of the colonizing power became a struggle to escape the gendered relations of male colonizer to female colonized" (5). To homogenize and masculinize a feminized national identity, "[James] Connolly's socialism and [Constance Markievicz's and Eva] Gore-Booth[']s feminism," along with " 'unmanly' homosexuality," were occluded in the new Irish Free State (6). Within such a framework, the novels on which I will focus — Iris Murdoch's *The Red and the Green* and Elizabeth Bowen's *The Last September,* Molly Keane's *Two Days in Aragon,* and Rosamond Jacob's forgotten novel, *The Troubled House* — can be read precisely as post-treaty recurrences of the suppressed Anglo-Irish feminism that Walshe identifies with Markievicz's armed resistance against British rule and Gore-Booth's trade unionism and lesbianism.

A mediating gothic vocabulary conventionally trading in occluded discourses repeatedly disrupts the realist surface of these novels. Moreover, the resurfacing of historical and familial secrets plays a significant role in their narrative structures. Domestic secrets which were conventionally projected outside the family via the gothic family romance and which served to bind children to the colonial structure via family bonds of secrecy and loyalty reemerge in these novels as anticolonial weapons. This resurfacing of domestic secrets such as sexual abuse, incest, and homosexuality, as well as a myriad of secret impulses, perceptions, political affiliations, and histories, reconfigures the gothic family romance into which "family secrets" were previously projected, signaling a shift from an unconscious disavowal of Anglo-Irish family dynamics to their conscious, if ambivalent and irony-prone, exploration.

Interwoven with the feminist critique that gothic conventions enable are strands of other suppressed discourses: homosexuality and republicanism. As in *Observe the Sons of Ulster* and *How Many Miles to Babylon?* a gothic-realist vocabulary and the dissenting viewpoints it encodes deploy the conventions of a well-established Anglo-Irish gothic tradition to make visible, rather than deny, relationships between domestic relations and larger political hierarchies. Bristling with gendered, sexual, and political dissent, the critical gothic-realist tradition these novels exemplify was too conventional to censor but too unorthodox to contain. Hence, these novels have been, with a few commendable exceptions, critically marginalized, celebrated in depoliticized contexts, or ignored.

Yeats's *Purgatory* and the Transforming Gothic Family Romance

If the Irish landlords had not deserved extinction for anything else, they would have deserved it for the treatment of their own women.
— Anna Parnell cited in Ward, *Unmanageable Revolutionaries*

According to Elizabeth Bowen, probably the Anglo-Irish Ascendancy's most astute commentator, an Anglo-Irish Big House was "something between a *raison d'être* and a predicament" (Kiberd, *Inventing Ireland* 376). The cultural ambivalence that Bowen's observation reveals has played out in the mid– to late twentieth century in an array of erupting fictional Anglo-Irish families and Big Houses that reenact but also intensify earlier representations of the self-devouring family. Of these the most well known is Yeats's *Purgatory*, a one-act play premiering in 1939, when the historical Big House burnings of the 1920s were still relatively recent. In *Purgatory*, a play that critics have frequently identified as eugenicist, Yeats ascribes the fall of the Big House to the unbridled sexual passions of an Ascendancy daughter who weds an Irish Catholic groom, thereby initiating a hybrid, bestial line figured in a parricidal and filacidal son (see Cullingford, *Gender and History* 279–86). *Purgatory* participates in, but also complicates, the tradition of autophagous families I have so far reviewed. Tellingly, the play depicts the death of a child at the hands of a parent without projecting its events onto a class or nation (wholly) other than the author's own. In the play, a Big House daughter's transgressive sexual desire for an Irish groom engulfs the future of her lineage. When she dies giving birth to her first child, she leaves the family house and its only heir, her son, in the hands of her dissolute husband. At sixteen, in a gothic epiphany, her son symbolically claims but literally loses his family legacy: as the Big House burns, set on fire by his drunken father, the boy stabs his father to death.

The play's action revolves around the return of this dispossessed heir, referred to in the play's stage directions as "Old Man," to the burned ruins of the family Big House. In the company of his own sixteen-year-old son, referred to as "Boy," the Old Man reveals the story of his origins, thus figuratively transmitting a legacy of loss. Subsequently, perceiving in his son the continuation of the degenerate lineage that dispossessed him of what he considers his rightful place, the Old Man kills the Boy with the same knife he once used to dispatch his father.

Purgatory depicts the burning of its emblematic Big House not as resulting from an external assault but as a form of self-immolation ignited by female sexual desire. The play thus depicts and simultaneously indicts a pattern of psychic and material collusion between Big House residents and the republican forces that historically burned Big Houses to break down settler colonial hegemony. Moreover, the play decisively absolves the Old Man of any collusion in the house's destruction by depicting him as twice seeking to expiate his mother's crime of miscegenation through the most drastic means possible.

The play's narrative structure reveals the significance of women within the Anglo-Irish settler colonial order and the particularly fraught relationship of Anglo-Irish women to the guilty secrets of settler colonial reproduction. A Big House daughter's transgression of constitutive sectarian boundaries initiates a chain of intergenerational autophagy when her marriage to a Catholic groom transmits Anglo-Irish property back into the hands of the native Irish, who are figured as *consuming* rather than intergenerationally *preserving* familial resources. The child resulting from this act of transgression in turn consumes his mother's life, the life of her husband, and ultimately the lineage itself when he kills his own son to prevent extension of the family's tainted legacy into the future.

Purgatory scapegoats Anglo-Irish women for the increasing hybridity of post-treaty Irish identity and the concomitant "fall" of the Big House from the center of Irish cultural life. But in light of Yeats's earlier work, and the larger tradition of Anglo-Irish representation, *Purgatory*'s positioning of women as the "weak link" in Anglo-Irish cultural transmission derives from a familiar representational pattern that is merely reworked in response to new historical pressures. For instance, *The Dreaming of the Bones,* in which Devorgilla's adulterous lust precipitates

England's original invasion of Ireland at the invitation of Devorgilla's abandoned husband, is an earlier, paradigmatic Yeatsian depiction of women's sexual desire as menacing the integrity of national groups. Similarly, "The Rose of Shadow" figures female sexuality as the aperture through which dangerous, liminal forces may gain entrance into the home.

Although *Purgatory* clearly indicts female transgressive sexual desire — summed up in the Old Man's lines, "Her mother never spoke to her again / And she did right" (227) — the play's specifics also invite a counterreading set within the Anglo-Irish material and social context. In the play, an economic and cultural system of accumulation is dependent for its perpetuation on the suppression of women's sexuality. As with the parables of reverse colonization that Stephen Arata has found everywhere in nineteenth-century British writing, *Purgatory*'s structure reveals a subliminal fear that women could justifiably relegate Anglo-Irish society to the same oblivion to which it has relegated them, disregarding its aims as it has ignored their desires and interests. Evidence in the play of a suppressed awareness of the appropriation of women's bodies and sexuality within the Anglo-Irish order may be found in the punishment that Yeats ordains for a woman who is sexually disloyal: entrapment within the bedroom of the family Big House, where she must perpetually relive the moment of conception.

Purgatory represents the reductio ad absurdum of an Anglo-Irish gothic tradition no longer able persuasively to deny its own implications. Hence, in *Purgatory,* untenable gendered and sexual contradictions endemic to the Anglo-Irish family give rise to an inevitable process of escalation that finds its logical end in the annihilation of the family itself. The other Big House novels I discuss similarly represent families whose destruction allegorically makes visible and editorializes on cultural changes or political upheaval; these narratives can no longer deny the Anglo-Irish family's relationship to the social pressures that have built up at its periphery. Read collectively, these "burning Big House" texts, starting with *Purgatory,* reveal an Anglo-Irish gothic family romance punctured by the force of external events, which must now be integrated rather than maintained as a dissociated cultural fantasy.

Compulsory Marriage and Broken Engagements
The Red and the Green and *The Last September*

In the late eighteenth and early nineteenth centuries, Anglo-Irish writers allegorized the anticipated benefits of the Act of Union (1800) in
novels enacting joyous marriages between British men and Irish women
which explicitly redress ancestral wrongs.[3] It is thus particularly apt
that beginning with *Purgatory,* Anglo-Irish narratives that reflect events
leading to the Act of Union's effective invalidation in the Anglo-Irish
Treaty of 1921 typically revolve around broken engagements or transgressive unions, thus building on a Yeatsian tradition figuring normative marriage as a metaphor for political quiescence. In *Kathleen ni
Houlihan,* for instance, Michael Gillane abandons his fiancée and the
domestic status quo (to which he would, in marrying her, symbolically
acquiesce) to join the 1798 rebellion. By a complementary, if politically opposed, logic, *Purgatory* depicts an Anglo-Irish woman's evasion of normative marriage as an allegory for the political ruination of
the Anglo-Irish. In women's post-treaty representations of transgressive
sexual alliances or disrupted marriage plans during periods of anticolonial insurgency, however, the fixed relationship of marriage as a meta-
phoric signifier for a preestablished signified — the colonial status quo
— is destabilized, as meaning begins to circulate more freely between
the two signifiers. Violations of gendered social norms and family decorum still allegorize decolonization, but anticolonial resistance also begins to represent the disruption of Anglo-Irish familial reproduction.
In the novels I consider in this chapter, secret pacts or bonds between
Anglo-Irish women and a series of republican volunteers and gunmen
constitute a chosen alternative to the secret of colonial misappropriation with which Anglo-Irish children were involuntarily burdened. In
this section, I focus on broken engagements in Iris Murdoch's *The Red
and the Green* and Elizabeth Bowen's *The Last September* as microcos-
mic representations of the more general disruption of the Anglo-Irish
social order heralded by the Easter Uprising and the Anglo-Irish War.

In *The Red and the Green* (1965), a broken engagement between a
British soldier and his Irish cousin figures the Easter Uprising's sym-

bolic rupture of British/Irish relations. Frances Bellman is an Anglo-Irish feminist and a nationalist sympathizer who believes that "being a woman is like being Irish. . . . Everyone says you're important and nice, but you take second place all the same" (29). In the week before the Uprising, she breaks a long-standing engagement to her English cousin Andrew Chase-White after telling her Uncle Barney that she would fall down and worship Andrew were he to become a conscientious objector rather than go to war in Europe (102). For his part, as the Uprising starts, Andrew realizes "he loved and he had always loved Pat Dumay," his cousin and an Irish Volunteer (264). Frances's profound reservations concerning Andrew's political allegiances and Andrew's epiphany concerning his desire for Pat (and presumably for men more generally) emphasize the bankruptcy of the original engagement and bear witness to the powerful social forces that initiate such contracts and (ordinarily) impel them to closure. Over the course of the novel, Murdoch depicts historical convulsions surrounding the Uprising as derailing the process through which marriage and reproduction have generationally sustained Anglo-Irish hegemony in Ireland.

In *The Last September* (1929), the Anglo-Irish Lois's broken engagement with Gerald, an English soldier, similarly symbolizes the impending breakdown of the long-standing bond between the British and the Anglo-Irish at the height of the Troubles. In Bowen's novel, the unspeakable wish on the part of Ascendancy women that the settler colonial system might disintegrate is encoded in Lois's crush on a female houseguest, Marda, with whom she wishes (ardently, if silently) she could leave, and in her Aunt Naylor's fascinated ruminations on disintegration within England ("But one does wonder sometimes whether there's really much there to disintegrate" [26]) and animated comparisons of the English underclass with the Irish tenantry. Lady Naylor tells an English friend, who argues that at least the English poor are "loyal," that "they hadn't got any alternative, and if they had an alternative [she] didn't suppose they'd see it" (27), a remark which betrays a strong if unconscious hope that her country's peasantry *will* discover an alternative. Like Lois's solitary encounters with ghostly IRA men and Lady Naylor's unconscious antipathy toward British imperialism, Lois's attraction to Marda gestures toward invisible seeds of change inherent in a crumbling colonial order.

In *The Red and the Green* and *The Last September,* the British soldiers whose marital hopes are blighted by their Anglo-Irish intendeds
represent modernist adaptations of the conventional type that Elizabeth Cullingford has identified in her essay "Gender, Sexuality, and
Englishness in Modern Irish Drama and Film" as "the stage Englishman" (159). The free, indirect dialogues and the omniscient narrators'
descriptions of the inner lives of Andrew Chase-White and Gerald Lesworth combine humor and horror in a manner that nominates the stage
Englishman as a forerunner of Beckett's earnest, deadpan, obsessive,
and terminally ingenuous characters. Both Andrew and Gerald embody
send-ups as well as gothic critiques of British imperialism. Compare,
for instance, the passages in which Andrew's and Gerald's characters
are first delineated. In *The Red and the Green,* Murdoch writes:

Andrew was a confused soldier. The role of soldier was perhaps the first
role in life into which he had made a positive attempt to fit. . . . The idea
of himself as a soldier, an idea which would have been entirely repugnant
to him in peacetime, was now, of course, backed up by the enthusiasm
of an entire community. . . . His persona as a soldier was still disparate,
composed partly of childish romanticism, partly of school-boy conscien-
tiousness, and partly of some yet veiled adult attitude of fear and resignation. (9)

In a parallel passage, Bowen's narrator reflects on Gerald's affections,
which are depicted as architectural structures that, like the British
company to which he belongs, define, delimit, and occupy their surroundings. They are "four-square—occurring like houses in a landscape" (40–41). Gerald's emotions have been regimented through their
systematic investment in a series of normative receptacles. He has
vested his emotions in "a few—he thought final—repositories[:] . . .
his mother, country, dog, school, a friend or two, now—crowningly—
Lois" (41). The word "repository" posits Lois as the consummate object
of heterosexual male desire, an empty vessel to be filled with projected,
inchoate desires—penetrated, impregnated, occupied.

Although Gerald differs from Andrew in his seamless identification
with the gendered social roles required of him, both descriptions emphasize the social regulation of emotions and these characters' concomitant estrangement from any dissenting impulses, which are no

more likely to arise in the uncomfortable, confused Andrew than in Gerald, for whom "life was a series of practical adjustments, into which the factor of personality did not enter at all. His reserve — to which one was apt to accord a too sensitive reverence — was an affair of convenience rather than protection" (41). Gerald has internalized the norms of his society more fully than has the tragicomically ill-at-ease Andrew, whose "knowledge of the facts of the trenches had not destroyed his attempt to make sense of it all by means of romanticism" (Murdoch 9). Both descriptions, however, emphasize the process by which compulsory heterosexuality accommodates the male subject to the requirements of an imperialist order.

The internal and external pressures of compulsory heterosexuality are extensively documented in both novels. In *The Red and the Green,* sexual subject formation is explicitly connected with Anglo-Irish ideological and biological reproduction through a recurring image pattern linking sex, procreation, imperialist aggression, and the annihilation of the subject. In *The Last September,* the establishment and maintenance of heteronormativity are depicted subjectively, in detailed descriptions of the novel's characters, especially Lois, as engaged in a persistent fending off of unauthorized reactions and feelings. Both novels make visible the social and intrapsychic processes by which their central characters, Andrew and Lois, are socially disciplined to accept their roles as gendered, heterosexual adults within the Anglo-Irish order.

In *The Red and the Green,* Andrew vacillates in his commitment to marry Frances Bellman, an Irish cousin to whom he is tacitly committed by "an understanding, dating from somewhere very remote in their childhood" (20). He finds himself passively resisting an air of collective expectation that he will marry Frances before he leaves for the fields of France. Sex and death — fear of and resistance to which are aroused by the force field of social coercion around him — converge in Andrew's "sense that people surrounding him, his family, perhaps society, expected him to make Frances pregnant before he was sent to the Front." He reflects that to marry and impregnate Frances represents a "sort of dubious 'survival', offered as a kind of duty" (21). On reflection, he concludes that "with the prospect of a return to the war opening before him like a black hole, he was prepared to settle gladly for a security in his personal life which seemed likely to exist nowhere else" (20). Still, obscurely resenting the societal double bind that compels him to marry and reproduce before sacrificing his life, Andrew finds himself curiously paralyzed with respect to Frances.

In *The Last September,* Bowen's characters articulate even more explicitly the cultural expectation that men must reproduce themselves and the family structure before sacrificing their lives in war, as a duty to their society, and to assuage the guilt of those they leave behind. In a conversation between two house guests, Mr. Montmorency and Marda, Marda recalls the loss of a ring given to her by Timothy, a suitor with whom she evidently broke an engagement. Mr. Montmorency observes, in remarks alluding obliquely to the broken engagement by way of the lost ring, "What a pity," and asks, "Did your—did Timothy mind?" Marda's answer refers directly to the engagement; she replies, "Not so much as the Naylors," thus indicating that social pressures had superseded personal preference for Timothy as well as for herself. "Later," she reflects, "he was killed on the Somme. But he had two sons first, so it all came right. I mean he married" (81). In *The Last September* and *The Red and the Green,* marriage and procreation, like fighting and dying, constitute the requisite consummation of a Burkean social pact; as Andrew Chase-White concludes, marriage to an approved partner "confirm[s] a settlement which seemed to have been so felicitously made long ago" (Murdoch 21–22).

The connections that emerge between war and procreation in *The Red and the Green* and *The Last September* relate the two both analogically and causally: fighting and procreation represent forms of bodily appropriation, but the fact that Anglo-Irish society is *at* war intensifes social and psychological pressures to procreate. Early in *The Last September,* soldiers and Anglo-Irish girls of marriageable age flirt at a tennis party that is saturated by and charged with the very political realities the party itself occludes. The soldiers' presence creates a frisson of actuality that both scandalizes and titillates the young women. For instance, when Gerald refers to his regiment as "all we jolly old army of occupation" and to "this jolly old war" (which he predicts the British will lose), Miss Hartigan denies that one would call his regiment *that* or that one would call this a *war*. But at the same time she and her sister inwardly "thought how daring it was of Mr. Lesworth to come so far to a party at all, and only hoped he would not be shot on the way home; though they couldn't help thinking how, if he should be, they would both feel so interesting afterward. 'Poor young fellow,' they thought with particular tenderness because he was so good-looking, and neither of them, with this tenderness in their eyes, dared to look at him" (38). The sexual titillation that the soldiers' proximity to death and to the unspoken facts of British/Irish social relations stir within the young women is made explicit in the responses of Livvy, a slightly overeager participant in the quasi-sexual intrigue that confirms female maturity. When she asks David, the soldier to whom she is attracted, why he missed a bicycle gymkhana, he responds, "with a mystic and obstinate look," that he was on duty "in those mountains on the other side of the Madder." Livvy felt in her spine, running down it from under her "waistband, a sharp little thrill. She felt all the soldiers' woman, and said in a glow: 'Well, I call that too awfully dangerous.' He told her: 'It's what we're here for.' They glanced at each other, then both were embarrassed — and showed it — at what they had seen" (39). This passage forges an explicit connection between the Anglo-Irish heterosexual contract and the forcible maintenance of social and economic relations in Ireland. Livvy eroticizes David and his company's policing of the Irish terrain, a patriotic "duty" that transmogrifies into sex in the course of the conversation. The pair's mutual embarrassment "at what they had seen" identifies the referent in David's assertion, "It's what we're here for," with the group sex signaled by Livvy's somatic reactions and thoughts.

At the same party, Lois's cousin Laurence, a student at Oxford with republican sympathies, stands apart from the heterosexual contract. Laurence seems to represent an array of political, educational, and ideological possibilities that are not available to Lois or even to the more sophisticated Marda, who is (after putting up, as we have seen, a good fight) "go[ing] off to get married in a mechanical sort of way" (191). Laurence's status in the novel as an expression of aspects of Lois's personality — the forceful perceptions, reservations, and convictions — that binary gender divisions have disallowed, is suggested by the depth of their largely unspoken bond.[4] Laurence's aversion to compulsory heterosexuality surfaces when he restrains himself from further goading Mr. Montmorency by reminding himself that Montmorency "was married, had given away his integrity, had not even a bed to himself." In the same conversation, in the midst of mingling soldiers and Anglo-Irish heiresses, he calls attention to the role the house is playing in the replication of colonial relations by coolly reflecting, "I should like to be here when this house burns" (44).

In *The Red and the Green,* a similar pattern connecting sex, procreation, and death recurs in imagery associated with Andrew and his family, the Chase-Whites. Andrew's free and indirect meditations on the relationship between sex, procreation, and death are, like Andrew's family and the Anglo-Irish people, bound up with and tensely situated between imperial warfare in Europe and the colonial status quo in Ireland. Images associated with Andrew's family emphasize the liminality of the Anglo-Irish position and frequently partake of the fascinated revulsion, verging on horror, that characterizes Andrew's feelings toward Ireland. The first hint of the origins of Andrew's aversion to Ireland occurs in a passage in which Millie, Andrew's aunt, equates the unique "complexity" of Anglo-Irish families with incestuousness; the image of incest, which concisely combines procreation, sex, and bodily appropriation, culminates in this passage with the figure of "the snake that eats its own tail" (13). This trope of the family as a self-devouring sexual "machine" (18) metaphorizes the nature of the family's connection to Ireland, for it is the ongoing production of bodies to be devoured by the British imperial order, as Andrew ultimately is, that makes the family both "complex" and "incestuous." Andrew reflects that "the sense that the family occupied or pervaded most of Ireland, managing to inhabit most of its corners, largely composed for him the sinister power of the island" (13). The terms "occupy" and "pervade" are structurally equated in this sentence, suggesting that (biological) pervasion constitutes occupation by another name and that this process of reproductive pervasion has imbued Ireland with a "sinister power" by which Andrew and his family are possessed.

This early imagery resurfaces at the novel's end, again in connection with Andrew's Aunt Millie, an aggressive, aristocratic nationalist with a penchant for guns and trousers. Millie's depiction as an oversexed exhibitionist suggests Yeats's reading of Constance Markievicz, spending her days in "ignorant good-will," shrill-voiced, her mind a "bitter, an abstract thing" (84–86), recast in a sexualized, Murdochian mode. In a decisive scene, however, Millie performs an act that is both heroic and repulsive, but above all stunningly effective. She prevents Andrew from alerting the British about the coming insurgency by threatening to send his mother, Hilda, evidence of an incestuous affair between herself and her brother, Andrew's father. Once again Andrew's life decisions and values are controlled by "a settlement . . . made long ago" (21–22). In this case, however, Millie unearths a domestic secret capable of locally interrupting vastly powerful historical forces that are coming to a head.[5] The secret of Millie's incestuous relationship with Andrew's father is a precisely inverted mirror image of the founding secret of colonial appropriation through reproduction: whereas the secret of colonial misappropriation is visible but denied, Millie's relationship to her brother is invisible and gains agency only when Millie threatens to make it known. And whereas the open secret of colonial misappropriation requires that Andrew fight for the British and sacrifice his life, the domestic secret that Millie sacrificially unveils requires that Andrew withhold assistance to the British so that Pat, en route to meet his regiment, need not kill him.

The political significance of "private" sexual and affectional choices is further emphasized in parallel scenes in which Andrew and Lois come to decisions about marriage at unlikely but telling moments. Their surroundings and thoughts in these pivotal scenes supply a social context for ostensibly "natural" and "personal" decisions. These scenes and the events leading up to them dramatize the centrality of heteronormativity within Anglo-Irish society via quintessentially gothic interactions between the external and the internal, the conscious and the unconscious, the social and the individual.

Murdoch's narrator observes that although Andrew was an "uninterested, almost entirely non-practicing Anglican" when in England, "he felt, on arrival in Ireland, his Protestant hackles rise" (6). This early representation of Protestantism as a political rather than spiritual ideology is developed when Andrew and Hilda pass a church "with quickened step and stiffened gait" as hundreds of children at a "Children's Special Service Mission" sing jubilantly of the love of Jesus. "Neither Andrew nor his mother referred to the phenomenon." Instead, Hilda, whose self-satisfied snobbery, venality, and blindness to the misfortunes of others exemplify the shortcomings of the Anglo-Irish Ascendancy, tells Andrew that he "really must fix things up properly with Frances." Andrew reflects silently that "in Ireland religion was a matter of choosing between one appalling vulgarity and another" and concludes sadly that if he lived there he would have to "be with the young people in the marquee and their boisterous mentors." As he realizes that his loyalties "have to be" with Ireland's vociferous Protestants, Andrew responds "absently" to his mother's insistence that he marry Frances, saying only, "Yes" (51). This scene implies an equivalency between Andrew's inner, sad commitment to Anglo-Irish Protestantism and his outer, "absent" commitment to Frances. It identifies the mass political indoctrination of children through zealous modes of religious worship as an embarrassingly flagrant, "vulgar" version of the ideological reproduction the Anglo-Irish ruling class carries on more discreetly, through marriage and childrearing.

In *The Last September*, Lois is similarly pressed by her schoolmate Viola to "do her bit" to perpetuate Anglo-Irish culture. Lois idealizes Viola as the type of perfect womanhood; her memories of their final day together arouse feelings of incompleteness and inadequacy, owing, in part, to Lois's inability as a female to retain Viola's attention: "They said goodbye in December, a slight day, anxious between the enormous past and future. The parting was hardly real, they had barely kissed. . . . They had left school the day before. Yet the new life had been impatient for Viola, drawing her away from Lois in the taxi, appropriating her with certainty."[6] Following their graduation, Viola is transformed overnight into a "completed" woman. "Her pigtail had been the one loose end there was of her. . . . Now the hair was woven in bright sleek circles over her ears, each strand round like an eel's body." Lois experiences a resurgence of the Oedipal crisis in the face of Viola's "completed" femininity; she realizes "she had been missing or else discounting something all these years." Experiencing her own femininity in terms of lack, Lois concludes that Viola must always have had a feminine essence or capacity that she lacks. She decides Viola "must have played at being a schoolgirl just as Lois would have to play at being a woman," and sets

out to live up to Viola's rendition of adult femininity with dogged for-
titude (50). In response to Viola's charming epistolary accounts of her
romantic conquests and her escalating demands for equivalent offer-
ings from Lois, Lois comically scrambles to assemble a suitable narrative of heterosexual intrigue. When Lois talks to Gerald at the tennis
party, she is thinking, "When next I write Viola, can I describe him?"
(50). When next she *does* write to Viola, she is still unsure what narrative, if any, she has to produce. "She thought a major had proposed
to her, though he seemed rather old, but he was so much confused and
had such a mumbly mustache she could not be certain." She considers a
few other equally desolate prospects, and finds herself "forced to state,
there *was* a man in the Rutlands, a Gerald Lesworth, whom she found
affecting" (51).

Lois's bond with Gerald, born of a correspondence with an admired
former schoolmate, progresses to the engagement stage in response to
pressures that she experiences in her relationship with Marda. Lois and
Marda's intense flirtation during Marda's stay is punctuated by the omniscient narrator's reportage of Lois's inner dialogue and affect. When
Marda first tells Lois she is engaged, for instance, "Lois had a shock
of flatness." Bucking up, however, she turns her attention to Marda's
clothes, asking, "Am I pawing things?" to which Marda responds, "I like
it" (96). As Marda looks at Lois's drawings, which Lois has brought to
her as a sort of homage, "Lois thought how in Marda's bedroom, when
she was married, there might be a dark blue carpet with a bloom on it
like a grape, and how this room, this hour would be forgotten. Already
the room seemed full of the dusk of oblivion. And she hoped that instead of fading to dust in summers of empty sunshine, the carpet would
burn with the house in a scarlet night to make one flaming call upon
Marda's memory" (98). This passage connects the colonial system of
ideological and biological reproduction that Danielstown upholds with
Marda's impending marriage, both of which are revealed as the objects
of intense unconscious rage in Lois's casual sacrifice of her home as a
means of imprinting herself on Marda's memory. The passage thus connects the burning of Danielstown with Lois's desire for Marda, even as
it simultaneously reflects Lois's disappointed "realis[ation] that no one
would come for her, after all." Watching Marda survey her drawings,

"with a jump of the heart [as] she heard every page turn over," Lois thinks, for the first time, "I must marry Gerald" (98).[7]

The words "I must marry Gerald" recur and seem to catch hold of Lois in a later scene that in certain respects resembles Andrew's exchange with his mother in front of a Protestant church revival. This later scene also takes place in a landscape that makes Irish history visible, opening with an evocation of pastoral tranquility, as Marda and Mr. Montmorency—a paradigmatic heterosexual dyad that subsequent events incrementally dismantle—walk in the Irish countryside. Mr. Montmorency appears infatuated with Marda and seems on the brink of baring his soul to her about his unhappy marriage. But as they round a bend in the valley, they come on an abandoned mill that "startled them all, staring, light-eyed, ghoulishly" just as Lois catches up to them.

Lois had to come hurrying up to explain how it frightened her. In fact, she wouldn't for worlds go into it, but liked to go as near it as she dared. It was a fear she didn't want to get over, a kind of deliciousness. Those dead mills—the country was full of them, never quite stripped and whitened to skeletons' decency: like corpses at their most horrible. "Another," Hugo declared, "of our national grievances. English law strangled the—" But Lois insisted on hurrying: she and Marda were now well ahead. (122–23)

The breaking off of Hugo Montmorency's reflections on the historical facts surrounding the mill's decline affirms rather than nullifies the political resonance of his truncated observations. What was to be a specific and lightly ironic disquisition on the effects of "English tariffs, custom levies, and shipping laws" at a particular moment in Irish history is left gaping, open-ended, as though all that English law strangled in Ireland were ultimately irreducible to words. As Julian Moynahan has noted, this scene turns on "a strongly Gothic work up of the ruined mill" (243). More specifically, the mill represents a virtuosic modernist and explicitly political reinvention of the Burkean sublime, with its "delightful horror" here representing a commingling of proscribed historical realities and sexual possibilities—a colonial primal scene—that Lois fears to "enter" but enjoys approaching. Intoxicated by the allure of this sublime unspeakable-made-visible, Lois spontaneously hijacks

Marda and they "hurry on ahead . . . avid to encounter a *worst* which the custom, ceremony, and privilege of Anglo-Irish life have conspired to cover up" (Moynahan 243).

When they come to the mill, Marda wants to enter it. She feels "'demoralized, girlish,'" and wants to hide from Mr. Montmorency. Lois is genuinely terrified at the prospect of going inside, but "Marda put an arm round her waist, and in an ecstacy at this compulsion Lois entered the mill" (123–24). Lois's response to this compelled entry into a forbidden space in Marda's arms is unmistakably erotic. Once inside, "fear heighten[s] her gratification." She imagines—perhaps anticipating some apocalyptic punishment for her transgressive feelings—that the cracks in the wall will widen and the walls will peel back from a cleft "like the House of Usher." On seeing a dead crow, she shudders and makes for Marda, "eager for comment, contempt, consolation. She was a little idiot—appealing, she felt quite certain, to a particular tenderness" (124). Their idyll is cut short, however, when Marda comes across a sleeping IRA volunteer, who wakes and holds them at gunpoint until he discovers who they are and how many others are about. Lois explains, "We're just out for a walk," and the gunman answers with a certain gentleness, "It is time . . . that yourselves gave up walking. If you have nothing better to do, you had better keep in the house while you have it." Lois "could not but agree with him"; she thinks "she had better be going—but where?" Overwhelmed by the emotions that the mill, Marda's presence, and the proximity of the gunman have aroused, Lois concludes, "'I must marry Gerald,'" while Marda holds her arm and "softly, satirically presse[s] it" (125). As with Andrew's decision to marry Frances in *The Red and the Green,* Lois's decision to marry Gerald is placed within an elaborate but uncommented on sociopolitical framework. While the insecurities of the wider world that the gunman's presence drives home undoubtedly influence Lois to seek whatever stability she can, equally compelling are the "soft, satiric" pressure of Marda's touch and the dissenting desires that are, in this scene, shot through with the dangerous allure of political insurgency.

Republican resistance and lesbian love are condensed in a single gothic image when Mr. Montmorency, hearing a shot, runs to the doorway of the mill. Marda puts her hand to her mouth and "in an incredible half-glimpse, he thought he saw blood round the lips" (126). The gunman has accidentally discharged his gun, and a bullet has grazed Marda's hand. The vampiric imagery of "blood around the lips," which also suggests a gothic deflowering, emphasizes the mill as a space of alterity, outside the conventions of domestic realism and its attendant political affiliations and heteronormativity. Mr. Montmorency's shocked glimpse of Marda wiping blood from her lips as she stands alone with Lois in the abandoned mill coalesces into an allegorical *tableau vivante* of sexual and political guilt and defiance. In the blood on Marda's lips, forbidden thirst for armed resistance and sexual satisfaction converge momentarily in the figure of the hunted, transgressive vampire.

In one of several episodes in these novels in which apparently apolitical Anglo-Irish women and men maneuver, when pushed, to protect republicans, Lois and Marda promise the gunman that they will keep their encounter a secret. And they do, even going so far as physically to block Mr. Montmorency from entering the mill to pursue the gunman. Later, confronted with Marda's impending departure, Lois begs her to keep their encounter with the gunman secret even from her fiancé. She asks anxiously, "A swear is a swear, isn't it, even in England?" unconsciously voicing a humorous nationalist double entendre by suggesting that the English might have different standards concerning the binding nature of promises. Marda agrees that she will keep the gunman's secret, because telling the story would only reinforce her English fiancé's belief that "her country was dangerous as well as demoralizing." The persistence of Marda's fiancé "upon the mental scene" is exorcised, however, only when Marda promises Lois, "I certainly won't tell," that the encounter will be "a perfect secret" (129). The secret through which Lois and Marda bind themselves in a pact that symbolically purges Marda's husband-to-be represents an act of virtually treasonous political collusion. In its violation of Anglo-Irish social norms, Lois and Marda's protection of an IRA gunman stands in for an unrealized sexual transgression that was, what with male houseguests and IRA operatives lurking about, perhaps more a logistical than a conceptual impossibility.

Lois's and Andrew's engagements are both ultimately broken in ways that make different but parallel political points. As Louise DeSalvo has persuasively argued, *The Red and the Green* was inspired in part by Murdoch's appalled response to U.S. intervention in Vietnam (122). Frances's breaking off of her tacit engagement to Andrew is both nationalist and anti-imperialist in its ramifications. That she breaks the engagement after saying she *would* love and respect Andrew if he had enough character to be a conscientious objector situates her refusal as a specific womanly and *rational* form of conscientious objection: Frances refuses to acquiesce to a system of imperial reproduction through which human sexuality is made to collude with death. This point is driven home in an epilogue in which the significance of the broken engagement—and Andrew's narrative centrality—are metaleptically recast. Frances reveals to her son in the novel's final lines that she too had been in love with Pat Dumay, who died in the Uprising. Frances's surprising disclosure reveals the depth of her emotional involvement with the cause of Irish nationalism and diminishes Andrew's overall significance within the narrative, symbolically moving the imperialist subjectivity that Andrew represents to the margins of the narrative and of Irish history.

Frances refuses Andrew's formal proposal of marriage after her Uncle Barney shares his (correct) assumption that Andrew will remove her to England as soon as they are married. Paralleling her early observation linking women and the Irish, Frances probably found such a plan unacceptable both for its national and its gendered chauvinism. Ironically, however, Frances, like Marda, "goes off to get married in a mechanical sort of way" shortly after the Uprising is quelled. Brokenhearted (as we learn only in the novel's final pages), Frances moves to England and marries a conservative Englishman who holds the Uprising and other acts of resistance against imperial domination in contempt. In the novel's final scene, as Frances's husband packs a newspaper with the headline "Franco Threatens Barcelona" into his briefcase, he declares: "[I]n this century, small nations have got to pack up, and the sooner they realize it the better. You've got to belong to a big show nowadays" (269). Frances, however, shares a quietly treasonous relationship with her adult son, who may be contemplating fighting with the International Brigade. When her husband leaves, trailing a stream of bigoted aspersions against the Irish in general and Frances's relatives in particular for their participation in "all that 1916 nonsense," her son declares that Easter 1916 was wonderful because "it was a reminder that people can't be enslaved forever. Tyrannies end sooner or later because people begin automatically to hit back" (270).

For a brief period, like the Volunteers who for six days in 1916 occupied the Dublin Post Office and other public buildings, Frances courageously held out against the onslaught of colonial and imperial pressures to reproduce the existing social order. But the devastating events of Easter week (including the death of the man she had silently loved) acted on her as the encounter with an IRA gunman did on Lois, impelling her blindly toward the safety of convention. Memories of that week return to Frances at the novel's end as a "drumming in her ears" in which she "hears, as she had heard it all through that dreadful week in nineteen-sixteen, battering and breaking her heart, the thunder of the English guns" (272). Fleeing to escape this primal scene of colonial horror, she "mechanically" immersed herself in the normalcy of British conservative domesticity. But her closing conversation with her son, who carries forward and indeed repeats the words of the most radical of the novel's characters—Cathal Dumay, Pat's younger brother—reveals that Frances's nationalist and anti-imperialist ideals have persisted in the unlikely setting of a Tory kitchen in a London suburb, in the heart of her revolutionary son.

Whereas the breaking off by Frances of her engagement to Andrew represents an act of personal agency—the very conscientious objection to imperial warfare of which she had wished Andrew capable—Lois's engagement to Gerald is broken off by her aunt, who objects to Gerald's undistinguished pedigree. Lois's broken engagement thus signifies more complexly than does the broken engagement between Frances and Andrew. It allows Bowen simultaneously to critique and to uphold Anglo-Irish heteronormativity, because as readers we are both appalled at Lady Naylor's snobby rejection of Gerald as a suitable husband for Lois and relieved on Lois's behalf. The Naylors' belief that Gerald, and most of the English, are beneath them and in fact dependent on them is part of a larger systemic denial of their subordinate place within the British colonial order. When Gerald is killed in an IRA ambush shortly after Lady Naylor has informed him (rightly, though she has no way of knowing it) that Lois does not love him, we overhear her revising Gerald's relationship to Lois and to the family in a conversation with Mrs. Trent of the neighboring Big House, Castle Trent. Her casual alterations are the culminating instance of a series of reversals throughout the novel in which the British are depicted as dependent on the Anglo-Irish. She recalls that Gerald "had been out here so much and seemed so glad to talk, and had come, in a way, to depend on one," reframing his relationship with Lois by saying that "they had played tennis so often and were beginning to be quite friends." She complains that Gerald's mother responded to Lady Naylor's letter, hypocritically claiming that the heartbroken Gerald had had "a happy life," by reflecting "that it was her *first* consolation to think he died in so noble a cause" (205).

Lady Naylor's easy repackaging of her severance of Lois's engagement enacts the same denial that ultimately leads to Danielstown's destruction, but it also leaves Lois free to pursue an open-ended future. Although Lois's desire to attend art school is foreclosed and ominously replaced by a more conventional tour of France with "such an interesting, cultivated family," at the novel's end her future remains, like that of Frances's son, unwritten. In both cases, the novels obtain epiphanic closures through the break-up or destruction of Anglo-Irish households. Whereas in *Purgatory* Yeats suggests that the destruction of the Anglo-Irish domestic sphere puts an end to everything in Irish history *but* cyclical violence, in these two novels the dissolution of Big House families paves the way, at least potentially, for the emergence of new, less deadening forms.

Prohibited Alliances and Domestic Secrets
Two Days in Aragon

Of this chapter's four "burning Big House" novels, Molly Keane's *Two Days in Aragon* (1941), set in 1920, most closely draws on and responds to *Purgatory.* Despite its Yeatsian resonances and its compelling gothic-realist style, this novel, originally published under the pen name M. J. Farrell, has not achieved the canonical status of *The Last September,* its most obvious counterpart. Keane's return to writing in the 1980s after a two-decade hiatus brought with it popular acclaim and the re-publication of many of her earlier works. Although a body of feminist and postcolonialist criticism is emerging around her novels, however, Keane's status within the Irish canon remains liminal. As Bowen's critical acceptance has grown and her work is increasingly set in relation to works outside the Big House subgenre, Keane appears to be inheriting the dubious honorific, "the best-known of the Big House novelists." Yet *Two Days in Aragon*'s dissenting relationship to the Irish literary canon through its subversive retelling of *Purgatory* and its brilliant redeployments of the Anglo-Irish gothic merit a more central position within twentieth-century Irish literary criticism.

Especially pertinent for my study of changes in the Anglo-Irish gothic family romance is the novel's status as a conscious "atonement for [Keane's] contemporaneous attitude" toward the Irish national struggle (Devlin ix). Given the role that I have shown families to play in the reproduction of colonial ideology, it is also relevant that Keane suggested the novel consciously rebels against the worldview cherished by her mother. Keane's mother, the author once reported, "couldn't think that the English had ever done anything wrong," to which she added, "whereas of course they had behaved appallingly for generation after generation." Keane wrote the novel in part for her husband, who was, she recalled, "far more open-minded than she, and saw things more clearly at the time they were happening." But she also wrote it to make amends to the Irish people for her earlier "condemnations and . . . lack of understanding" (ix). Keane's open acknowledgment of her motivations for writing the novel testify to her conscious and deliberate use of gothic conventions to make visible elements of Anglo-Irish family life that such conventions had, in earlier cultural productions such as *Purgatory*, served to occlude.

Two Days in Aragon rewrites *Purgatory* in its depiction of an affair between Grania, the younger daughter of the Foxes of the Big House Aragon, and Foley O'Neill, a Catholic groom. Unlike Yeats's groom, however, Foley is himself the product of an act of Big House miscegenation. He is the son of Aragon's governess, Nan—who is the daughter of a Big House maid and Grania's grandfather—and is therefore Grania's first cousin. Grania becomes (or believes she is) pregnant, and her illicit and unwittingly incestuous affair and feared pregnancy reenact in reverse an intergenerational pattern of sexual abuse inflicted on Aragon's Irish maids. When Foley is arrested for his part in the abduction of two British officers, Grania reveals her pregnancy and Foley's paternity, thereby scandalously exposing an intergenerational web of sexual abuse that heretofore has remained submerged. An image of the house's sexual secrets as literally submerged embodies the consequences of this intergenerational web of silence: "babies' bones . . . little and green scattered skeletons on the river bottom" (122).

Grania and Foley's union, like the marital union of the Big House daughter and the Irish groom in *Purgatory*, allegorizes a reversal in Anglo-Irish/Irish power relations. Keane, however, refigures Yeats's dissipated Irish groom as the dispossessed grandson of the Big House who inherited his mean streak from the Anglo-Irish landowner who raped his grandmother. In doing so, she works to compensate not only for her own earlier misunderstanding of the nationalist struggle but also for the gothic distortions inherent within the Anglo-Irish literary tradition. Grania's voluntary reversal of exploitative sex/gender roles at a time of political crisis signals the downfall of a transgenerational system of male and Anglo-Irish domination. In contrast to *Purgatory*, Grania's sexual betrayal of her class and culture enacts the end rather than the onset of barbarism. Keane answers Yeats's chronic concerns about the politically undermining potential of female lust by calling attention to the more pervasive and toxic influences of male sexual abuse and betrayal within a system of colonial domination that perpetuates itself under the seemingly benign and natural auspices of the patriarchal nuclear family.

Although Grania and Foley's love affair is neither the only nor the most shocking of the secret relationships that incrementally emerge in the course of the narrative, its explicit grounding in historical, gendered crimes against the Irish by the Anglo-Irish makes it a paradigm for other, similar reversals in the novel. Grania is irresistibly drawn to the cruelty that Foley inherited from her own bloodlines, while Foley is attracted to Grania because she represents that of which he, as the grandson of a Fox patriarch, has been dispossessed. Parallel reversals of historical patterns of exploitation and affiliation emerge in the extraordinary bond formed between Sylvia, Grania's older and more punctilious sister, and the leader of the IRA men who burn down the house, and in the secret torture of Aragon's Aunt Pidgie by Nan.

Aunt Pidgie, a character in whom the comic and the grotesque intermingle, first appears as a dotty, atavistic, and attractively pagan female forerunner to certain characters in the plays of Brian Friel, such as Uncle Jack in *Dancing at Lughnasa*. Dressed in absurd, shabby old clothes and thick boots, immersed in an ongoing magical relationship with invisible creatures she calls the Diblins, and known to have "terrible fancies when she got a glass of port," Pidgie is an object of mirth in the family (10). Yet in the reader's first encounter with Pidgie, when Grania comes on her unexpectedly in the woods, Pidgie appears disquietingly outside her assigned role as a laughably eccentric old woman: "Finding her this evening in the darkness of the towering rhododendron, among the glossy darkness of the laurel leaves, Grania had a chill moment before the customary way of seeing Aunt Pidgie came back to her, and she was blinded again by custom to that moment's vision of a different creature: alive, rather wild, strong in its desires" (10). As this passage suggests, Pidgie is not what she seems. The family's "customary way of seeing" Pidgie obscures not only the cronish powers attributed to her in this passage but her pain as well. The narrative gradually connects Pidgie's erratic behavior and deteriorating sanity to Nan's secretive—but not secret, since Frazer, the butler, can tell by looking that Pidgie is being starved (79)—program of systematic deprivation and torture.

Pidgie's utterly dominated and dependent position within Aragon emblematizes the vulnerability of women within the Anglo-Irish Big House. Her incarceration, starvation, and torture represent the abjection to which even ruling-class women have been liable in the name of an aggressively masculinist imperial project. Pidgie's own disenfranchisement from this project is especially evident in her hatred of Aragon's commanding view. She "hated the beauty and isolation of the prospect with all her heart. She would look down on the wildness and beauty she had always known, with her heart mourning for that dream cottage . . . where she could be her own mistress and lie half the morning in a hot bath if it pleased her" (225). Unlike the male imperialist, who in the words of Joseph Addison seeks " 'a spacious Horizon . . . where the Eye has Room to range abroad, to expatiate at large on the Immensity of its Views' " (cited in Gibbons, "Topographies" 28), Pidgie identifies personal autonomy with a restricted and humble setting where she would no longer be caught in the crossfire of covert imperial warfare waged within the Anglo-Irish domestic sphere via emotional blackmail, sabotage, and hidden abuse. The visual motif that places the heroic, masculine ideals of grandeur, expansion, and the sublime associated with Aragon's unimpeded prospect in opposition to women's best interests is reiterated toward the end of the novel, in a passing reference to "the poor Aragon bride who had once gone crashing and hurtling down through the tree tops to her death," a tragic event in response to which "her widower . . . built the little wall before he had married again. It was not quite high enough to be much use, but why hide so lovely a prospect because of one stupid little bride?" (229). An undercurrent of sadism toward and victimization of women, both Irish and Anglo-Irish, flows through the novel, erupting most shockingly in Nan's systematic torture of Pidgie. Nan displaces onto Pidgie's frail, inoffensive person rage that must be hidden even from herself if she is punctiliously to fulfill the position of domestic authority that can never quite compensate for the filial status of which she has been dispossessed. Nan's ritualized persecutions free her to act as an otherwise flawlessly faithful servant; indeed, she ultimately sacrifices her very life in the service of the "God of Aragon" (156).

When Nan learns of Grania's plans to save Foley by making her pregnancy public, her previous desperation to save her son evaporates, and she can think only of Grania and the Fox family's reputation. Hence she reenacts an intergenerational pattern of child sacrifice, as often literal as symbolic, in the name of Aragon's reputation. Nan is wholeheartedly devoted to the maintenance of Aragon's cleanliness and purity, which symbolically compensate for her illegitimacy, a defiling wound that Aragon itself inflicted. In desperation, she wonders:

Was the high giving of her life to be twisted to nothingness in an hour? A Fox daughter in vulgar trouble with a servant's child. In just such trouble as the poor country girls who worked in the house had been in with the bad Fox's [*sic*] of all times, and they had been despised and aborted, their babies, dead or dying thrown to the river, unless they were lucky like Nan's own mother and found some man to put shoes on a Fox's pleasure. All these things have happened, all these things were true and strong in the past. They have happened again and again. Cruelty and pain and tears and death had been common mates to childbirth at Aragon. (156)

Nan thinks of the purity of the house as relying on the unilateral flow of pollution arising from sexual transgression "outward" onto the Irish, and never inward, from the Irish into the house. This paradigm is shaped by Nan's own life experience. She was expelled from Aragon in utero as the abject, as waste material to be thrown to the river or pawned off on a man sufficiently gullible or sentimental to accept "damaged goods," only to return later to oversee the work of maintaining Aragon's literal and symbolic cleanliness, a project to which her life was, from the outset, dedicated. Nan's assumptions concerning Aragon's purity are also shaped by her mother's treatment as a tainted element to be purged from the house after she was made pregnant by her employer.

Reflecting on her mother's experience during her years of service at Aragon and her own connection to the house and its family, Nan concludes that "it was hard to tell whether it was as hell or as heaven that [Nan's mother] looked toward the house. Her life had been somewhere between hell and heaven, a glorious and dramatic purgatory, before she married one of the keepers and settled in the lonely house where Nan was born" (107). Keane thus introduces a subversive substitute for *Purgatory*'s central image of a Big House daughter reenacting the bliss and shame of her wedding night with a drunken Irish groom. In her place we find an Irish servant irrevocably entangled genetically, economically, and sexually with the Big House family she was born to serve, suffering "a glorious and dramatic purgatory" consisting of repetitive involuntary acts of copulation within an intoxicating realm of wealth, power, and plenty from which she is, once visibly pregnant, banished.

At the generative center of the novel's topoi of hidden and twisted relations is the architecture of the house itself, which is fully revealed to the reader only late in the novel. In an elaborate orientalist passage reminiscent of Oscar Wilde's description of the ornate box in which Dorian Gray keeps his opium, Keane gradually reveals a hidden base of domination, expropriation, and murder at the center of Aragon. This passage occurs as the ongoing, damaging effects of Aragon's history are violently surfacing in the lives of various characters. It directly follows an analysis of the effects of Irish and Anglo-Irish genetics on the character of the now-incarcerated Foley that reads like Matthew Arnold under the influence of Edgar Allan Poe. The omniscient narrator veers abruptly from a meditation on Foley's sadistic nature to a passageway that runs underneath the Big House in which Foley's mother was conceived:

In Aragon's basements there was a passage that ran its length to reach one room only, a room distant from any other, a room whose lonely window looked straight out over the river, deaf sailing ships might pass below but no other traffic. This room was unused for many years. There had been an effort made once to turn it into a butler's bedroom, but butlers less austere than Frazer could not enjoy a quiet sleep in airs so shaken and petrified by long past doing. The walls of this room had been papered over in blue and white, but where the paper had peeled in the damp air from the near river, you could see underneath one of old chinese design, a most peculiar design, perhaps rightly hidden and in parts purposely defaced. About this room there remained still an air of past luxuries. White and gold pelmets over the windows, an Italian decoration on the ceiling, a thin marble mantel and steel basket grate—a strange room to find in the basements of Aragon where the hordes of servants had slept in dirt and confusion. Once the room had been hung with mirrors. Other curious contrivances were set in the wall. There was still an old ottoman covered in faded *petit-point,* white rose wreaths on a shadowy blue background. And it was locked. It was fifty years now since any one had opened it and closed it, sick and shuddering at a half-understanding of delicate ivory-headed cutting whips and other fine and very curious instruments. (192–93)

This passage is followed by the exclamation, "It must be burnt. . . . It must be burnt immediately." These are the disembodied words of an ancestral "Mrs. Fox," apparently the most recent family member to have —some fifty years earlier—opened the telltale ottoman and happened upon its horrible secrets. This ancestor, we learn, was rendered unable to speak to her husband of her terrible knowledge, "for it was his grandfather who had used such dreadful tools, who had built this far-off room for his pleasures. . . . *It was Mr. Fox's own grandfather*" (193). This scene of discovery and the repetition of the name Mr. Fox seem deliberately to recall the folktale "Mr. Fox," in which a young woman finds a hidden room in her fiancé's mansion filled with the dismembered bodies of previous brides.[8] Unlike the plucky virginal protagonist of "Mr. Fox," however, Mrs. Fox, having already made her marital commitments, bears the terrible secrets of her husband's house in silence to protect her husband from the incriminating knowledge of the torture that secured his family's fortunes and to maintain at least an external semblance of her own entitlement to the family's property and resources.

Two Days in Aragon explicitly incorporates gothic tropes previously projected onto Europe's Catholic periphery or, in some cases, as in *The Picture of Dorian Gray* and "The Demon Lover," onto England, back into the Anglo-Irish domestic sphere. The novel refutes Yeats's (and Nan's) construction of a morally, culturally, and sexually pristine Anglo-Irish domestic sphere by visually revealing the violence of physical dispossession on which Anglo-Irish settler colonial relations are based. The novel's various subplots reach a feverish pitch as Grania, driving back from dropping a coolly indifferent Foley at the boat that will ferry him to safety in England, catches a glimpse of Aragon in flames. Grania is aware that Pidgie is locked in the upstairs nursery, where Grania too was recently held captive by Nan. "No one can hear what goes on in the nursery," Pidgie told Grania sadly when Grania first sought a means of escape from the unfamiliar (or long-forgotten) world of the nursery and its occluded sufferings (160). Having escaped, leaving Pidgie to suffer the consequences of Nan's wrath, Grania is in the process of convincing herself that the hellish secret world of Pidgie's sufferings she had entered that afternoon was "a slight matter, not the horrifying tragedy it had [seemed]" (215), when she catches sight of the house in flames. Still miles from the house, she careens heedlessly forward on the curving road, only to veer into a ditch as she swerves to avoid a puppy. Nan, meanwhile, is tied, bound and gagged, to a tree in the mountain avenue leading to the house. She has undergone a mock hanging ordered by Killer Denny in retribution for having liberated the two British soldiers, one Sylvia's fiancé, who Foley helped to abduct, and also for older, more personal crimes against Denny himself. At the same time, Pidgie, aware that the house is burning and that she has no means of escape, is taking heroic measures to save Grania's little dog, Soo.

One final and particularly compelling rewriting of *Purgatory*'s central theme of illicit bonding occurs in the novel when Sylvia, Grania's immaculately proper older sister, assists in the escape of Killer Denny, the IRA officer who oversees the burning of her family's house. The narrative backtracks to cover the initial encounter of Sylvia—who believes her fiancé dead—with Killer Denny and his men as they enter the house to set it on fire. Denny was once a pantry boy at Aragon; beaten and blackballed among local Big Houses by Nan for the crimes of drinking cream and handling a china ornament, he is filled with conflicted hatred and grief. Still gripped by the enforced deference beaten into him as a child, Denny "turn[s] his head . . . and sp[its] on the carpet," then feels ashamed of himself. Sylvia, sensing his shame, "recover[s] some of her horrid composure" and belittles him with words similar to those which must have been used against him as a child: "childish and dirty, don't you think so, hardly what one expects from an officer of the IRA" (237). Sylvia intuitively identifies with Denny's childhood experiences, however, when, gazing wildly around at all that is to burn, she looks at the china on the mantelpiece and "felt again the ache to touch that bright china gives to children," just before Denny tells her of the beating he received from Nan when, as a child, he was caught touching one such piece. Sylvia and Denny are thus set in opposition: she wishes to save the china because ownership of it represents the redemption of the frustrated childhood yearnings it elicited in her, whereas Denny seeks to destroy the china because it represents that which he can never touch, thereby emblematizing the material maldistribution that has shaped his life. After hurling the piece of china that he was beaten for holding—the image of an aristocratic little boy with a hen in a basket—to the floor, Denny picks it up again, "fitting the broken pieces together," saying, "Nothing I do . . . would divide me from that little boy" (238). This statement lays claim to the validity of Denny's childhood experiences, perceptions, and wishes. As a pantry boy, he was beaten for daring even to touch the image of an aristocratic child whose condition was constituted, by the beating, as infinitely divided from his own. Denny's memory juxtaposes the social invulnerability of the Anglo-Irish with the supreme violability of the Irish. His determination that nothing divide him from that little boy suggests both a fierce loyalty to his own body and his own perceptions and an acute awareness of all that the Anglo-Irish colonial order has declared off-limits to him. When Sylvia attempts to place Denny in her own life and fails, saying she does not remember him, he answers resignedly, "One dirty pantry boy is very like another" (238).

As fire rages through the house, Sylvia tries desperately to free Pidgie from the locked nursery. To her surprise she looks up to see that Denny, having set the house alight with his men and fled, has reentered the burning house. Denny's return to save Pidgie resembles his mock, rather than actual, execution of Nan; his regret after spitting on the floor before Sylvia; and his impulse to put back together the china figurine after throwing it on the floor. His collaboration with Sylvia, until now a cold and dislikable character, is negotiated in the vocabulary of melodrama:

"You came back. But you'll be caught."
He gave her a direct look. A look that
crossed fire and death and their opposite ways of
living. A look straight from a tough guy to a tough girl.
There was a streak of divine humour in the soft way he said:
"Ah, no. You'll get me off, now see, won't
you?" "I will," Sylvia said, and the promise was
given. She would do as much for his safety now as for
Aunt Pidgie or for her dog's safety. (244)

Forgetting the fire, Sylvia watches the methodical, intelligent way in which Denny's workingman's hands "picked cleverly and slowly at the bared lock." Later, from the base of the stairs, where she has been pouring water to keep an escape route open, she sees the stairs on the brink of collapse and "scream[s] upwards to the man she could not see" to come down, but there is no answer. Making an effort "she did not know she had in her," she climbs the six steps to where the fire is coming through, pours two cans of water on them, and screams out again. "Then she saw him. He came down the dark corridor, and he carried in his arms a bundle as small as a six-year-old child. . . . He tightened his grip on Aunt Pidgie and ran down into the smoke and flames" (245).

Outside, with Aunt Pidgie alive but now completely mad, "the bond of death and fear loosen[s]" as Sylvia questions Denny about her fiancé's fate. He tells her the two soldiers are "safe back in barracks, when they should be cooling in the heather." When British soldiers arrive on the scene, Sylvia assures them that the IRA has "cleared off." We learn later that one of the soldiers' lorries hit and killed Nan, in a scene similar to the inadvertent slaying of Afro-British soldier Jody by an onrushing personnel carrier in Neil Jordan's film *The Crying Game*. The soldier's oblique allusions to Nan's death increase tensions between Sylvia and Denny, but she hides him in a stable in which she tells the soldiers she has a young horse "half-cracked with the smoke and the smell" (248). As the soldiers search the area, she stands in a box stall with Denny, speaking "idiotic words of horse comfort and love, while Denny watche[s] her with fierce, bright eyes, the look of the cornered wolf . . . on him." When the soldiers move on, she puts out her hand to him and he holds it "in the smooth, dry grip of unnervous people" and tells her, "I didn't do Nan in." Sylvia urges him to flee, feeling "that even Nan's death was less important than his escape" (249).

But when he went, dropping off the window-sill into the night, she felt the hour empty, she was drained of all purpose. She was left with a sense of horror at what she had done, and a sense of triumph because she had done it. She had let a dangerous man go free, because he had chanced his life to save a cracked little old woman. He had nearly murdered her lover today and tonight she had his life in her hands and she had held it safe for him. Who would understand, no one, no one, least of all her lover. She sat in the dark, forgetting Aragon, forgetting Nan, crying over her secret she must never tell. Crying because her heart had shrunk so that there was not even room in it for relief and joy that her lover was safe. Because of what she had done, she had lessened her love to herself. Because of this past hour of peril with a tough stranger her importances were changed. She had played traitor to them and in their betrayal she had known an hour of truth. For that hour she had been closer, more obedient to one from whom by every law of her nature she was divided, than she had ever been to any man or woman in her life. And now the hour and the man were lost to her. Before she became once more the Sylvia of tennis parties and white hunting ties and blue habits, the Sylvia meet and right for her Norfolk lover (heir to a respectable old baronetcy) she must know tears for all that was lost to her. (250)

This lovely passage owes an unmistakable debt to the forlorn cries of Pegeen Mike in the final moments of Synge's *Playboy of the Western World*. Like Pegeen, Sylvia is a callow, superficial young woman who achieves momentary greatness through her bond with a killer. Killer Denny, like Christy Mahon, is rendered both heroic and horrifying through his proximity to serial acts of Oedipal violence that awaken an answering desire in the heart of a young woman engaged to marry a man who represents her society's rather than her own (undeveloped) ideals. But, in answer to Yeats's *Purgatory,* this passage makes visible the endless alienation from her own experiences and perceptions, from "truth," that is required of the Big House daughter. Denny and the occluded truths that his experiences and perceptions represent, rather than the Big House and its material contents, are the "all that was lost" for which Sylvia is now obliged to mourn. The burning of Aragon did not inflict this loss, it merely broke through Sylvia's endless domestic rituals and made their loss tangible. This passage opposes the narrowly materialistic view that Yeats asserts when the Old Man in *Purgatory* declares, "To kill a house / where great men grew up, married, died, I here declare a capital offence" (227). As the passage makes clear, the loss of Aragon will not rob Sylvia of her privileged future as wife of a British baronet. But the events surrounding the Big House's burning have created a rupture at the center of Sylvia's previously seamless identification with her socially mandated roles. It is adherence to these roles, not the burning of Aragon, that has robbed Sylvia's life of its meaning.

Recovering an Unsanitized History in *The Troubled House*

Set in 1921, *The Troubled House* represents Rosamond Jacob's sensitive account of the shattering of a Big House family under the pressures of historical necessity. Jacob situates Margaret Cullen, a mother whose stately Dublin home only technically escapes the designation "Big House" owing to its urban setting, in a self-consciously sacrificial position, torn between her loyalty to her husband, a unionist lawyer, and her love for her anticolonialist sons, Theo, Liam, and Roddy. Emerging bonds of sympathy and solidarity between Margaret and, respectively, her politically divided sons, a lesbian couple, and an IRA commanding officer recall the heterogenous *communitas* that supported Irish decolonization.

Jacob's now virtually forgotten novel was published in 1938, the year after the approval of De Valera's new constitution, which, in its infamous Article 41, "underpinned discriminatory measures against women, like the ban on married women working in the public service and a raft of discriminatory regulations in the social welfare area" (Coulter 26). Overtly seeking to limit women's participation in Irish society to their "life within the home," the constitution was doubly offensive to nationalist women such as Jacob for its marginalization of women, including many who had "devoted decades of their lives to the creation of a different society and political system in Ireland," and because it represented a servile "aping [of] their imperial masters" on the part of "Ireland's new rulers." As Carol Coulter points out, "The ban on women working in the civil service paralleled a similar British regulation which was in force in the United Kingdom until the 1960s" (27). The constitution was "opposed by many of the female veterans of the nationalist movement," including Hanna Sheehy-Skeffington, who "organized a public campaign against it" (26). As a republican, it is possible that Jacob would have followed Cumann na mBan and other republican organizations in standing "aloof from the debates on the grounds that [she] did not recognize the state anyway" (26). But it is *not* possible, on reading it, to evade Damian Doyle's conclusion that the novel is Jacob's rejoinder to the constitution's conservative rewriting of the War of Independence and its associated aspirations. As Doyle, to whom we owe the novel's recovery, has pointed out, the novel re-invokes the artistic, sexual, spiritual, and political demi-monde to which the Irish state in part owes its existence.

The Troubled House reverses many of the conventions of the "burning Big House" novels I discussed above, which focus on the experiences of artistic, sensitive young people within Anglo-Irish families and on their reactions to republican volunteers who, while significant to the novels' meanings, are situated spatially at their periphery. In *The Troubled House,* republicanism is placed at the center, within the Dublin family home to which Margaret Cullen, the narrator, is returning in the opening scenes. Conversely, the novel's sensitive artists — Nix and Josie, lesbian nationalists who befriend Margaret and her sons — occupy a more conventionally gothic, peripheral space. Paradigmatic of the novel's strategies of reversed conventions is the opening scene, in which Margaret returns from Australia, where she has spent over three years caring for her desperately ill sister, a stay she repeatedly prolonged to enable her niece to stay in college. Margaret's entry into the text as a female nationalist returning from Australia to a country that has, in her absence, risen in arms reverses conventional folkloric images of nationalist men deported to Australia. Central to this novel are Margaret's and her sons' struggles to define their political ideals and practices during a time of social upheaval. In what could be termed an antigothic gesture, anticolonial politics and their relationship to family relations and subjectivity take center stage here; they become the direct, immediate, and nearly ceaseless concern of Big House residents, who are, in this case, not merely sympathetic observers but also active agents of historical change.

The Troubled House represents the fulfillment of a trajectory that begins with *Purgatory*'s admission of gothic autophagy into the Anglo-Irish domestic sphere. Yeats's play, however, lays the blame for intergenerational hostilities on that all-purpose scapegoat, female lust, and on the domestic sphere's contamination by the consuming native Irish. *The Red and the Green, The Last September,* and *Two Days in Aragon* connect the autophagous patterns they depict to Anglo-Irish intergenerational family dynamics, but although their gothic vocabularies symbolize the internal, familial origins of these dynamics, their realist plotlines situate the forces that break down these gothic cycles outside the family. But in *The Troubled House*, IRA resistance arises within an ideologically and denominationally "mixed" family (Margaret is a Unitarian with republican leanings, and her husband, Jim, is a Catholic unionist lawyer). The text's gothic moments occur outside the house, while members of the family speak openly of those intrafamilial dynamics of sexuality and abuse that are typically gothicized in earlier Anglo-Irish literature.

Whereas the central characters in the other novels discussed in this chapter were unmarried and (except for Grania) virgins, in *The Troubled House* Margaret is the mother of grown sons and the wife of a husband whom she had been finding "a bit tiresome, sometimes, when [she] left home." In chapter 1, Margaret struggles with her eagerness to see her sons and her relative indifference to her husband, reminding herself "your boys are growing old enough to do without you," whereas "Jim will need you more than ever" (9). Significantly, she escapes these lectures from her "inward monitor" during her encounters with Miss (Josie) Carroll, a Dublin artist with whom she has made friends onboard the ship. Miss Carroll uninhibitedly expresses her observations concerning the destructive nature of family relations, declaring that it was probably good for Margaret's sons to be without her, as "every mother either weakens or worries her children when they're beginning to grow up" (11). Margaret reflects, "I wouldn't have left them alone enough, I suppose," and Miss Carroll reassures her, "Don't worry . . . the two elder ones, at least, will be able to cope with you by now" (12).

The voice of Josie Carroll, who we later learn lives with and loves fellow painter Nix Ogilvie, is that of an intelligent outsider who is not herself entangled within the bonds of heteronormative reproduction. Her perspectives come to stand in opposition to "the warnings" of Margaret's "inward voice," from which Margaret deliberately takes refuge in her company. Miss Carroll's critical analysis of family relations comes accompanied with firm political beliefs, which surface when Margaret speaks of her fear that Theo and Liam, her two eldest sons, will have joined the fight against the British. She admits, "I'm glad I have no sons. But if I had one, I should like him to be in that fight." The novel's condensed account of their extended shipboard conversation ends with

Margaret's oblique account of Jim's beating of Liam, their middle son, when at fifteen he "ran off and spent five days spying and carrying messages for the Volunteers" during the Easter Uprising (13). Josie, having told Margaret that she had seen Jim in Dublin and sometimes wanted to paint his portrait, identifies with Liam, implying a common opposition to patriarchal authority among lesbians and republicans. She muses, "Judging by the look of him, I shouldn't care to have him angry with me, if he was my father" (14).

Upon her return, Margaret learns from Theo that Liam, whom Theo believes was emotionally damaged by the violence done him by his ill-disciplined father, has been thrown out of the house for his membership in the IRA. Of the scene that led to Liam's expulsion, Theo jokes, "They say it's bad to repress yourself, so maybe it was a healthy form of self-expression, but I'm glad you weren't at home for it" (19). When she arrives at her family home, Margaret experiences a gothic epiphany that resembles the final scene in *Observe the Sons of Ulster,* in which the younger and elder Pypers embrace, figuring a temporal paralysis in which the past devours the present. Encountering her eldest son side by side with her husband after an absence of three years, it seemed to Margaret "it was not Theo that entered, but the Jim of twenty-five years ago, come to join the Jim of to-day. The likeness had increased amazingly. . . . I had a dazed sense of living simultaneously in two epochs, or seeing a ghost and a living man together." She makes them stand before the mirror together, and Jim laughs and says, " 'There can't be much doubt of your paternity, my lad,' with a slight emphasis on the 'your' " (22). A series of standard gothic tropes — intergenerational violence, doubles, ghosts, and illegitimacy — arise, but as in the above passage, they are rapidly and often humorously dispelled. Similarly, Margaret deflates the sentimental hand-wringing of Jim's sister-in-law, who laments, in consideration of Liam's banishment from the house, "It's a hard thing to be a mother in Ireland now," observing that "mothers must take their chance like other people" (29).

Since before her return to Ireland, Margaret has been struggling to define her own political position. She comments on the "disadvantages" of her sister-in-law's "prudent" course of "talking . . . of women's matters" as a way of avoiding the tensions inherent in political discussions among Jim and their sons (Liam is in the house for the occasion), "for I badly wanted to hear what Jim and Theo were saying." She quickly concludes that "Jim spoke from the same old Home Rule Party standpoint as ever" but that Theo's opinions "were sweeping and crude enough, but they had a hopeful idealism very becoming at his age, and also, I thought, a touch of originality" (29). The novel documents the refinement of Margaret's own political position, which takes place as she negotiates between Theo's (evolving) pacificism and Liam's militancy and through a series of meetings with Clancy O'Hagan, Liam's commanding officer.

O'Hagan enters the text as a stereotype indistinguishable from the sexy but two-dimensional gunman in *The Last September* and Killer Denny in *Two Days in Aragon*. Indeed, with his first appearance as a "tall, dark figure" alluded to as "it" rather than "he," Jacob's depiction of O'Hagan draws as much from vampire lore as from conventional depictions of the IRA. Margaret encounters O'Hagan while she is visiting Liam following the Bloody Sunday shooting of fourteen British officers, in which, she has just learned, Liam participated.

"There's a gentleman here to see him," said Mrs. O'Neill's voice in the darkness. "It's all right, he knows him." I saw behind her a tall, dark figure, which moved forward as she whispered to it. I opened the door wider, and a man came in, taking off a black felt hat and making me a little bow. If I had been asked to point to a man who looked as if he might well have been concerned in the killing of the fourteen officers, I would not have searched further. He was tall and lean and powerfully built, shabbily dressed, with just the long, tanned, black-browed, strong-featured, sinister face I should expect to find connected with a well-managed revolutionary assassination. At first sight I thought him ugly, but before he had been ten minutes in the room I saw that he was handsome, in a harsh style of his own. (87–88)

This scene of recognition, in which Margaret encounters a sort of person she has never seen before — a person whose identity is itself a transgression of the dominant order — also occurs earlier, when Margaret first meets Josie Carroll's partner, Nix. Nix's depiction too owes something to the conventions of vampire literature. As with O'Hagan, Margaret assesses Nix visually and recalls that "the impression I received at that first look was of something subtle, cold and strange. I felt afraid of her" (56). This pattern is reenacted when Margaret views Nix's artwork, which seems to her simultaneously beautiful and appalling. Later, Josie recommends that Margaret keep the evidently love-smitten Theo from seeing Nix, saying Nix could "love a woman, but I doubt if she could ever love a man." Josie warns her that the bonds Nix forms, like the bond between vampire and victim, are eternal, and she casts Nix's effects as themselves slightly vampiric: "if you once like Nix, she does seem to take the colour out of other people." Margaret, who has evidently revised her assessment of Nix's appeal, tries to imagine what effect Nix would have on her, were she a man, and finds herself "inclined to agree with Miss Carroll" (108).

More than Nix, who emerges as a lovable and politically courageous but dangerously temperamental vamp, Clancy O'Hagan is gradually and movingly revealed as a sensitive, intellectual man whose political ideals place him, as do those of Margaret and Theo, the pacifist, in a painful, contradictory position that he can maintain only at immense personal cost. This Christian trope of sacrifice recurs throughout the novel: when Theo's hat is knocked off him by soldiers and he restrains himself from hitting back (96); in the destruction of Josie's and Nix's paintings by Black and Tans in search of the ailing Liam, whom they have nursed back to health (157–64); and in a culminating moment of political crisis that converts Margaret Cullen to armed resistance and permanently divides her politically heterogenous household against itself.

The pacifistic Theo saves the life of Liam and many others by bending his code of nonviolence and transmitting an IRA message that warns of an ambush. Resultantly, he is incorrectly identified as an IRA member and is dragged beaten and half-conscious from the family's ransacked home by Black and Tans. This raid on the Cullen household represents an apocalyptic destruction of the Anglo-Irish domestic sphere parallel to the burning of Danielstown and Aragon. The behavior of the British soldiers who conduct the raid, however, compares unfavorably with the behavior of, for instance, Killer Denny, who is ashamed of having spit on the floor of a house he is about to burn. Margaret emphasizes "the atmosphere of brutish hostility" that the soldiers exude, adding "my first impression was that every man was half drunk" (145–46). Jacob makes resonant the scene of the intrusion of a throng of British soldiers into the home of a unionist lawyer by using the same strategies that Ernesto Cardenal and the campesinos of the fishing village of Solentiname would later use to make visible to themselves and the world the nature of oppression in Nicaragua; she places the scene she describes in the context of a key event in the New Testament. Her representation of the raid implicitly compares the capture of Theo by Black and Tans to Jesus's arrest: "The sense of utter defenselessness, the blinding, sickening, freezing terror which must be controlled because there was nowhere any possibility of help, I shall always shiver to recall, and through it I was half-consciously aware that once, somewhere, it had happened to me before; that this was not the first time I had seen a crowd of soldiers with gleaming weapons rush into a lighted hall and violently make prisoner one unresisting man" (146). Viewing modern oppression through the filter of events in the New Testament shockingly restores a political dimension to New Testament narratives, simultaneously restoring to contemporary victims the dignity and humanity of which they have been stripped by such oppression. In this case Jacob, a republican and a Christian, creates an uncanny effect by situating Theo's arrest as the reenactment of a primal scene of imperial power of which Christ's Passion is paradigmatic.

The Troubled House culminates in the killing of Jim, the unionist father, by Liam, the republican son, in an act that is constituted as one of grievous necessity. Jim has seized hold of an IRA man in the midst of an ambush by the British army on a Dublin street corner, and Liam, unaware of Jim's identity, shoots him to free his comrade. Obeying a narrative logic familiar to vampire fans, Jim's relatively peaceful final moments enable a cleansing reconciliation between himself and Liam unattainable to them so long as Jim was buoyed up by the powers of imperial capital. At the threshold of death, Jim assures Liam that he knows Liam was unaware of his identity when he shot him, adding, with spontaneous dry wit, "You'd have fired a bit lower, I think, if you had" (248). While alive, Jim was unable to stop himself from attempting to sap his son's political will. Dying, however, he acknowledges Liam's right to distribute his life energies for himself and admits to the damage that he has done to Liam by seeking to control his behavior through insults, threats, and beatings. He asks Liam whether, if he dies, Liam will quit the IRA, and Liam answers no, "in a tone that sounded sullen from sheer unhappiness." Jim smiles and answers, "I'm just as well pleased. . . . You wouldn't have meant it if you'd promised. You're honest, anyhow. . . . I'm sorry if I was sometimes hard on you." His final words suggest his acceptance that his years of dominating and intimidating Liam have justly, if unintentionally, come home to roost. Allegorically, they bespeak an analogous attitude of comprehending resignation on the part of the Anglo-Irish settler colonial order toward republicanism, which seeks to redress the maldistribution the settler colonial order has so long upheld: "You've got your own back now anyhow" (249).

"I Should Like to Be Here When This House Burns"

The destruction of the Anglo-Irish domestic sphere in these "burning Big House" texts represents the only possible end to intergenerational cycles of exploitation and abuse perpetuated by the intergenerational denial of colonial appropriation within the settler colonialist order. In image patterns in the texts, this order is connected with the somatization of women and the Irish brought about through a familial system of mandatory heterosexuality in which masculine agency is identified with and brought into being through British colonial structures. The novels, however, refute *Purgatory*'s indictment of female sexuality by representing violations of the Anglo-Irish system of compulsory heterosexuality as symbolically ending rather than precipitating cycles of intrafamilial violence and exploitation.

Anglo-Irish women suffered all the epistemic pressures and lacerations inflicted on Anglo-Irish children, but they never escaped the humiliating conditions of material dependency that rendered the psyches and bodies of Anglo-Irish males overtly appropriable only as children and in time of political crisis. The enforced dependency of Anglo-Irish women confined them within the domestic sphere, where their uninterrupted presence perpetuated private cultural practices which sustained the life of that order and which maintained the economically and politically crucial distinction between the Anglo-Irish and the surrounding Irish. As these women were acutely aware, "a house [is] never a mere setting, but a coded set of instructions as to how its occupants should behave" (Kiberd, *Inventing Ireland* 376).

Perhaps as a result of their enforced confinement within Big Houses, Anglo-Irish women often depict the burning of such houses during the Troubles with an astonishing degree of complacency, if not enthusiasm. To the readings above, I wish to add one final representative passage from Elizabeth (Countess) Fingall's *Seventy Years Young,* published in 1939. Countess Fingall recalls that at the height of the Troubles, in 1920–21, "the country houses lit a chain of bonfires through the nights of late summer and autumn and winter and early spring. . . . People whose families had lived in the country for three or four hundred years realised suddenly that they were still strangers and that the mystery of it was not to be revealed to them—the secret lying as deep as the hidden valleys in the Irish hills, the barriers they had tried to break down standing as strong and immoveable as those hills, brooding over an age-old wrong" (414). This passage's gothic touches—a buried secret, insurmountable barriers, and an age-old wrong—project aspects of the Anglo-Irish family's structural position within Irish society onto the Irish countryside. These gothic elements echo the sublime conventions of eighteenth-century landscape descriptions that Luke Gibbons describes in his article "Topographies of Terror," attributing the secret of colonial appropriation and the strong and immovable economic, social, and physical barriers that had, prior to the burnings, separated the demesne from its social surroundings to the Irish landscape itself. Conversely, the passage is also notable for its characteristic aestheticization of the Big House burnings, which runs counter to the emphasis on human loss and suffering that we might reasonably expect in the reminiscences of a member of an ousted ruling class. Above all, it is characteristic of such reflections that the countess takes the opportunity to break the taboos of the Anglo-Irish domestic sphere and acknowledge "an age-old wrong," thus calling attention to the primal scene of colonial violence in a passage that could easily, through an emphasis on the specifics of anticolonial violence, have diverted our attention elsewhere.

Few twentieth-century Anglo-Irish women writers have joined Anna

Parnell in explicitly indicting the settler colonial order's maintenance of its own women and Irish tenants in positions of parallel dependency and exploitation. Yet many, such as Countess Fingall and the burning Big House authors, express considerable (if sometimes unconscious) aggression toward the houses and social relations that in blatant or subtle ways were continuing to "asser[t an] absolute right to shape" the lives of women and children in Ireland (Kiberd, *Inventing Ireland* 371).

Chapter 7
"Perhaps I May Come Alive"
Mother Ireland and the Unfinished Revolution

Soldiers kicked down the door, called her a whore
while he lingered in Castlereagh.
Internment tore them apart, brought her to the heart
of resistance in Belfast today
Her struggle is long, it's hard to be strong
but she's determined deep down inside
to be part of the unfinished revolution.
. . . She holds the key to the unfinished revolution.
— Christy Moore, *Christy Moore Songbook*

As I argued in Chapter 6, women who broke away from the settler colonial social order at a moment of historical opportunity were rapidly recontained in the post-treaty Free State. The cycles of appropriation and exploitation that the War for Independence set out to end merely continued in slightly different forms and with different players in key positions. In writing a contemporary "fall of the Big House" novel, however, Jennifer Johnston appears to suggest that while systems of familial and colonial appropriation remain powerfully entrenched in the contemporary Irish Republic, women in Ireland continue to "hold the key to the unfinished revolution."

In the first six chapters I have examined narratives in which the subject is consumed by an a priori order: the patriarchal family, the monastery, the prison, imperialist warfare, history itself. These narratives enact the relationship of the Anglo-Irish child and, as the settler colonialist order became entrenched, of all Irish children to that order. The figuration of Ireland as a mother who habitually devours her children will be familiar to most readers through such famous literary tropes as Joyce's "old sow who eats her farrow." In this chapter I explore representations of the historical consumption of the subject from a different vantage point, focusing on "the old sow" herself and considering gothic reconfigurations of "Mother Ireland" as the victim of paternal incest.

As I have argued, children are sacrificed within the settler colonial family in a variety of ways. This pattern of sacrifice, moreover, spread outward from the settler colony itself into Irish society at large, as British colonialism moved from its dominant to its hegemonic phase. Central and prior to the production and interpellation of children, however, is the oppression of women. The societal mechanisms that push women into marriage and motherhood in both the six counties of the North and in the Republic date from changes in the law and social structure that originated or worsened with the onset of British colonial rule. If Irish children continue to be symbolically sacrificed to the needs of a neocolonial order, women are sacrificed twice: once as children, and once as producers of children.

Arguably, the perpetuation of social mechanisms containing women within families is attributable to the Irish and British states' continuing need to enforce the production of children. Evidence for a neocolonial order with an ongoing stake in confining Irish women within a single, prescribed, and legally and economically enforced role may be found in the fact that, although the influence of the Catholic Church is frequently cited as the main force militating against the liberation of women in the Republic, abortion, while legal in England, is unavailable in the North of Ireland (Fairweather, McDonough, and McFadyean 126). The extensive participation of Catholic women in the North and in the Republic in the struggle for women's rights and services and in all areas of the struggle against imperialism (militarily; in the prisons, through electoral politics and neighborhood organizing; and on the streets, through nonviolent creative action groups such as Derry's Bloody Sunday Initiative) [1] also exposes the conventional fallacy that Catholicism is chiefly responsible for women's restricted role in Irish society.

The neocolonial Irish and British states have an obvious stake in promoting both the mother and the land as scapegoats for colonialism's ongoing maldistributions. Irish women's lack of access to birth control information and technology, abortion, and (until recently in the Republic) divorce symbolically affiliates women with nature, constituting all women, including victims of rape and incest, as "natural" mothers who, if they are unable to mother adequately owing to their lack of choice or to the economic or social stresses of their material circumstances, are themselves at fault.

In this chapter I explore two noncanonical representations of the gothic family romance that flamboyantly break with canonical Irish literature's constitution of the mother as scapegoat. My focus will be on the figure of the incest survivor—as this figure mirrors the symbolic position of women in Irish society—in Frank McGuinness's overtly allegorical 1985 play, *Baglady,* and in Jennifer Johnston's gothic-realist 1991 novel, *The Invisible Worm.*

"This Woman Has Received a Blow That Will Shut Her Up Forever"

In "The Politics of the Possible," Kumkum Sangari describes Gabriel García Márquez's *One Hundred Years of Solitude* as encoding the mutual construction and interpenetration of the colonizer's historical temporality with that of the colonized. She writes:

The narratives are obsessed with . . . time and derive a special intensity from prolonging stagnation, oppression, decay. On a political level the stagnant time in *One Hundred Years of Solitude* is imposed by a determining history that puts Latin America out-of-date, keeps it in thrall, fixes it in another time. Stagnant time is both indigenous time *and* alien time, in the sense that it is *re*-imposed by foreign domination. Further, such linear time is also embedded in Macondo as the history of European intrusions in some form, and so as its *own* history, there is no such thing as pure or uncontaminated time. It is significant that the concurrent or circular time of Macondo is not only invaded or interrupted by gypsies who bring alchemy, but also exists in dialectical relation with several entries of linear time. Thus the banana company builds a separate enclave within

Macondo, fences off circular time in order to exploit it. Linear time is as "impure" and as oppressive as circular time. (175)

As Sangari points out, there is no such thing as pure or uncontaminated time in *One Hundred Years of Solitude*. The *wish* for such a pure temporal space outside history is a metropolitan precept, imposed and reimposed by foreign domination. The association of the mother with a pre-Oedipal time of pure and uncontaminated bliss is itself tainted through the implantation into the colony of a capitalist symbolic order within which both "the woman" and "the colonized" are constituted as impure "sites of nature" that are supposed to produce and nurture both children and surplus value. The imposition of English notions of "pure" exchange value, constituted in opposition to "contaminated" use value associated with self-maintenance and the production and nurturance of children, produces repulsion against the body of the mother and, indirectly, against the body of the child, where once the body would itself have constituted the "space outside time."

The constitution of the child as a gendered object offered up within the settler colonial family as a means through which to extend a colonialist symbolic order is figured, in Sangari's analysis as well as in much of Irish literature, as incest. Sangari speculates that "if circular time is a metaphor for historical inevitability, then it is important to notice that it does come to an end. Pilar Ternera perceives incest as a cyclic retardation of linear time: 'the history of the family was a machine with unavoidable repetitions, a turning wheel that would have gone on spilling into eternity, were it not for the progressive and irremediable wearing of the axle' " (175). In Sangari's analysis I find a model that accounts for the way in which otherwise inexorable systems, such as those that replicate sexual abuse within families or colonial hierarchies, might, over generations, wear down through the accumulated resistance to which their repetitions give rise. The colonial machinery of subject production under such exploitative conditions wears like an axle, as Gabriel García Márquez suggests. While the periodic breakdown of such family systems is, in real life, sporadic and asynchronous, Márquez's intuition that the larger political and economic systems that such family systems collectively uphold must also inevitably spawn their own contradictions is enacted allegorically within each of the texts that I discuss in Chapters 6 and 7. The "fall" of the Big House depicted in modern Irish novels represents the inevitable end result of a "wearing of the axle" that occurs at the site of subjectivity itself. This site "wears" because the means by which the subject is accommodated to society by their nature provoke resistance and friction and because the intrasubjective and historical orders this process of subject formation seeks to make congruent themselves, over centuries, wear and grind away at each other.

In his one-act play *Baglady*, Frank McGuinness provides an allegorical representation of the trajectory that such a wearing of the axle might take. An extended monologue that McGuinness says "tries to suggest that an individual is not a fixed entity, but always fluid" (O'Toole, Interview 19), the play premiered in 1985. The play's central figure, the Baglady, is reminiscent of the Tarot figure "the Fool." Like the well-known Fool of the Ryder Tarot deck, the Baglady carries a mysterious sack. Like the Ryder image, she represents a figure stepping into a historical/spatial void. As do Pyper and Dido in *Carthaginians*, two other fool figures from McGuinness's oeuvre, the Baglady represents the discontinuity of the "self" and the simultaneity of past and present in the constitution of the subject.

In *Baglady*, for the first time McGuinness directly challenges stable constructions of gender as a binary code. In *Observe the Sons of Ulster*, McGuinness critiques the social production of "masculinity," as the main character transgresses against masculine coding in ways that clearly amount to a form of (unsuccessful) political resistance. But in *Baglady*, gender itself is thrown into question. According to McGuinness's stage directions, the Baglady "wears the heavy clothes of a farmer, rough trousers, dark overcoat, boots," and "she is feminized only by a grey scarf protecting her head, covering her hair completely" (73). McGuinness seems to want the audience to experience a moment of uncertainty concerning the actress's gender. Moreover, from the first moment of dialogue, the Baglady is continually paralleled in her monologue by male figures who are clearly herself. Her first lines are: "I saw someone drown once. I was carrying them in my arms. When I looked behind me, there was nobody there" (73). The figure the Baglady carries in her arms is herself, as well as the illegitimate son that she drowns. The gender of the figure is specifically withheld here.[2] In the next section of monologue, the Baglady sings: "Who's at the window, who? Who's at the window, who? A bad, bad man with a bag on his back" (73). The "bad, bad man" who threatens to carry the Baglady away *is* the Baglady, as well as the Baglady's father. The bag on his back identifies him with her, and the action of carrying her away refers back reflexively to the image of the Baglady carrying someone whom she watched drown. Identity continues to proliferate reflexively throughout the monologue in a manner which at once suggests that all subjects in patriarchal cultures have fully internalized the characteristics of both genders and that the Baglady has internalized her oppressor (the father who raped her and whose child she bore) and his oppression lives on, in the present, within her.

The factors silencing the Baglady include the false belief that the past is "over and done with" — a belief that represents an internalized colonization of time as well as space, because the Baglady's inability to *confront* her past, for fear of punishment in the present, prevents her from liberating herself from the past's impact on her present — and the culturally constituted confusion between her own memories and experiences and the narratives of others. She holds up the five of clubs and muses:

The five of clubs. A bad card. Don't worry, it's over. It's youth. But it stands for suffering, because it means sorrow. . . . It happened long ago. Somebody did something and you did. Did whoever it was tell you to say nothing, or did you imagine their voice was your own? When you tried to tell eventually did nobody believe you, so you stopped believing too although you saw it all happening?" (79–80)

The Baglady's narrative is overlaid with the fairy-tale narrative of the queen of hearts, who also had a son. "He was taken. The queen left her country in disguise as beggarman, searching for her son. Every time she came to a place where she might find him all she found instead was the same answer. Your son is dead, his father killed him. She couldn't say my son is father and my father is my son. She couldn't say it, but it was all she possessed, the truth" (80). This passage suggests a rereading of Yeats's *Kathleen ni Houlihan* allegory, in which the mother (Mother Ire-

land), a disinherited queen in the garb of a beggar, seeks after sons sacrificed not by her but by the colonial father, who demands the perpetual
sacrifice of sons, his own and those of the colonized Other. Here, the
father begets and sacrifices the body of his son on the brutalized body
of his colonized daughter. The line "your son is dead, his father killed
him," may be read as an indictment of Ireland's literary fathers, who,
dressed in drag as "Mother Ireland," have projected the child sacrifice
intrinsic to the colonial order onto Ireland and Irish mothers, as well as
a broad burlesque of the dilemma of Our Lady, who, impregnated by
her heavenly "Father," bears him the son whom he forsakes and kills.[3]

In the figure of the Baglady, McGuinness conflates the silent *mater
dolorosa,* the grieving figure of Mary that came to prominence in Ireland in the wake of the famine, with Mother Ireland, to construct an
archetypal mother who figures Mary and Mother Ireland as silenced
incest survivors and also represents both the literal injuries sustained
by all incest survivors and the figurative injuries sustained by women
within the Irish social order. Like *Purgatory* and the other "burning
Big House" texts, *Baglady* plays out another possible variation of the
breakdown of a Burkean system of cultural and economic replication.
As does *Purgatory*'s Boy, the Baglady embodies the final link in a chain
of historical causality that she does not comprehend and can no longer
contain. Like so many of the children in the narratives I examine in
this book, the Baglady is left "holding the bag" for the transgressions of
her forebears; her suicide represents the ultimate triumph of the father
over the daughter. Indeed, it constitutes by extension the ultimate triumph of the Oedipal configuration, which exhibits at all moments the
passionate desire to suppress and silence, to render up the body of
the female as perfectly and uncontestedly material. Yet the death of the
Baglady and her child also exacts the final and (within a patriarchal
and misogynist society) the only revenge that the daughter can take
against the father to whom she belongs as property by Oedipal logic
and by Irish law. Through the destruction of her biologically female
body, the Baglady removes from her father and her society the means
by which they have marked her out as a discursive space on which all of
society may write but that may never be claimed for her own use. Above
all, however, the drowning of the Baglady represents the end point of

an unconscious quest backward toward the site of an injury that was, retroactively, discovered to be fatal.

The violent emergence of the past into the present is represented in McGuinness's use of Tarot symbolism, through which the Baglady divines both her past and her future, only to discover that they are identical. Tarot imagery is invoked through the Baglady's reading of a series of playing cards, in the systematic references to the four elements, and in the play's ritualistic invocations of the subject positions "Mother," "Father," "Daughter," and "Son" as the Baglady reads the cards.[4] Her reading of cards, along with her ritualized references to burying, drowning, burning, and suffocation (the constitutive symbolic elements of the Tarot are earth, water, fire, and air), violently conflate the past and present. Through imagery associated with historical forms of punishment for witchcraft (the crushing of witches under enormous rocks, a form of live burial, was favored in Scotland; hanging, a form of suffocation, was preferred in England; death by fire and water was more widespread on the Continent and in North America, respectively), the Baglady's litany connects the four elements associated with a pre-Christian, earth-centered spirituality with the fate of the pre-Christian European tribes at the hands of hegemonic Christianity. The "circularity" of pre-Christian reverence for the seasons, associated with the pagan figure of the god who dies and is reborn, collides, in the Baglady's monologue, with what Porter Abbot has identified as the imperialist "trope of onwardness," which constructs a linear and binary cosmology through which the body of the countryside is "cleansed" in the genocidal clearing away of the old religion and its supposed impurities. The historical subtext of the Baglady's monologue connects the early destruction of indigenous religious practices throughout Europe to the colonial destruction of Irish culture (embodied in the Baglady's connections to the conventional portrayal of colonized Ireland as a violated woman) and to the symbolically and sometimes literally violated position of women within the patriarchal family that was instituted in Ireland through colonial processes.

A further figuration of the persistence of the past into the present occurs in the river that the Baglady says "is everywhere you look about you" (73) and in which she is destined to drown. In the monologue's water imagery, emotions are identified with history, both of which are ubiquitous. In her reading of the cards, the narrative and figurative collapse of emotions and history, of generational positioning, and of gender coalesce, pushing the audience toward an encounter with the monologue's elegized historical object: the lived truth of the Baglady's personal narrative, which has been brutally silenced.

Finally, the queen of hearts is transformed into the queen of spades, "the quiet card." The queen of spades has the face of a corpse: "This woman has received a blow that will shut her up forever, but she's with you for all your life" (80–81). The last word of dialogue is the Baglady's ambiguous "Drown." Fintan O'Toole has written that *Baglady* "reaches towards expiation," reading this final word as addressed to the symbolic objects — the cards, the dress, the scarf, and the ring — of which she has divested herself (Interview 19). I read these objects as pulling the Baglady down with them, although I agree that the scene, in its profound ambiguity, certainly reaches for expiation. The wedding ceremony that precedes the Baglady's final gesture — the dropping of the ring — formalizes an ongoing *Liebestöd,* and her final gesture resonates with the import of Cleopatra's final words: "Bridegroom, I come."

In *Baglady,* we see the denial of history in the face of its contemporary persistence operating at its fatal worst. The connection that the play forges between the sacrificial colonial order and the loss of memory is figured in the Baglady, an amnesiac rape victim searching hopelessly for her slaughtered son. Mother Ireland, as she appears in the figure of the Baglady, is a fool who drowns in an ocean the nature of which she does not understand, pulled under by objects symbolizing Ireland's church-imposed gender relations.

The destruction of the Baglady by an internalized oppressor who began his work in the enforced silence of her childhood and finishes it off through an internalized system of remote control is reminiscent of the fate of actual incest survivors such as Virginia Woolf. As Louise DeSalvo has shown, Woolf was a survivor whose internalized identification with her childhood oppressor silenced her forever, finishing her off as she was writing the childhood memoirs in which she at last named her violators and admitted the significance of the past within her present consciousness. The Baglady's death by immersion is also, however, a complex metaphor for the ways in which the colonial violation of national boundaries may produce its own disastrous and self-destructive silences. McGuinness illustrates the ways in which the maintenance of a suppressed and abject female subject position through the legal and political enforcement of the Oedipal family symbolizes but also literally perpetuates the colonized spaces out of which the deadly compulsion to silence and repeat the traumas of Ireland's historical past continually proceeds.

"I Don't Know Which Tense I Live In"
Jennifer Johnston's *The Invisible Worm*

Like the burning Big House novels, *Baglady* enacts the withdrawal of the subject's bodily or emotional loyalty from a sacrificial system at a moment of revolutionary opportunity. Jennifer Johnston's *The Invisible Worm* (1991) parallels the allegorical narrative of *Baglady* without requiring the death of the subject to bring the system to an end. Johnston examines the post-treaty dispossession of women from the point of view of a culturally (although not economically) marginal woman within the twenty-six counties. Johnston's work, like that of other Protestant women in the Irish Republic, has either been disparaged as the archaic emanations of a residual class or celebrated in splendid isolation by apolitical feminist critics. I hope to show that *The Invisible Worm* holds an important place within the largely neglected body of work that identifies the sacrificial position of women within the settler colonial order and represents the struggle of women to "undo" the very symbolic conditions of their existence within an order that appropriates and scapegoats them. Because much of the small body of criticism that does justice to the work of Irish women writers strips that work of all political significance save that of gender, I hope that my inclusion of Johnston's work within a broader spectrum can help to destabilize a monological, sanitized, static construction of Irish women as (once again) apolitical or "natural" bystanders caught in the crossfire of "male" political violence. Much of what is most painful in the lives of women in both the six and the twenty-six counties today has little to do with overt forms of "terrorist" violence. As the protagonists of the above, female-authored Big House novels demonstrate, many women have actively *supported* violence as the only viable means by which to break out of a thoroughly sacrificial position within a system that continues, vampirelike, to appropriate their bodies and their energies to its own ends.

In *The Invisible Worm,* Johnston recuperates two figures familiar from the paranoid gothic—an incest survivor confined within the domestic sphere and defined by those around her as mentally ill, and a Catholic son disinherited by his family when he renounces his priesthood—in order to depict the ongoing influence of history within the crucible of Irish postcolonial society. As in *Baglady* and other contemporary Irish texts, such as Timothy O'Grady's *Motherland* and Brian Friel's *Dancing at Lughnasa,* subjects in movement in Johnston's novel figure dispossession. The protagonist's recurring visions of a running woman here represent the dispossession of women within the Irish Free State. Dispossession in Johnston's narrative, however, does not take the form of economic or class-imposed exile but of cultural and social exile experienced by a woman who, although the daughter of a popular statesman and hero of the 1916 Uprising, experiences herself as an outcast by reason of her dual parentage (her mother is a Protestant) and her sexual violation by her father.

Schematically, the family romance of Johnston's protagonist, Laura Quinlan, reenacts the evolution of the southern Irish state: a marriage between a middle-class Catholic "revolutionary" and an Ascendancy heiress produces a daughter who is historically displaced (within a national narrative that makes Catholicism and masculinity synonymous with "true" Irishness) and sexually violated. Laura's narcissistic father exploits her entrapment within the patriarchal, bourgeois domestic sphere for his own gratification. In doing so, he strips his daughter of all subjectivity and constitutes her as an exchange value, reducing her, in a manner that mimics both the Catholic Church's and the Irish constitution's reduction of women, to her sexuality: "Laura Quinlan's father liked things to have their uses, and people too. 'No use to me,' he would say. And that was that . . . sometimes even people would never be seen again" (81). The reference to "people . . . never . . . seen again" seems to allude to women, who "disappear" throughout the book, silenced, coerced into "protective coloration," or, like Laura's mother, fatally crushed under the weight of insupportable knowledge. The phrase also alludes, however, to internment, torture, and political assassination. These references not only point to the environment within which the conservative structure of the modern Free State was formed but also to the tactics by which it accrued power to itself. In *The Begrudger's Guide to Irish Politics,* Breandán OhEithir describes the Civil War period:

The Free State decided that the new state needed a blood bath and it set out to put down Republicanism with a reign of terror. . . . [S]pecial emergency powers which allowed military courts to impose the death penalty . . . for a range of offenses, seem draconian even by contemporary South African standards, but variations on such laws became part of the paraphernalia of the new state, under different governments, up to the present day. . . . Ernest Blythe . . . tried to bring institutionalized savagery to its logical conclusion by suggesting that the killing of prisoners in retaliation for the killing of Free State soldiers should be carried out secretly. (15–19)

OhEithir sums up his characterization of the birth of the Free State with the pronouncement, "A terrible beauty was certainly not born in the early 1920's but terrible precedents were certainly created in both states" (18).

Laura's father, O'Meara (his first name is never mentioned), represents both the misogynist and repressive characteristics of the post-treaty Free State government. Laura's descriptions of her father evoke a popular figure, possibly a fantasy composite of several early Free State leaders. She reflects that "he brandished his charm and energy like a conjurer brandishes his brightly coloured silk scarves. People loved the flamboyant insincerity of my father; the smiles, the jokes, the promises flourished in front of their eyes; sleight of hand, magic tricks" (19). Although the Free State rapidly sent women, many of whom had paid very high personal prices to rid Ireland of British colonial rule, back to their homes and in other ways enforced policies that resulted in "people who were never seen again," the careers of bourgeois nationalist leaders such as O'Meara were seldom imperiled by their association with these events. The "open secret" that the Free State was formed through a series of egregious violations of the values for which many volunteers in the War for Independence had fought embodies, in the figure of O'Meara, the essential allure of the southern political structure.

As in earlier gothic-realist novels, Johnson realizes the trope of the open secret in the figure of the ghost, envisioning a ghostly realm into which inassimilable elements of Irish and Anglo-Irish history are repressed. The novel's central haunting — Laura's incestuous abuse by her father — is the "invisible worm" of the title. Through its allusion to Blake's "The Sick Rose," the title links the ghostly, invisible worm that has eaten away at Laura's sanity to Yeats's allegorical rose of Ireland, thus situating Laura as a figure for Ireland who is also, however, a literal incest survivor. The novel recurrently moves between realist and allegorical registers, persistently reminding the reader of allegorical and causal connections between the ghost of incest that haunts Laura's family and the ghosts of Irish history. At one point, for instance, Laura reflects that the Anglo-Irish "live fairly comfortably with [their] ghosts of the past," adding that this comfort in the company of ghosts is "quite seductive" (121). This passage suggests that Laura's father sought to position himself at the head of an Anglo-Irish family because he is *not* comfortable with his own ghosts. In an attempt to put to rest the ghosts of Irish history, Laura's father reenacts the dispossession by which Anglo-Irish society originally came into being. Seeking to enter the charmed circle in which the ghosts of colonialism have been domesticated and rendered "comfortable," he spawns a new generation of shades that continue to eat out the hearts of both Ireland and its children.

Laura's rape by her father, the sexual betrayal that constitutes the novel's paradigmatic "open secret," leads directly to her mother's (or symbolically, the Protestant Ascendancy's) death. Rather than remain as an actor within an increasingly distorted and abusive family romance, Laura's mother conveniently arranges to bow out via a "boating accident" when Laura seeks her help by revealing that she has been raped by her father. "You killed your mother," her father tells her. "I warned you" (38). Figuratively, Johnston suggests that the Free State government opportunistically used the subjugation of women to set a precedent for articulations of Catholicism to "Irishness" and the state. De Valera's constitutional "rape" of Irish women helped to weld in place a comprador Catholic Ascendancy. Drastic constitutional restrictions on women's rights represented one final social and religious nail in the coffin of Ascendancy Protestants, already deflated economically by the Land Acts and politically by Irish independence, within a political power structure that was retained and appropriated by a new generation of bourgeois Catholic nationalists. What leadership remained among the old-guard Ascendancy chose not to "waste" the bargaining powers it had left on the rights of women,[5] thereby colluding in its own suicide rather than fighting to protect the mixed-blood daughters of a new Irish house over which Irish Protestants could no longer rule unilaterally.

Laura's inner quest for healing begins when she meets and is befriended by another cultural outsider, Dominic O'Hara, intellectual and "spoiled priest." "I mustn't run. I have to stop running," she thinks, when he drops in unexpectedly (21). Laura and Dominic share a common resistance to fundamentalist interpretations of their respective religions and to their families. In both cases, intersections between religious bigotry and gender seem to have been responsible for their sufferings as children: as a Catholic boy, Dominic was singled out to ensure his parents' salvation and social status by becoming a priest, whereas Laura, as a Protestant girl, received the full brunt of her father's conflicted desire for and hatred of the Protestant Ascendancy. Dominic says of his parents, who, like his siblings, rejected all contact with him after he resigned from the priesthood, "I was impaled on the spike of their ambitions for me, right from the word go. I found that painful always, and not very love inspiring" (84). Dominic's candor about his position as "the chosen victim" (26) in his family enables Laura gradually to admit to herself her own sacrificial position.

At their second meeting, Laura tells Dominic about her great-grandfather, who collected jade and traveled around the world. When she mentions him, Dominic responds, "Empire building. That's what Mr. Quinlan said" (22). Laura replies with an alternate narrative to that of her husband, Maurice Quinlan:

"Oh, no. He was just a traveler. He was lucky, my great grandmother could keep things going here. There was a mill, you know. He didn't fancy sitting here being a miller. . . . He had this man . . . well, servant I suppose, called Markey, who seemed to have the same notion in *his* head and they both spent all their time traveling. They came home from time to time and their wives had babies nine months later. Both of them." She laughed. "I always used to think that was funny . . . all those little Markeys and all those little Hansons, almost like twins. And their mothers, managing. Weren't women amazing, that they could cope with all that?" (22–23)

"Mr. Quinlan said empire building," Dominic repeats stubbornly (23). Laura, it is clear, identifies with both the Catholic and the Ascendancy women in the stories that are handed down in her family. Her account also emphasizes the parallel positions of Anglo-Irish and Irish women and (especially) children, while acknowledging Irish women's lack of agency. She reflects that "it would have been easy enough for my great-grandmother, but I often used to wonder if Mrs. Markey hated my great-grandfather for taking her husband away like that" (23). "Mr. Quinlan" (Laura's husband, Maurice) relates only to the dominant male in the narrative, coding Laura's great-grandfather's penchant for travel, with a mixture of rancor and veiled pride, as "empire building." In constructing Laura's ancestors as empire builders, Maurice configures himself as their successor, for in truth, Maurice's own activities are explicitly oriented toward empire building in the new world of global capital. Dominic too seems anxious to uphold Maurice's account, even trying to reinstate it once Laura has debunked it. Laura tells him, "Maurice isn't always right, you know. He has odd notions about my family. My father was the same" (23). And O'Meara is, in a sense, "the same" as Maurice Quinlan. Both, as nouveau (bourgeois, Catholic) empire builders, married into the Anglo-Irish Ascendancy that they purported to despise, and both reduce into sensational cartoon outline the history of the family into which they married. The grandeur and wickedness they attribute to their wives' families may be seen as proportional to the power each himself hopes to wield within the emerging twenty-six-county state.

The intense hostility that O'Meara bears toward his wife and what she stands for and his simultaneous identification with Maurice Quinlan's family are expressed when, as Laura recalls, her father responded with rage to his wife's remark that Maurice Quinlan's father "look[ed] like a crook." He spat back, "My dear woman, you've no idea what you're talking about. You expect people to have thin faces and ride horses . . . speak with marbles in their mouths . . . let me tell you something about that lot . . . they're crooks too, only they're unsuccessful. They've lost. Your swanky lot. Lost. And about time too" (116). Later, Laura remarks to Dominic that she is surprised her father never remarried after *she* married and ordered him out of the family house, which was legally hers. This move was, incidentally, upsetting to Maurice, whose marital intentions were directed principally toward Senator O'Meara rather than his seemingly "mad" daughter. Laura muses that "some county lady fallen on hard times would have suited him nicely," since "he could have railed at her for being a Prod and at the same time he'd have had the benefits" (121). "Benefits?" Dominic queries.

Yes. You know . . . that mythological edge they have over everyone else. The glamour of being an endangered species. But what he liked was the air of history, of knowing where you came from . . . crests on spoons, book plates, family portraits, all those museumlike objects collected down the years. . . . We use those artefacts every day. We live fairly comfortably with our ghosts of the past. It's quite seductive, that. You can't buy that. He became a part of it through me, not through my mother. I was part of that chain and I was also his, so I made him. . . . (121)

The line trails off, but Laura's account makes clear that in producing a daughter of the Protestant Ascendancy who was also his own offspring and then by sexually "possessing" her, Laura's father pursued and secured his own longed-for position as an heir to the settler colonialist hierarchy. O'Meara attempted to come to grips with the historic problem of dispossession through an abuse of patriarchal and parental power. He utilized the avenues available to him within the bourgeois family to embed himself within the colonial structures of power that gave rise to that family model and to his own historical dispossession in the first place.

  Within Johnston's sociosymbolic order, daughters of the Protestant Ascendancy are coded as "high-born women" (see Theweleit 294–300) who confer on their husbands "the air of history, of knowing where you came from . . . crests on spoons, book plates, family portraits, all those museumlike objects collected down the years," at the same time that their continued specialized status serves as a bitter reminder that the chains of a colonial past still bind the hearts and minds of contemporary Irish subjects. While Johnston has not been able to offer a literal solution to this intransigent dilemma, she does provide an allegorical remedy. She recounts one woman's symbolic confrontation with the means by which a comprador Ascendancy has maintained the colonial power structure in Ireland to benefit members of its own class and sex. In Laura's burning of a symbol for the "open secret" through which she was silenced and effaced—the summerhouse in which her father raped her—Johnston offers up a utopian gesture, a symbolic expression of hope.

A turning point comes for Laura as Dominic ponders the question of his dying father, who has refused to see or communicate with him since Dominic left the priesthood. He tells her that his sisters are now standing guard around their father, whom they "protect . . . from the likes of me." Laura animatedly urges him to fight, telling him, "Barge in. . . . Don't let them stop you. . . . Knock them down if need be. Fight." The narrator observes, "The word echoed in her head" (86). Later in the conversation, Laura connects the idea of resistance with forgiveness; she tells Dominic, "You see, we need to know how to forgive as well as be forgiven" (86). Through her empathy for Dominic's abject position within his family, Laura conceives an important axiom concerning resistance as a prerequisite to forgiveness; at both the political and the personal levels, Laura recognizes, we cannot forgive those we are still allowing to dominate us.

After Dominic has departed to confront his dying father, Laura sets about unearthing the overgrown summerhouse, "stripp[ing it] of its protection" (90). In this process of excavation, she remembers conversations and interchanges with her parents, mundane and momentous. The recollections that attend her labors emphasize the tacit complicity of parents in the abuse of children and the intergenerational repression of secrets that the nuclear family's replication entails. Laura recalls her mother's complicity in her sexual exploitation. When she begs her mother to allow her to attend boarding school to avoid escalating abuse by her classmates as a "Prod," which her mother knows about, and to escape her father's sexual abuse, of which her mother is only technically ignorant, her mother responds mechanically that her father had said no. When Laura blurts out in desperation, "I know why he said no," her mother silences her, saying curtly that she does not want to hear any more about it. Laura remembers, "The world split into fragments as the tears burst from my eyes" (91). She recalls her father's prohibitions against speech — "Treading on dangerous ground there, Laura" (91) — and these memories are interlaced with her husband's muted warnings against revealing anything that might embarrass her father: " 'Just take care,' he said, and lifted the fork to his mouth. He chewed in silence. . . . Silence was like the splint that held a broken limb tight, she thought — prevented pain, prevented truth, prevented dislocation, falling apart. Long live silence!" (102).

Laura symbolically breaks the silence, however, acting decisively in a way that she has been continually pressured not to, when she burns down the summer home in which her father raped her. She tells Dominic, who helps her, "I don't want you to speak. Not a word. I am generalissimo. I am in charge" (167). She instructs him where to pour gasoline, then herself lights a rolled-up tube of paper and tosses it in: "For a moment he thought the flame was going to go out as it hit the balcony floor, but after a pause there was a cracking noise and the door began to blaze" (168). She tells him, "You can talk now. Recriminate, if you wish. You've been so good not to try and stop me" (168). Dominic's contribution to Laura's healing, which amounts to the fact that he has (unlike other men in Laura's life) not "tried to stop" her from addressing and symbolically redressing the trauma of her past, may seem disappointingly minimal to some readers. Yet as a dissenting Catholic who has broken away from the demands of his own patriarchal line, his participation in Laura's ritual destruction of a structure that should have been eradicated at the moment of decolonization is necessary. The summerhouse, an extension of the ancestral Big House of Laura's mother, which she characterizes as "a mad museum" where she resides as "the curator of [her] ancestor's folly" (24), embodies the material surfeit, amassed through the process of colonization, that continues to shape Irish society. Such emblems of economic and cul-

234 The Gothic Family Romance

tural centrality—"crests on spoons, book plates, family portraits"—
aroused her father's acquisitiveness in the face of a gnawing feeling of
continuing displacement, while the maintenance of the Big House as a
privileged, patriarchally dominated sphere also supplied him with the
power boundlessly to impose his appetite for belonging on his wife and
daughter. Through her "violation" of the summerhouse, a representative piece of socially authorizing cultural capital, Laura strikes back at
the system that both motivated and enabled her own violation. The
burning of an Ascendancy outbuilding by the daughter of a Big House
and a dissenting priest also recalls the republican burning of Big Houses
during the revolution and symbolically suggests that the colonial system against which feminist and socialist republicans struggled at that
time requires further dismantling.

In *The Invisible Worm*, Johnston depicts two paradigmatic figures of
the paranoid gothic—the son sacrificed to the priesthood and the in-
cestuously violated daughter—joining forces to stop autophagous processes within their respective families. In so doing, she creates an astonishing emblem for intersectarian political and affective alliance that
is simultaneously contemporary and realist and profoundly historical
and allegorical in its symbolizing of an end to the gothic family romance. The uniting of Dominic and Laura to speak their truths to each
other marks an end to centuries of sectarian separation, silence, isolation, and disorientation inflicted on children in the name of a long past
military conquest that lacks relevance for anyone in Ireland except insofar as it continues to shape present-day financial disparities and the
experiences of children within contemporary families.

In this novel's narrative trajectory the urgent implications of numerous earlier narratives are made good. Such transgressive alliances as
Laura and Dominic's, which cross religion or class boundaries or which
violate the rules of compulsory heterosexuality by forging primary
bonds between members of the same sex, are precisely those which the
capitalist nuclear family has maintained the colonial status quo by pro-
hibiting. Such alliances, whether they are formed at the individual or
larger community and national levels, can serve to undo the bonds that
have held the autophagous nuclear family in place across generations.
They represent the literal as well as allegorical means by which the

reproductive powers of family and community that have been intransigently harnessed in the service of colonial appropriation may be recovered and harnessed anew in the service of alternative social structures. Through the cultivation of alternate bonds, the autophagous appetites that settler colonialism installed at the heart of the nuclear family in Ireland may at last be sated.

Laura's quest ends when she symbolically catches up with the running woman she has viewed from a distance throughout the narrative and finds herself, at fifteen, raped and bleeding, running along the beach before a failed suicide attempt. She catches up to or symbolically "stops" the running girl by finally piecing her narrative together in the sympathetic presence of Dominic, after the burning of the summerhouse. Having symbolically united her past and present selves, Laura is now able to consider the possibility that she will have a future: "Out of this window I see the night white and empty. Like my future—an empty page on which I will begin to write my life. I will try to embellish the emptiness of living. Perhaps I may come alive" (181). For Laura, a woman in a state that legislates misogyny, a Protestant in a state that has stricken her from the official record, and an incest survivor whose body and past have been colonized in a continuing spiral of injury spinning out from the original and ongoing colonial violation of Ireland, the quest has been inward toward self-possession, toward an active, conscious inhabitation of her own body, her own present, her own familial house, her own marriage, and her own country. Although she loves Dominic, and their chosen, intersectarian alliance has allowed for the interruption of ongoing patterns of familial replication, entrapment, and silence on both sides, in the end she sends him away. This gesture asserts her continued determination to resist the dominion of the past through her refusal to reconstitute its forms. She thinks, "I will never mention Dominic again out loud, but I will mention him in my prayers" (182).

Laura's quest is backward, into the past, toward the geographic or narrative locus of dispossession. As in the earlier Big House narratives, the text's apocalyptic encounter with the past is characterized by violence. In this case, however, it is the locus of violence itself, rather than the traumatized subject, that is destroyed. As do Millie in *The Red and the Green* and Grania in *Two Days in Aragon,* Laura is able to turn the Anglo-Irish family's characteristic repression of the past against the structure itself. She reflects: "Tomorrow Maurice will come home and I will explain to him how I brought down petrol and matches and set fire to the summerhouse. I will describe the flames, smoke, sparks, cracking, splintering, the explosion of violence in which the door burst into flames. He may not believe me. He may consider my story to be a manifestation of my madness, but he will not question it" (181–82).

The narrative ends with an incantation:

Dominic.
Laura.
She will not run again.
The woman.
Whoever she may be.
Away.
Never away again.
Prehaps. (182)

The form and rhythm of this incantation recalls the final passage in Beckett's *Malone Dies,* with which I believe it is in dialogue. Beckett's final passage is preceded by a discussion of "two islands, separated by a gulf, narrow at first, then wider and wider as the centuries slip by" (286). The characters in this passage are journeying from one island to the other:

Lemuel is in charge, he raises his hatchet on which the blood will never dry, but not to hit anyone, he will not hit anyone, he will not hit anyone any more, he will not touch anyone any more, either with it or with it or with it or with or

or with it or with his hammer or with his stick or with his fist or in thought in dream I mean never he will never

or with his pencil or with his stick or
or light light I mean
never there he will never

never anything
there
any more. (288)

While Beckett's closing incantation enacts an exorcism of male and, arguably, of English and Protestant violence, Johnston's represents the expiation of both women's and children's roles as victims. *The Invisible Worm* stands as an important addition to earlier depictions of the destruction of Big Houses because of Johnston's explicit focus on the sacrifice of women and children within the settler colonialist order and her emphasis on the important role that breaking the silence concerning abuse and domination within the nuclear family plays in opposing that order. While the earlier texts I have discussed typically find closure in the image of material destruction or in violent death, *The Invisible Worm* ends with a manifesto that resembles that of Canadian novelist Margaret Atwood's unnamed protagonist in *Surfacing:* "This above all, to refuse to be a victim" (35).

The final word in Laura's incantation, "prehaps," is a word of Dominic's, a mispronunciation of "perhaps" that takes on increasingly utopian or visionary overtones through the course of the narrative. "Prehaps" seems to represent, in the words of Moya Cannon's poem "Toam," one of the "small unassailable words / that diminish caesars" (13–14). It is unassailable both because it is "wrong," a mispronunciation, a made-up word, and therefore not contradictable through existing rationalistic discourses, and because it is radically ambiguous, saying neither yes nor no, neither always nor never, but also saying neither "definitely" nor "perhaps." The narrative space that the destruction of the summerhouse has made available is now open, just as the space once occupied — or colonized — by Lemuel, Beckett's captain who sailed from one island to another to commit acts of violence, is opened up at the end of *Malone Dies.* The advantage that Johnston's "weak," ambiguously visionary ending has over Beckett's "strong," assertive ending is that the latter is prone over time to transform into that which it once opposed, as the Irish anticolonial movement was appropriated and co-opted by a bourgeois Catholic leadership that perpetuated the economic and social wrongs of an old order under a new flag.

Johnston's emphasis on refusing domination so that one may forgive resituates the image of the burning Big House. Through an emphasis on a goal beyond catharsis, Johnston defends the right of all people to self-defense and to self-definition, while reminding the reader that the aim of such a struggle must be an open and indeterminate *forgiveness* if prior dynamics of domination and exploitation are not to reassert themselves. A new story, Johnston's final passage suggests, may (perhaps) begin if the social vocabulary through which we tell our stories can be altered from a semantics of assertion, defensiveness, and hopelessness to one of indeterminacy and vulnerability—if, that is, we are able to develop a narrative vocabulary which is adequate to the intersubjectivity and heterogeneity of historical experience.

Conclusion

If you consider Ireland as a large family house and a garden, and the story taking place in the early 1920's after the "War of Independence" [*sic*]. Some members of the family take the skeleton hidden in the cupboard and bury it secretly in the garden. As the years pass, those who hid the skeleton die off and its whereabouts becomes unclear. Most of the following generations don't know there is a skeleton or indeed that it is buried in the garden. What they do know is . . . that digging is not encouraged, and it is better not to use the ground to its full potential. The skeleton and its identity must be kept secret from the collective memory. If you don't like it you can leave! — Joe Comerford, "The Skeleton in the Garden"

" 'That corpse you planted last year in your garden,
Has it begun to sprout?' "
— T. S. Eliot, "The Waste Land"

In this book's introduction, I offered up the despairing question asked by Glenn Patterson's character Alex in response to the cycles of violence and emotional bullying to which she is subjected in her middle-class unionist family—"Why did we have to get born here? Here of all places" (136)—as my central point of entry. Over the course of the book I have explored literary representations of Anglo-Irish family life from the perspective of numerous children who did indeed have to be born in Ireland, within families that considered themselves to be British rather than Irish.

The various gothic and quasi-gothic texts that I have mined for their representations of family life bear out W. J. McCormack's assertion, in his introduction to *The Field Day Anthology*'s section on the gothic, that Irish gothicism is an impure and heterogenous genre (833). From the standpoint of the family, however, the two major gothic impulses that I identify in this book—the paranoid gothic and gothic realism—

are semantically opposed. While the paranoid gothic reifies and totalizes the nuclear family as society's untranscendable horizon, gothic realism representationally undermines the family. As the conventions of a critical gothic have developed, gothic-realist texts have privileged homosexual and cross-class social alliances that pointedly undermine the family cell's ability to replicate itself.

As I have tried to show, the political meaning of Irish gothic representation is closely tied to a writer's (imagined) relationship not only to the system of economic and social privilege originally established in Ireland during early modern colonization but also to the nuclear family structure that has been central to that system's perpetuation. Within contemporary Irish political culture, as I will argue, the conventions of the critical gothic have enabled those most ideologically and structurally removed from the comforts and confines of bourgeois domesticity to call into being alternative social identities that may, over time, be contributing to the emergence of a more egalitarian, communitarian vision of Irish society.

Inside the Anglo-Irish Settler Colonial Order

As Albert Memmi points out in his classic volume *The Colonizer and the Colonized,* children born into a colonial social order are entrapped within an inescapable moral quandary. The colonizer who attempts to wash his (or her) hands of the colonial enterprise is, over time, confronted with a bleak revelation:

Colonial relations do not stem from individual good will or actions; they exist before his arrival or his birth, and whether he accepts or rejects them matters little. It is they, on the contrary, which, like any institution, determine a priori his place and that of the colonized, and, in the final analysis, their true relationship. No matter how he may reassure himself, "I have always been this way or that with the colonized," he suspects, even if he is in no way guilty as an individual, that he shares a collective responsibility by the fact of membership in a national oppressor group. (Memmi 38–39)

In his well-known description of the dilemma faced by the colonizer who refuses his or her ordained position within the colonial order,

Memmi calls attention to an aspect of colonial relations that I have, in writing this book, sought to plumb to its depths: the reliance of colonial relations on economic and social prescription established through the production of children and the intergenerational transmission of guilt.

The precise nature of the collective culpability that Anglo-Irish children share from their birth is made explicit in Terry Eagleton's summary of Edmund Burke's defense of the transmission of power and property through hereditary prescription. Eagleton sums up Burke's position concisely: "it is the temporal lapse between an origin and the present which retrospectively justifies that origin," or more pragmatically, "my right to the peerage or property I fraudulently acquired today will become luminously evident in two hundred years' time" (*Heathcliff* 42). Neither Eagleton nor Memmi, however, explores the role of familial reproduction in the creation and maintenance of the social institutions that "determine a priori" the position of the colonizer, "that of the colonized, and, in the final analysis, their true relationship."

The family has, in fact, been a neglected component of the overall sociocultural makeup of the colonial machine. The absence of discussion concerning the role of the family within colonialism is especially notable in the field of English literature, where we have a particular interest in the production and dissemination of narratives. Edmund Burke's intergenerational pact, central to my exploration of Anglo-Irish colonialism's inscription in Irish literature, is, as Eagleton maintains, validated "by the recounting of a certain narrative" (*Heathcliff* 42). A serious argument for a foreign-identified people's retroactive entitlement to colonially expropriated land and resources could not be made without the transgenerational perpetuation in Ireland of a narrative that continually renews and reaffirms British identity in Ireland. At the center of the reproduction of such a narrative is familial reproduction and childrearing. It is the inscription of this widely neglected aspect of social reproduction within Anglo-Irish literature that I have sought to elucidate.

In Ireland, according to Eagleton, the "illicit source or aboriginal crime" (43) that Burke's necromantic depictions of a gloriously veiled English past are meant to hide is not difficult to name (46). But within the Anglo-Irish household, naming this crime would have been not only difficult but also taboo. A central, constitutive taboo against any inquiry, observation, or discussion that would connect the material origins of the family or of Anglo-Irish society with an everywhere impinging colonial primal scene secured the Anglo-Irish subject's position within a transgenerational epistemological contract.

The Anglo-Irish settler colonial epistemology appropriated children's minds and bodies through an elaborate extension of compulsory heterosexuality. In Gayle Rubin's memorable formulation, the Oedipal crisis commences when "the child comprehends the [sex/gender] system and his or her place in it" and realizes that he or she will be constrained to a fraction of "all . . . sexual possibilities" to which humanity is heir (92). The Anglo-Irish child's coming to consciousness, however, entails a more extensive and impinging range of interpenetrating epistemological and sexual restrictions, all of which revolved around the maintenance of a particular, internally contradictory narrative: "we are not Irish, and we are not English."

Viewed from within, such a pervasive system would inevitably have appeared monolithic, majestically indifferent to any resistance short of self-annihilation or apocalypse. Children raised within the Anglo-Irish settler colonial order thus grew up to represent their experience of that order via devouring gothic systems most notable for their inescapability. Read as a figurative displacement or critique of literal circumstances, the apparent all-pervasiveness of the gothic family romance that I examine in this volume represents this structure's most disturbing feature. But it is in the interplay between realism and gothicism to which I have alluded throughout the book that the limits of the system of familial appropriation obsessively inscribed within the gothic family romance are delineated.

Central to the constitutive opposition between realism and gothicism that has implicitly informed this book are the fundamentally different postures of the two traditions toward the capitalist family cell. Whereas realism characteristically disavows all knowledge of "unauthorized versions" of the family, in the gothic such patterns of familial transgression are inescapable. These opposing stances self-evidently serve complementary ends, however: both assert an absolute disjunction between all forms of deviance and bourgeois reality. Such deviations may occur in geographically and cultural remote fantasies, but never in real life. Significantly, it is through a particular synthesis of the two, in the work of twentieth-century Irish gothic realists, that alternative spaces outside the self-replicating nightmare of the gothic family romance have become increasingly visible.

As gothic-realist narratives frequently dramatize, mere awareness of and resistance to the system of imbricated biology, social norms, and economic carrots and sticks that perpetuates colonial dispossession in Ireland is insufficient to provide those who resist that system with viable alternatives. McGuinness's Pyper and Johnston's Alec may clearly see the double binds of the imperial system by which they are entrapped, but they play out their assigned parts to the end all the same. Paradoxically, however, as the burning Big House narratives and Johnston's *The Invisible Worm* suggest, the untenability of this system itself gives rise to forbidden alliances that can crystalize at unlikely moments. Particularly in Northern Ireland, where there remains acute consciousness of historical trauma that the social order must repress to maintain its coherence, contemporary Irish gothicism of both the paranoid and critical stripes spectacularly calls attention to the precariousness of settler colonial economic and social prescriptions, which have been, over the past two decades in particular, radically challenged precisely by those who, like Patterson's Francy O'Hagan, are most marginal to the ongoing system of settler colonial reproduction.

Outside the Pale

Gothic Figuration in Contemporary Northern Ireland

A crucial point that emerges in this book is the significant difference in meaning that identical literary conventions may take on in differing places and at different moments. As Kevin Whelan has observed, Edmund Burke's conservative political philosophy "became subversive once transposed to the narrow ground of Ireland. In England the past was a stabilizing, even a sedating, political presence. In Ireland an appeal to the past inevitably worried old wounds on which the scar tissue had never fully congealed" (37). In Ireland the gothic, with its necromantic interest in the transmission of things — property, capital, curses, guilt — across generations, has had precisely the effect of "worrying old wounds."

In tracing the shifting meaning of gothic conventions in Ireland as the genre emerged out of Swift's blighting irony, evolving through the nineteenth-century paranoid gothic into the critical strains of twentieth-century gothic realism, it is clear that within Ireland, Irish gothicism's necromantic capacities have been deployed to serve a range of purposes. But regardless of the political context in which the Irish gothic emerges, wherever its characteristic images or narrative patterns are invoked, the past is always being renegotiated.

As Joe Comerford parodically suggests in this chapter's epigraph, the contemporary Irish social order continues to direct considerable collective energy into the management of a traumatic past. The yearly marching season in the North, commemorating events establishing Protestant hegemony, exemplifies the cyclical management or suppression of colonial history in Ireland. Marches marking the anniversaries of the Battle of the Boyne and the Battle of the Somme are accompanied by ritual burnings of Catholic symbols, along with the more formally ritualized burning in Derry of a figure for Protestant compromise, an effigy of the traitor Lundy. The dedication of northern unionists to a policy of historical repression is also evident in the unionist slogan, "Not an Inch," which equates political compromise with the literal loss of land but which also suggests the physical rigidity associated with psychic repression.[1] The persistence of a Burkean aversion to potentially disruptive historical material continues to condition Irish cultural production, perpetuating within the present an ongoing, collective gothic family romance. Subjected to ongoing representational repression, "the ground" of Irish culture cannot, as Comerford puts it, be used "to its full potential."

As Comerford's casual satire suggests, however, the critical strand of gothic is growing ever more vital in Irish culture. In the North, especially within nationalist culture, gothic conventions continue to cross-pollinate with folkloric native Irish narrative strands that have been informing Irish gothicism since the time of Maturin.[2] In my closing reflections on the meaning of the gothic in contemporary Irish culture, I would like to explore briefly the relationship between Irish folklore and the conventions of the gothic in republican cultural and political production.

Beginning in the early 1980s and continuing up to the time of the Good Friday Accord in 1998, an uncomfortable awareness of the inner, buried, ongoing lives of the imprisoned "men behind the wire" and of irretrievably "blocked off" (Sedgwick, *Coherence* 12) Irishmen "sleeping rough" on the streets of London has emerged into journalistic prose and academic and political analyses. Strip searches of women prisoners in Armagh and Brixton Prisons have weighed subliminally or acutely on the minds of many Irish men and women on both sides of the border.[3] The Dirty Protest and the 1981 Hunger Strikes, along with the wrongful imprisonment of the Guildford Four, the Maguires, and the Birmingham Six, brought images of suffering selves "hidden, buried," and above all "isolated" from the communities to which they "properly, naturally, necessarily" belong (Sedgwick, *Coherence* 13), to the awareness of all the people of Ireland.

The use of gothic conventions by republican cultural producers and their supporters, who surmounted extraordinary obstacles to make these issues visible and comprehensible, may be responsible to some extent for the extensive transformation that these years have wrought in the Irish political landscape. A salient example of the power of gothic conventions in transmitting a particular sensibility that transcends the individualist ethos of the bourgeois family is "The Voyage," a ballad by Bobby Sands. Written "for his comrades from Derry who were in the H-Blocks" (Moore 77) and set in 1803 on a ship of Irish transportees bound for Australia, the lyrics use gothic/folkloric imagery to express grief for the destruction of Irish community. When I was traveling in the Irish Republic in 1989, I heard this song in nearly every pub I visited. Although most citizens of the Republic I spoke to were highly critical of the IRA, at that time Sands clearly represented a powerful contemporary embodiment of the rebel martyr. Sands's hero status, as it is disseminated and reinforced via performances of this song, may be related in part to the ways in which his lyrics interweave powerful and familiar gothic/folkloric imagery with a poignant (and narratively conventional) consciousness of repetitive cycles of oppression and injustice in Irish history.

I cursed them to hell as our bow fought the swell
And we danced like a moth in the firelight.
White horses rode by as the devil passed by
Taking ten souls to Hades in the twilight. . . .
Twenty long years have gone by and I've ended my bond
And my comrades' ghosts walk behind me.
A rebel I came and I'll die just the same
It's on the cold wind at night that you'll find me. . . .
Oh, oh, I wish I was back home in Derry
Oh, oh, I wish I was back home in Derry. (125–26)

In Sands's lyrics, gothic conventions signal the presence of a colonially instituted separation of the subject from the community. The narrative's preoccupation with community and enforced separation is expressed most overtly in the choric, repetitive wish to return home.

In the song's folkloric rendition of the devil's pact, the living dead appear as supernatural figures — "alive," but already "claimed" by death — so that their "lives," as historical and social agents, are radically restricted. Because the devil here is *able* to take the protagonist's innocent comrades, this image transforms the paranoid gothic tradition by secularizing and socializing "the devil" within a postcolonial context. The force that separates his comrade's souls from their bodies through the strategic, social manipulation of the natural and immutable threshold between life and death is a historically and politically produced devil whose appropriation of souls may be contested. These figures allegorize a devil's bargain born in the violence of colonial onset, a covenant with the forces of death which may often be involuntary or unconscious but which effectively forecloses personal agency.

The inexorable force of history is expressed in the figuration of the comrades' ghosts and highlighted by an extratextual awareness of the conditions under which the song was written. As many scholars and critics of Irish literature and culture (notably Julian Moynahan, Roy Foster, and Allen Feldman) have observed, representations of the living dead as ghosts frequently figure a return of repressed or unresolved historical events. The dirty protesters and hunger strikers, whose suffering the British government tried to repress, have remained, like ghosts, irrepressibly visible. Their uncanny persistence in photographs, recordings, written statements, memorial ceremonies, and spontaneous popular performances of Bobby Sands's songs has represented a "formidable barrier" within colonial epistemology (Gibbons, "Topographies" 41).

Through the song's performance, the image of the 1803 transportee who longs to reunite with the comrades whose souls have been appropriated by the devil in the course of their voyage is superimposed on the image of Sands singing this song to his comrades in the H-Blocks, with his voice as the last vestige through which human connections could be established. It emerges as a more general image of a stifled, enclosed, separated voice, a voice of historical, mythical, and political significance that has reunited against all odds with its rightful community, which in turn enacts the restoration of communal bonds through the song's performance.

"The Voyage" was, via the elaborate information networks of republican prisoners, liberated from the H-Blocks, although Sands himself never was. As a performed narrative, Sands's song calls attention to the existence of a semiotic space (in Julia Kristeva's sense) that transcends colonial law. Like the invisible networks of IRA communication that the song itself makes tangible, its performance bears witness to a network of historico-social bonds that, while invisible from within the dominant symbolic order, nonetheless hold in place a web of Irish community which colonialism has never entirely effaced or severed.

Although the system of colonial appropriation cannot be overthrown by those writing from within the settler colonial order, critical gothic texts lay claim to a semiotic space outside the reproductive power of the Big House, forge alliances that breach the restrictive boundaries of the family cell, and offer possibilities for genuine change. The logic that underlies the self-conscious strain of gothic realism promotes a relational rather than essential analysis of interactions between individuals, groups, and institutions. As the narratives discussed in Chapters 5–7 indicate, those voices which the colonial family's compulsory heterosexuality and sectarianism have long buried represent a genuine challenge to the settler colonial order. Their increasingly clear and unified articulation within Irish gothic narrative represents a strong and progressive trend. In contemporary Ireland the marginalized voices of the critical gothic are serving, like T. S. Eliot's dog "that's friend to men," to dig "the corpse in the garden . . . up again" (32).

The Coat of Arms of the City of Derry/Londonderry

Notes

Introduction

1 It was during this period that the growth of anti-Catholic intimidation led to the deployment of British troops to Northern Ireland and the subsequent reemergence in the North of the Irish Republican Army.

2 In this book, the term "Anglo-Irish" designates the Protestant English and Scottish settlers in Ireland during or following the colonial plantation period, from 1601, and their descendants. By Anglo-Irish literature I do *not* mean anglophone Irish literature but the literature of the Anglo-Irish. I also use the terms "English and Scots settlers," "Irish Protestants," or sometimes "colonizer(s)" or "settler colonizers" more or less interchangeably for the same group in various contexts. The political and economic system by which this group was authorized and organized I refer to as "the Anglo-Irish settler colonial order." The "Old English" (many of whom were Normans), integrated into Irish society and, unless they converted to Protestantism, fall into the group that I will refer to interchangeably as the Irish, the native Irish, Irish Catholics, or sometimes "the colonized." At times I also designate groups according to political beliefs or national loyalties or both (for example, nationalists/republicans, unionists/loyalists). I do not take the subject position "Anglo-Irish" to be identical to the political affiliations "unionist" or "loyalist," nor do I mistake all Irish Catholics for nationalists.

3 See Fairweather, McDonough, and McFadyean, *Only the Rivers* 14.

4 I use Adrienne Rich's term "compulsory heterosexuality" to designate the network of forces which compel and naturalize normative heterosexual courtship, marriage, and reproduction within the Anglo-Irish settler colonial order and which punish transgressions against the heterosexual norm. My use of this term encompasses a wider complex of gendered dynamics than those originally embraced by Rich. A comparison of our respective uses of the term will immediately show that I apply the term in ways that Rich herself deliberately set out to avoid, although in doing so, I hope I extend her essay's original aim: to posit the compulsory nature of women's heterosexuality as a system with widespread implications for all women, not only lesbians and bisexuals, and hence as a matter of immediate con-

cern for all feminists. My most evident and potentially disturbing deviation from Rich's original model resides in my broadening of the term's definition to encompass the experience of men, which could be seen as risking the reinscription of a spurious "inclusion" of lesbians as "female versions of male homosexuality." In interrogating the experiences of both men and women whose existences make up, like Rich's lesbian existence, "the breaking of a taboo and the rejection of a compulsory way of life" (52) — even if such breaches and rejections are tentative, brief, or symbolic in nature — I expand my definition of her heteronormativity, as well as the array of possible transgressions against it, by taking into consideration not only gender but also class and ethnicity. I do so because I believe that such a broadening of definitions is politically useful, if not essential, and that this model promotes an accurate understanding of the ways in which children originally internalize object choice and the spirit in which object choice has been enforced. I thus intend "compulsory heterosexuality" to designate an expanded and related network of requirements and prohibitions and to make visible literary depictions of breaches against them. I hope to honor the spirit of Rich's watershed essay, which, for many of us, first provided a vocabulary with which to comprehend the compulsory nature of heterosexual orientation.

5 This concept was first defined in Orlando Patterson's magisterial *Slavery and Social Death,* as the condition of subjects who have been deprived of civil rights and protections to such an extent that their lives have been made contingent on the good will of a dominant order from which they are excluded.

6 From a keynote address delivered at the conference "Gender and Colonialism," U.C.-Galway May 1985.

7 Compare Backus, " 'Looking for the Dead Girl' " 424–25.

8 In her fine study *Art of Darkness: A Poetics of Gothic,* Anne Williams identifies this pattern of inexorable breakdown with gothic elements in a Freudian family romance that simultaneously expresses "the desire to escape the 'reality' of the family and the impossibility of doing so." This contradiction is implicit in the form of the family romance, because "the 'escape fantasy' of the 'family romance' remains itself organized by the structure one desires to escape" (12). Williams credits Horace Walpole with "grafting — or perhaps fusing — a dynastic, a family plot onto the Gothic atmosphere and setting already familiar in other modes." Williams suggests that Walpole's *The Castle of Otranto,* like the narratives on which I focus, "generated the possibility of a narrative operating within the rules that govern the patriarchal family, and by extension, government and the Church, and yet at the same time threatening their destruction" (24).

1 The Other Half of the Story
English and Irish Social Formations, 1550–1700

1 Cited as the epigraph for Nancy Armstrong and Leonard Tennenhouse, "Gender and the Work of Words," *Cultural Critique,* no. 13 (Fall 1989): 229.

2 As Ann Rosalind Jones and Peter Stallybrass have shown, the policies of absolute "otherization" that accompanied the intensification of English efforts to control Irish society in the late sixteenth century contradict English policies established earlier in the century. Emerging constructions of the Irish as "barbarically/heroically resistant to all change" (161) are, as Jones and Stallybrass argue, at variance with the absolute assimilation that is the apparent goal of "An Act for the English Order, Habit and Language," a 1537 act that attempts to legislate differences between the English and Irish out of existence (157). While English constructions of and approaches toward the Irish appear to have done a complete about-face within a few decades in the sixteenth century, however, the goal of imposing "order" on Irish social forms did not vary, although it does seem to have intensified.

3 See especially R. F. Foster, "Plantation: Theory and Practice," chap. 3 in *Modern Ireland.*

4 Vincent Gookin, an adviser to Cromwell, explicitly cautioned that the Irish should not be allowed to "kni[t] together again like worms their divided septs and amities" (Allen 49–50).

5 Examples of this ongoing process of displacement are given in Des Wilson, *An End to Silence* 17–19, and in *Fortnight,* no. 313 January 1993: 16.

6 As Henry Kamen writes in his compendious study of this period, *The Iron Century:* "The stage at which ordinary European folk magic became irrational was the stage at which the devil entered history. It was when the doctrine of the witches' Sabbath began to be taken seriously in the fourteenth and fifteenth centuries that the witchcraft problem really materialized" (239).

7 According to William Monter, "both sixteenth-century reformations, Protestant and Catholic," abruptly embarked on a massive educational campaign that centered around fear of the devil and equated residual pagan beliefs with diabolism (212). Monter's analysis reaffirms Christina Larner's contention that during the period of the Reformation and Counter-Reformation, the personal religious beliefs of peasants, which had never before been of serious concern to the metropolitan clerical hierarchy, were suddenly of crucial interest to the Catholic and the Protestant leadership (118–19). In a pattern that became increasingly well established throughout the history of imperial expansion, the twin gazes of competing metropolitan churches did not bode well for the peasantry on whom they were trained.

8 R. Williams 38. See also Marx, *Capital*, vol. 1, pt. 8, esp. chaps. 26–28, for additional discussion of this period.

9 Clearly the state of affairs that Adrienne Rich terms "compulsory hetero-sexuality" has been implicit in some form in many sex/gender systems. In premodern societies, however, it would have existed as the de facto conse-quence of a kinship system aimed not (predominantly) at reinforcing an abstract sexual orientation but at bringing into being new kinship bonds among men (Rubin 85). Through the changes that I outline in this chapter, however, compulsory heterosexuality emerged as an autonomous, explicit norm rather than the incidental effect of a patriarchal kinship system.

10 Although vivid literary depictions of emotionally claustrophilic, invasive families began to emerge only with the literary-realist novel in the mid–eighteenth century, Henry Kamen's account of the "leading part played by children" in the witch persecutions offers a suggestive glimpse of the inter-generational strife that would have characterized this period (244). His catalogue of cases in which "children denounc[ed] their own parents"—a woman accused by her son, an eight-year-old girl who accused her father, an outbreak in Essex that appeared "to have started with a sick child's accu-sations," and "the famous Warboys case," in which "the evidence for the prosecution rested principally on the evidence of three children"—suggests the intense climate of acrimony and invasion that would have character-ized the family environment at this time (244).

11 See Louise Kaplan's *Female Perversions* for an extraordinary explication of the psychic and particularly the sexual consequences of the imposition of compulsory heterosexuality and its attendant binary gender norms on chil-dren.

2 "Does She Not Deserve to Pay for All This?"
Compulsory Romance in the Constricting Family Cell

1 I use the term "bourgeois" throughout this chapter to denote a cultural rather than an economic category. The term identifies family members, families, and all class strata exhibiting the nuclear, constricted family for-mation that originated with the emergent European middle class in the early modern period.

2 See Castle, "Lovelace's Dream," in *Female Thermometer*.

3 See MacCannell 23; Foucault, *History of Sexuality* 1: 108; Backus, "Dis-course and Silence"; and Stone, "The Growth of Affective Individualism," in *Family*.

4 In "From Immodesty to Innocence" in *Centuries of Childhood*, Philippe Ariès discusses the transition from medieval to modern conceptions of

childhood, with an emphasis on the emergence of new conceptions of children as valorized (and indeed fetishized) for their sexual purity. The visual representations of children that Aries describes in the chapter "Pictures of the Family" however, tell a different story, suggesting that a growing emphasis on the child's body as a site of, at minimum, visual erotic gratification accompanied the verbal de-emphasis of children's sexuality.

5 See Lillian Faderman, *Surpassing the Love of Men.*

6 This gendered structure helps to make sense of the fascinating role played in the novel by the Godot-like cousin Morden. Owing to his absence throughout the whole of the action (he returns from his interminable Continental travels only in time for Clarissa's funeral), Morden stands in as a sort of absented principle of masculine justice who, like the deist's Clockwork God or the giant, flaming letter *Aleph* in Tony Kushner's *Angels in America,* has wandered off, leaving flawed humanity to find its own way as best it may.

7 Sussman's recurring figuration of female subjectivity as "hemmed in" by threats of violence and spawning, in self-defense, strong compensatory aspirations to connubial bliss supplies an explicit gloss on Ian Watt's arresting representation of the Georgian closet (the English equivalent of the French boudoir) as the "new forcing-house of the female sensibility" (*Rise of the Novel* 188).

3 "Something Valuable of Their Own"
Children, Reproduction, and Irony in Swift, Burke, and Edgeworth

1 This elegantly, absurdly Wildean dictum was outlined for the Irish Bar in the eighteenth century by Chief Justice Robinson and Chief Chancellor Bowes (Moynahan 4–5).

2 See chapter 1 of Trumpener, *Bardic Nationalism.*

3 See JanMohamed, "The Economy of Manichean Allegory."

4 The hybrid seventeenth-century origins of the Anglo-Irish have been incorporated into Anglo-Irish writing and self-construction in various ways as originary myths. For instance, in volume 4 of *Memoirs of Sir Walter Scott,* J. G. Lockhart recounts a myth of familial origins that was ceremonially narrated to Scott's party during Scott's first extended trip to Ireland (in July 1825) by the party's host, a Protestant Loyalist whom Lockhart casts as "our little Irish Squireen" (283). In the best stage Irish tradition — drunk, obstreperous, sentimental, and bellicose by turns — Lockhart's "Squireen" proudly narrativizes his descent "from a sergeant in Cromwell's army" (284). His Cromwellian ancestor behaved, in the squire's estimation, like a real gentleman, accepting the land ceded him with assurances to its pre-

vious owner, "the widow," that "he would neither turn out her nor the best-looking of her daughters; so get the best dinner you can, old lady . . . and parade the whole lot of them, and I'll pick" (284). Clearly Scott's host was boasting not of his Irish Catholic ancestry but of his impeccably legitimate claim to his estate, secured through the unimpeachable bloodlines of Cromwell, on the one side, and the "gentlemanly" forced marriage of his forefather to a thoroughly nullified daughter of the house, on the other.

5 Dympna McLoughlin, in an article entitled "Exploding the Nuclear Family," dates the widespread normalization of the middle-class nuclear family in Ireland to the late nineteenth century, after the progressive erosion of women's employment horizons and increasing hostility toward women's presence in the public sphere had, over the course of the century, curtailed the "flexibility of the pauper family" (8).

6 I have heard only a brief summary of Luke Gibbons' work on this subject, at the NYU conference on famine in June 1994. I have been unable to obtain a published copy of the full-length essay.

7 See especially Laura Brown's essay, in which she argues that defamiliarizing figurations of female corporeality in *Gulliver's Travels* attack the bourgeois woman as an emblem for British imperialism.

8 See Theodore W. Allen, *Invention of the White Race* 1: 87–88.

9 As Maggie Kilgour observes in *Communion,* the image of cannibalism "replac[es] more orthodox though indirect means of communication," signaling "the failure of words as a medium [and] suggesting that people who cannot *talk* to each other *bite* each other" (16). The paradoxical thrust of Swift's rhetorical technique—according to Edward Said, "to become the thing he attacks" ("Swift as Intellectual" 87)—reaches its apogee in "A Modest Proposal" with the deployment of cannibalism: a symbol that obliterates meaning and turns conventional language back on itself.

10 Moreover, the narrator's neutral observation that "Papists" are the "principal breeders of the nation" confirms that Catholics would not constitute the only but merely the *principal* casualties of his plan. The economist's strenuous emphasis on the advantages of massive Catholic mortality reveals that the children of the Protestant poor would constitute acceptable (but de-emphasized) collateral casualties. In this passage the reader's attention is diverted from the implied sacrifice of Protestant children by the economist's coldly rational expressions of sectarian hatred. Viewed through Swift's annihilating lens, the excessive space of colonial mayhem that Michael Taussig alludes to as the "space of death" expands to devour a wider range of victims than either the atavistic impulses of sectarian hatred or economic interests would individually have justified (*Shamanism* 4).

11 See McCormack, *From Burke,* chap. 1.

12 The Irish hedge school, taught by "peripatetic Catholic primary school masters," has been immortalized in Brian Friel's 1981 play *Translations.*

Emerging out of older Gaelic traditions of itinerant scholarship, the hedge schools kept alive Gaelic culture and learning—Latin, Greek, mathematics, and other subjects—when, as during Burke's childhood, "Catholics were forbidden to keep a school, to act as ushers or private tutors or to send their children to be educated abroad" (C. O'Brien 39).

13 My decision to jump in and label Burke bisexual is variously motivated. I find the anachronistic "bisexual" sufficiently useful to risk the inevitable objections of colleagues because it marks a sexuality that has historically gone unmarked or been subsumed under its adjoining "heterosexual" and "homosexual" rubrics. While there is, inevitably, a lack of watertight evidence concerning Burke's dual sexual orientation, we certainly have in Burke one of the likeliest starting points for a study of eighteenth-century bisexuality. To fail to specify Burke's apparent sexuality is to render his sexual "ec-centricity"—Ed Cohen's useful term ("Double Lives" 354)—invisible or to flirt with the idea of it in a way that almost inevitably reverts into a reductive psychology that equates bisexuality with unresolved Oedipal tensions and immaturity. By foregrounding Burke's bisexual orientation, I treat his sexuality, like his nationality and religious upbringing, as a material fact that situated him in certain specifiable ways relative to the dominant discourses of his time. I consider his rhetorical strategies as the material means by which he negotiated these discourses.

14 By situating Burke's writing within a social context that takes account of the family as a social institution, I do not mean to replicate Kramnick's Oedipal history of Burke, which tends, like much of psychoanalytic analysis, to occlude the larger social system out of which families emerge. Instead, I explore the influence of the nuclearizing and bourgeoisifying Anglo-Irish family, a consolidating system of compulsory heterosexuality, and colonial relations within Ireland on Burke's representations of a normative cultural contract underlying English national subjectivity.

15 *A Vindication of Natural Society* (1756) was written during what Burke's biographers sometimes refer to as the "missing years," a "dark period" to which he was afterward "exceedingly unwilling to refer" (Kramnick 69). He spent these years living and traveling with his long-time companion, Will Burke, a man he disingenuously introduced to others as his cousin. Journal entries and unpublished poems from this period suggest that Burke experienced tremendous conflict between his desire for earthly success, which he equated with marriage and procreation, and his desire for Will (Kramnick 70-79). Born of a period of intense personal ambivalence, *A Vindication*—which became, like the years that produced it, a gap in Burke's later self-construction—is an odd, ambivalent work through which Burke seems to have exorcized his dissenting political beliefs in the form of a wildly unsuccessful "parody" of free thinking.

16 The bifurcated subjectivity inscribed throughout Burke's oeuvre also, how-

ever, reflects what Burke referred to in "The Muse Divorced," an unpublished poem dated November 1750, as his "Lazy side," which he associates with his aversion for "the Marriage Noose" but which, roused by thoughts of professional and social success, he "lash[es]" before lapsing once more into "boyish dreams" and "play" in the company of his male companion (cited in O'Donnell, Appendix, 1).

17 See Haraway, *Primate Visions.*

18 For reflections on the ways in which Burke used the figure of the family to negotiate relations between modernity and tradition and between collective versus individual values and obligations, see "Phantasmal France, Unreal Ireland: Sobering Reflections," chap. 1 of Seamus Deane's *Strange Country.*

19 See, for instance, his representations of India as a deceived lady, preyed on by Warren Hastings and his henchman (cited in De Bruyn), and his justly famous depiction of Marie Antoinette in *Reflections* (Burke 2: 343–44). For a great discussion of Burke's deployment of gender and family roles, see Corbett, "Public Affections and Familial Politics."

20 Talia Schaffer has undertaken a particularly wonderful analysis of this phenomenon in Bram Stoker's oeuvre, but Oscar Wilde, W. B. Yeats, Elizabeth Bowen, and Jennifer Johnston, in their representations of seductively but catastrophically divided selves (see Chapters 5 and 7, this volume), delineate and (with the exception of Johnston) celebrate similar patterns of subjectivity in their writings.

21 Burke's prohibition against investigating the origins of institutions and social structures broke down periodically within England, but it was in a continual state of crisis at the colonial periphery. As Conor Cruise O'Brien's biography documents, Burke reacted explosively but unpredictably wherever the provenance of state authority was in the process of being established or contested, in colonial settings as well as in France. In the cases of India and France, he argued vociferously for the resumption of prior forms of state authority, while his responses to colonial power struggles in Ireland and North America (which he did not, for ideological reasons, perceive as having *had* precolonial modes of governance) were more complex and tortured.

4 "A Very Strange Agony"
Parables of Sexual Subject Formation in
Melmoth the Wanderer, Carmilla, and *Dracula*

1 In "Protestant Magic," R. F. Foster observes that "from the inside of the demesne wall, a sense of threat was inevitable" during this period. He also

suggests a connection between the precariousness of the Anglo-Irish position and the emergence of the paranoid gothic, pointing out that "as the
nineteenth century wore on," the Anglo-Irish, experiencing themselves as
marginalized in Irish society, produced increasingly paranoid persecution
scenarios (247–48).

2 See Johnson, "Gaps and Gothic Sensibility.

3 Monçada's terse and elliptical allusion to horrendous and indeed unspeakable actions that left him "delirious with rage, shame and fear" resembles
Thomas Clarke's account of a fifteen-year term in British prisons, beginning in 1883, in which he reports, in addition to continuous harassment
and episodes of "crude brutality," punishment "of a more refined kind that
seemed inspired by a spirit of devilry and aimed at galling the finer feelings of a man's nature and was calculated to blur and deaden the moral
sense" (2: 285). As an example, he mentions a " 'Special Search' which occurred frequently—about twice a month through all the years." Again this
account is reticent, mirroring, in fact, the pattern of Monçada's account in
its studied and even foregrounded silences.

On these occasions we would be stripped stark naked and subjected to the
most minute examination of our persons—so minute that often the bull's
eye lamp was used. Had this search stopped short at a minute examination
of the hands and between the fingers, of the soles of the feet and between
the toes, of the mouth and inside the jaws and under the tongue, it would
be disagreeable enough; but it went further and to such a disgustingly in-
decent extent that I must not here do more than imply the nature of it. This
search would sometimes be carried out to the officers' accompaniment of
a running fire of comments *in keeping with the nature of the work they were
engaged on.* (285; emphasis added)

Like Monçada, Clarke emphasizes devilry, offenses against decency and
human nature, and the sense that he must not compound the crime by explicitly repeating it or reinhabiting the thoughts or feelings it elicited in
him. As indicated by Monçada, one of the aims of this regimen of punishment was, as Clarke asserts, to drive prisoners mad, for while these "Special Searches" went on, along with other forms of torture, Clarke "saw my
fellow-prisoners break down and go mad under the terrible strain—some
slowly and by degrees, others suddenly and without warning" (282).

4 In what Gulliver deems "the greatest Danger I ever underwent in [Brob-
dingnag]," he is abducted by a monkey that painfully squeezes him, induces him to suckle at its breast, forcibly feeds him from "Victuals he had
squeezed out of the Bag on one Side of his Chaps," and exposes him to public ridicule. The act of forcible suckling is obliquely inscribed in Gulliver's
account of his "submission" to the monkey, which "took me for a young

one of his own Species" (Swift 123); the humiliation that accompanies this act of transspecific submission is inscribed both in the reticence with which it is alluded to and in the affective shame and physiological retching with which Gulliver responds in the episode's aftermath (124): "He took me up in his right Fore-foot, and held me as a Nurse doth a Child she is going to suckle. . . . And when I offered to struggle, he squeezed me so hard, that I thought it more prudent to submit" (123).

5 Monçada's account also resembles in its brevity if not its evasiveness Bobby Sands's description of an assault against several prisoners in the H-Blocks in 1981. While the descriptions of abuses against Republican prisoners written by Sands and his comrades to inform one another and, ideally, to document abuse within the prison were ordinarily extremely detailed, one such communication, included in David Beresford's *Ten Men Dead,* has a memorable impact owing to its uncharacteristic conciseness. It gives only the names of the victims, a one-sentence description of the event ("they all were fired over a table and the cheeks of their behinds torn apart by the screws' hands"), and the terse remark, "Comrade, this is sexual assault" (52).

6 I am indebted to Ann Cvetkovich for these concise formulations, made in her responses to an early version of this book.

7 See Love, *Emotional Incest Syndrome.*

8 Significantly, an ancestral crime does, in fact, give rise to the system of subjectivity that Carmilla and her activities figure. Its nature is revealed in the conclusion, by the Baron Vordenburg, whose vast knowledge of vampirism lore enables the discovery of the Countess Mircalla's grave. "Assume, at starting, a territory perfectly free from that pest. How does it begin, and how does it multiply itself? I will tell you. A person, more or less wicked, puts an end to himself. A suicide, under certain circumstances, becomes a vampire. That spectre visits living people in their slumbers; *they* die, and almost invariably, in the grave, develop into vampires" (137). The crime of suicide, which represents an act of transgressive violence within a "territory" heretofore "perfectly free," figures a crime that is both familial and, as it is represented here, territorial. Thus this figuration of a Burkean "ancestral crime" draws together both imperial and familial transgression as the two become bound up when children are sexually consumed within a family system built to both deny and extend a primordial violation.

9 I am referring to the logic that underwrites events such as Massachusetts governor Michael Dukakis's 1986 decision to remove two children from foster care when the sexual orientation of the couple parenting them was sensationalized in the press, as though the exclusion of homosexuals from the state's foster care system would magically rid the system of sexual abuse. Even Freud's preoccupation with the "vagaries" by which maturing children evade heteronormativity can be read — like the drive theory — as a

screen for his earlier, unbankable findings on the prevalence of childhood sexual abuse among his patients.

10 Evidence for *Dracula*'s connection to Irish history, as well as to the other texts I consider in this chapter, may be found in the novel's omitted opening chapter, "Dracula's Guest." This chapter retains a vestige of the 150-year devil's compact that frames both *Melmoth* and *Carmilla;* as Joseph Spence points out, "the tomb of the vampire countess records that," like the Anglo-Irish Ascendancy in the Act of Union, "she sought and found death in 1801" (56).

11 See Moretti, "Dialectic of Fear."

12 As Raymond Gillespie points out in "The Image of Death, 1500–1700," the Reformation and Counter-Reformation sought to put a stop to many communal elements of Catholic practice in Ireland, for instance, banning keening, "which symbolized communal grief," at funerals and suppressing local cults of saints (9).

13 See Foster, "Protestant Magic."

14 *Dracula* — in which the splendid isolation of the aristocratic count is countered by a collectivity of bourgeois men in a manner that prefigures the displacement of aristocratic vestiges within industrial capitalism by multinational corporations — obviously deviates from this pattern. The novel nonetheless enacts a characteristic Anglo-Irish fascination with isolated power, perhaps more fully than the other texts I discuss in this chapter, in its representation of Dracula himself as a highly attractive and compelling monster.

5 Irish Gothic Realism and the Great War
The Devil's Bargain and the Demon Lover

1 This observation was made by Frank McConnell in a keynote address at the "Sub/Versions" graduate conference, University of Colorado, Boulder, March 1990.

2 It is by design that I have begun to drop "Anglo" from the modifier that defines these texts' national/cultural context. As I have suggested in the book's earlier chapters, the Anglo-Irish family and its attendant historical ideology came to shape social dynamics and narrative representation within the Irish social order as a whole. This fusion becomes evident in the late twentieth century when, as can be seen in this chapter, a Catholic author such as Frank McGuinness may use conventions originating with Anglo-Irish gothicism to make points concerning Irish history nearly identical to those made by Protestant author Jennifer Johnston.

3 In *Writing Ireland,* David Cairns and Shaun Richards discuss Arnoldian

hegemonic constructions of "the Celt" as "peculiarly disposed to feel the spell of the feminine idiosyncracy" and examine the interrelationships between gender, race, and colonialism. They make use of Ashis Nandy's excellent work on colonialism in the Indian context, *The Intimate Enemy,* concurring with Nandy that "naturalized" gender constructions that offer up "an aggressive, warrior-like masculinity and a submissive, passive femininity" entrap a colonized group into a set of gender constructions that seem to offer power to some members (the men), while at the same time rationalizing the entire group's continued subjugation by a "masculine" colonizing power (49).

4 I have chosen several comparisons from the Chicano context not only to acknowledge my own historical relationship to the land I currently inhabit but also because certain parallels between the Irish and the Chicano experience are striking. Especially notable are similarities between the construction of the Mexican bandit and that of the Irish woodkern, both forced off their land and representationally "born again" as criminals at the moment of their own dispossession, and in the asymmetrical significatory strategies both groups adopted to combat this representational (as well as literal) reframing.

5 See Brian Inglis, 358–59. For an entertaining and informative account of the posthumous life of Roger Casement, see also Lucy McDiarmid, "The Posthumous Life of Roger Casement."

6 In "Myth and Bonding" in Frank McGuinness's *Observe the Sons of Ulster Marching toward the Somme,"* for instance, Helen Lojek remarks that "even a casual awareness of Irish literature and history discovers a pervasive tendency to use the past to excuse or explain the present" (46). In "The War against the Past," Declan Kiberd argues bitterly and convincingly that a mythologized version of the past overtook and derailed Irish decolonization, and Robert P. Forbes, in "Eliade, Joyce, and the Terror of History," finds in *Finnegan's Wake* a cosmogonic "abolition of time" arising in response to Joyce's horror at the cyclical ravages of Irish history.

7 As Porter Abbot has pointed out, *English* historiography is obsessed not with circularity but with linearity, with what Abbot has called "the trope of onwardness."

8 It is worth noting that Edward Carson, the father of contemporary Ulster Loyalist Protestantism and chief architect of the modern northern statelet, was also the lawyer who prosecuted Oscar Wilde. McGuinness is undoubtedly aware of this further irony in Pyper's enforced, convenanted show of loyalty to Carson. He may be suggesting that "the sons of Ulster" who marched into German artillery at the Somme were betrayed and destroyed by Carson as systematically and cold-bloodedly as was Wilde, through an identical logic linking Britishness to bourgeois male heterosexuality in opposition to a scapegoated homosexual, Anglo-Irish subject position.

9 Pyper, in what could be read as a reenactment of Peter's denial of Jesus (because he is attempting to deny what is the central social relation out of which his subjectivity springs), tries at first to deny his relationship to Ulster by saying "it's not mine," refusing the sash three times. He snatches it when Anderson "threatens" to "put it round" him (78), as if to avoid this last show of homosocial (as opposed to homosexual) bonding which would mark him as finally and irrevocably "of Ulster" and which would mock the chosen and life-affirming bond of love and eroticism he shares with David Craig.

10 In "Jennifer Johnston's Irish Troubles," Christine St. Peter has demonstrated convincingly that Johnston's (predominantly male) critics have been almost inconceivably blind to the historical and political ramifications of Johnston's novels. St. Peter herself, however, identifies Johnston with her Big House protagonists at unlikely moments, especially when she thinks Johnston sympathizes with the ascendancy lady who blithely tells her London friends "when there's no food in the house [the Irish poor] boil the baby" (119–20). Moreover, St. Peter seems too ready to deplore Johnston's recurring themes of "flight" and "failed friendships across boundaries," both of which can as easily be read as critiques, as I read the failed friendship in *How Many Miles to Babylon?* Surely among the most dangerous of cultural artifacts are those which suggest that alliances across class, cultural, or national lines and across historical divisions are readily made and easily maintained. It is in such texts that the wounds of history are most effaced. If Johnston's novels provide few happy endings, they quite explicitly depict the historical, economic, and cultural conditions that impinge on their characters' desire to touch across the historical demarcations that invisibly separate them.

In her chapter on Jennifer Johnston in *Irish Women Writers,* Ann Owens Weekes also outlines the critiques that have been made against Johnston, especially Seamus Deane's assertion that Johnston has not explored "the wider questions about fiction, its nature and status, its methods and its philosophy" (191). She implicitly refutes perennial masculine assertions of the "smallness" of Johnston's literature in her excellent discussion of the Anglo-Irish symbol of "the orphan," abandoned by England (the "natural" parent), as this figure relates to Alexander, who is "stripped of his genealogy, country, tradition, history" and who "by default embraces the traditions of his mother" (196).

6 Somebody Else's Troubles
Posttreaty Retrenchment and the (Burning) Big House Novel

1 Yeats's "The Dolls" evidently expresses male insecurities in the face of female reproductive capacities, which unintentionally belittle the doll-maker's creations by making them appear lifeless in comparison. Yet the dolls' reaction also evinces revulsion toward birth and babies, which unavoidably confront socialized adults with the spontaneous, messy, unregulated aspects of life that Anglo-Irish customs are geared to repress (see Kiberd, "Elizabeth Bowen: The Dandy in Revolt," in *Inventing Ireland*). Like Yeats's *Purgatory* (*Selected Poems*), "The Dolls" holds women responsible for procreation (in the poem's final line, the doll-maker's wife laments, "It was an accident"). In both cases, procreation is related to a guilty secret, the "evil" that "no man can report," owing to the ongoing suppression of the colonial primal scene as it shamefully recurs in "generations of [the baby's] sort" (*Variorum Edition* 319).

2 See Hull, "Scribbling Females and Serious Males."

3 The simultaneous emergence of the Anglo-Irish family and "national tales" in late-eighteenth- and early-nineteenth-century novels by Anglo-Irish women, Marilyn Butler suggests, hints at the mutually informing character of two contemporary projects: the making visible of Irish identity and female identity. "The imagined community and the empowered woman tend to appear in a symbiotic relation, each needing the other as a condition of existence" (Introduction 50). This mutual dependence of the visible, empowered female subject and the construction of a tenable national identity is particularly identified with narratives in which marriage serves as a nationalist allegory of intersectarian reconciliation. In writings of this period such as Lady Morgan's *The Wild Irish Girl,* Sir Walter Scott's metrical romance "Rokeby," and Maria Edgeworth's *The Absentee* and *Ennui,* intersectarian marriages enact reconfigured national social contracts through which historically hostile or estranged groups are symbolically reconciled, and historical wrongs, palliated. Typically in such marital dyads a woman emblematizes Irish culture, although in "Rokeby," a Scottish nation-building romance, a male Irish hero (who turns out to be Scottish) embodies Celtic courage and resourcefulness. Female characters during this period appear to have grown increasingly intelligent, cultured, moral, and, above all, significant in response to a cultural initiative to resymbolize earlier representations of Ireland through allegorical marriages between culturally differentiated equals. Edgeworth's *Castle Rackrent,* which I discuss at length in Chapter 3, characteristically deforms the antiquarian precepts of such nationalist allegories, prefiguring elements of the gothic-

realist novels that I explore in this chapter. Edgeworth's first novel includes two failed intersectarian romances: the crassly exploitative marriage of Sir Kit to the Jewish woman whom Gilbert and Gubar have identified as the original "madwoman in the attic," and an intersectarian romance between Sir Condy and Judy McQuirk that fails owing to character deficiencies on both sides.

4 That Lois and Laurence are gendered halves of one whole hypothetical person is especially clear when Lois reflects that, while she hates being a woman, she " 'would hate to be a man. So much fuss about doing things. Except Laurence' " (99).

5 In this case, the mounting social and historical forces that compel Andrew to alert his superiors or die trying include a disastrously displaced homo-eroticism that persuades him he should have fought Pat to the death as an expression of his love (264).

6 Especially telling is the similarity between Lois's memory of the final loss of Viola to heterosexual womanhood and the wonderfully comic and overtly lesbian passage in Bowen's later novel *Eva Trout* that Patricia Coughlan uses as the epigraph for her essay "Women and Desire in the Work of Elizabeth Bowen":

"She abandoned me. She betrayed me."
"Had you a sapphic relationship?"
"What?"
"Did you exchange embraces of any kind?"
"No. She was always in a hurry." (103)

7 Shortly after this ideological hiccup—a form of flight from rejection—Marda and Lois discuss Lois's future. Lois observes that she likes "to be in a pattern . . . to be related," and Marda remarks that then she will like to be a wife and mother, adding, "It's a good thing we can always be women" (98). "I hate women," Lois bursts out. "But I can't think how to begin to be anything else." She adds that she would also hate to be a man, "except Laurence." Marda asks Lois if she had ever been abroad, in a question that indirectly posits "abroad" as an alternative to being either a woman or a man—as a way, perhaps, to "begin to be" something else. Lois thinks to herself that "she liked unmarried sorts of places" (99). Later, watching as Marda writes a letter to her fiancé, Lois thinks "how anxious to marry Marda must really be, how anxious not to frighten Leslie away from her," and announces, "I think . . . I must be a woman's woman." Lois's un-wanted engagement is, however, inexorably advanced in Marda's letter to her fiancé, in which she writes that Gerald wants to marry Lois. Lois asks if this will "give . . . a good impression," and Marda responds, "Well, it furnishes you rather." This exchange, which flags Marda's letter writing as

a paradigmatic exercise in heteronormative epistolary composition, demonstrates the generativity of homosexuality's conventional unspeakability: Marda, like Lois, invents a heteronormative romance between Gerald and Lois because she " 'can't think what else to say' " about Lois (101). In one last, comic vacillation, Laurence shows up and suggests that Lois has been boring Marda. Marda stands up for Lois spiritedly. She tells Laurence, who is competing with Lois for Marda's attention, "If I were not going to marry I should ask [Lois] to come abroad with me. I have never been less bored." Lois is "intoxicated by being told she was charming and by Laurence's disapproval"; she feels "movement, a wind in her face as though she were on the prow of a ship. . . . She felt certain that Leslie would die or break off the engagement." Laurence crushes her immediately by casting her as a bridesmaid at Marda's wedding, and Lois envisions herself "forlorn in the aisle, with hot air coming up her legs from a grating and tears dripping off her nose into a bunch of chrysanthemums." The thought of Marda's marriage causes the desperate thought of marriage to Gerald to recur in greater detail: "She would keep the ribbon from her bouquet and show it to Gerald in confidence while she unpacked on their wedding night." Aloud, she tells Laurence, "I am thinking of going abroad quite soon" (103).

8   Interestingly, "Mr. Fox" is an oral folktale that predates Perrault's "Bluebeard," published in 1697, a tale that Anne Williams has brilliantly explicated as exemplifying gothic's "uncanny" reenactment of the Law of the Father within the patriarchal family (46), with "the contents of the [forbidden] room represent[ing] patriarchy's secret, founding 'truth' about the female: women as mortal, expendable matter/*mater*" (43). The earlier oral tale enacts not the new wife's culpably curious transgression of her husband's arbitrary and absolute power but a young woman's courageous inquiry into an injustice of unthinkably massive proportions. In drawing on "Mr. Fox" rather than "Bluebeard" as a spatially and temporally organizing mythos for her work, Keane emphasizes the constructed nature of the double bind in which the ancestral "Mrs. Fox" finds herself, while dramatizing a *zero-sum* relationship between Anglo-Irish women and the Irish by substituting Irish bodies, labor, and land for the bodies and minds of women as the suppressed "mortal, expendable matter/*mater*" at the heart of power relations, epistemology, and speakability in the Anglo-Irish family.

7   "Perhaps I May Come Alive"
Mother Ireland and the Unfinished Revolution

1   *Fortnight*, no. 312, December 1992, 20–21.

2   She refers to the figure in her arms as "them," suggesting both a specific

withholding of gender and that the figure represents more than one person.

3 I am grateful to Elizabeth Cullingford for pointing out the resemblance between the Baglady, Our Lady of the Sorrows, and Kathleen ni Houlihan in her responses to an early draft of this chapter.

4 The "court" cards (Queen, King, Page, Knight) signify woman and man, girl and boy of each element.

5 Yeats, of course, in his famously intemperate speech decrying the ban on divorce, represents an exception to this general apathy. Yeats clearly took the ban on divorce to represent precisely the sort of impediment to any future recuperation of a heterogenous Irish Republic that it has turned out to be, but he argued from the unstrategic position that Irish Protestants are too talented and brilliant and gifted to be so callously politically marginalized. This perspective, inviting, as it did, memories of a too recent past in which Irish Protestants did not find Catholics "too good" to marginalize, won few converts.

Conclusion

1 Perhaps Ulster's most intriguing representations of historical trauma occur in official emblems of state entities, in the symbol of Ulster itself, and in the seal of Londonderry. The image of the red hand of Ulster, originating in Irish mythology but enthusiastically embraced as a unionist emblem, figures a founding act of mutilation on which the northern state is figuratively founded. The image of the red hand commemorates mythic brothers who agreed to race by boat to the Kingdom of Ulster, with the first one to touch land to be king. The slower brother, in a gesture in which the figurative and the literal are gruesomely conflated, won the race by cutting off his hand and hurling it to the shore before his brother was able to land. The image of the dismembered hand, like the annual commemoration of the Battle of the Somme, celebrates an act of self-mutilation through which northern Protestant identity was magically and permanently established in Northern Ireland. Most explicitly, the seal of the City of Derry flaunts precisely the secret that Comerford claims continues to hold the whole of Irish society in a state of paralysis: its representation of a skeleton interred in a basement visually reassures the viewer that the state's secrets remain safely buried.

2 I am thinking, for instance, of Maturin's incorporation of a *Sean Bean Bocht* figure in the person of Biddy Brannigan in the frame narrative of *Melmoth the Wanderer*. See Innes 15–17 for a brief discussion of this native Irish narrative convention. Work exploring the cross-germination of Irish folklore and the gothic is already under way. In a paper delivered at the 1998 International Association for the Study of Irish Literatures, for instance, Margarita Gimenez Bon persuasively outlined the relationship of Le Fanu's

Carmilla to Irish fairy lore. It also seems probable that Angela Bourke's incredible readings of fairy lore and specific fairy narratives will enable more sophisticated consideration of the impact of Irish folklore on the development of Anglo-Irish gothicism.

3 In *Passing the Time in Ballymenone,* Henry Glassie describes the following interactions between a pianist and customers in a pub in Fermanagh, a small town in the south of Ulster: "Again and again, the men around him, their ages between eighteen and thirty five, ask for 'The Men behind the Wire,' a current hit heard often on the radio, anthem of the internees held without charge in Long Kesh near Belfast, where eerie light at night whips barbed wire into the eyes of motorists on the swift highway" (82). Several of Christy Moore's songs, including "Ninety Miles from Dublin" and "On the Bridge," attest to the massive energy that the average resident of Belfast or Dublin must put into repressing the awareness of the suffering of detainees in northern prisons in order to remain emotionally and psychologically functional.

Bibliography

Abbot, Porter. "Preserving Beckett's Unfamiliarity." Paper presented at the 1989 Yeats International Summer School, Sligo, Ireland, 18 August 1989.

Alarcón, Norma. "Making Família from Scratch: Split Subjectivities in the Work of Helena María Viramontes and Cherrie Moraga." *Chicana Creativity and Criticism*. Ed. María Herrera-Sobek and Helena María Viramontes. Houston: Arte Publico, 1988. 220–32.

Allen, Theodore W. *The Invention of the White Race*. Vol. 1, *Racial Oppression and Social Control*. London: Verso, 1994.

Althusser, Louis. "Ideology and Ideological State Apparatuses." *Lenin and Philosophy and Other Essays*. New York: Monthly Review Press, 1971. 127–86.

Arata, Stephen D. "The Occidental Tourist: *Dracula* and the Anxiety of Reverse Colonization." *Victorian Studies* 33, no. 4 (Summer 1990): 621–45.

Ariès, Philippe. *Centuries of Childhood: A Social History of Family Life*. Trans. Robert Baldick. New York: Vintage, 1962.

Armstrong, Nancy. *Desire and Domestic Fiction*. New York. Oxford University Press, 1987.

Armstrong, Nancy, and Leonard Tennenhouse. "Gender and the Work of Words." *Cultural Critique*, no. 13 (Fall 1989): 229–78.

Atwood, Margaret. *Surfacing*. New York: Fawcett Crest, 1972.

Auerbach, Nina. *Our Vampires, Ourselves*. Chicago: University of Chicago Press, 1995.

Azim, Firdous. *The Colonial Rise of the Novel*. New York: Routledge, 1993.

Backus, Margot Gayle. "Discourse and Silence in the Victorian Family Cell: Problems of Subjectivity in *The History of Sexuality, Vol. 1*." *Victorian Literature and Culture* 24 (1997): 159–74.

———. " 'Looking for the Dead Girl': Incest, Pornography, and the Capitalist Family Romance in *Nightwood, the Years, and Tarbaby*." *American Imago* 51, no. 4 (Winter 1994): 421–45.

Baldick, Chris. Introduction. *Melmoth the Wanderer*. By Charles Maturin. New York: Oxford University Press, 1989.

Barringer, Carol. "Breaking Silence about Childhood Sexual Abuse: The Survivor's Voice." Unpublished paper completed in the Women's Studies Program, University of New Hampshire, Durham, 1990.

Beckett, Samuel. *"Molloy," "Malone Dies," "The Unnamable": Three Novels by*

Samuel Beckett. Trans. Samuel Beckett and Patrick Bowles. New York: Grove, 1958.

Bell, Catherine. *Ritual Theory, Ritual Practice.* New York: Oxford University Press, 1992.

Bercovitch, Sacvan. *The American Puritan Imagination.* New York: Cambridge University Press, 1974.

Beresford, David. *Ten Men Dead: The Story of the 1981 Hunger Strike.* London: Grafton, 1987.

Bon, Margarita Gimenez. "An Early Fright by a Fairy Guest." Paper presented at the 1998 International Association for the Study of Irish Literatures Annual Conference, University of Limerick, July 1998.

Boswell, John. *Same-Sex Unions in Premodern Europe.* New York: Villard, 1994.

Bourke, Angela. "Reading in a Woman's Death: Colonial Text and Oral Tradition in Nineteenth-Century Ireland." *Feminist Studies* 21, no. 3 (Fall 1995): 553–86.

———. "The Virtual Reality of Irish Fairy Legend." *Eire/Ireland* 31, nos. 1–2 (Spring–Summer 1996): 7–25.

Bowen, Elizabeth. *Bowen's Court.* New York: Alfred A. Knopf, 1942.

———. "The Demon Lover." *The Collected Stories of Elizabeth Bowen.* Ed. Angus Wilson. New York: Ecco Press, 1989. 661–66.

———. *The Last September.* 1929. London: Penguin, 1987.

———. *Seven Winters: Memories of a Dublin Childhood.* London: Longmans, Green, 1943.

Brown, Laura. "Reading Race and Gender: Jonathan Swift." *Eighteenth-Century Studies* 23, no. 4 (Summer 1990): 425–43.

Burke, Edmund. *The Works of Edmund Burke. Vols. 1 and 2.* Boston: Little, Brown, 1894.

Butler, Marilyn. Introduction. *"Castle Rackrent" and "Ennui."* By Maria Edgeworth. London: Penguin, 1992. 1–54.

———. *Maria Edgeworth: A Literary Biography.* Oxford: Clarendon, 1972.

Cairns, David, and Shaun Richards. *Writing Ireland: Colonialism, Nationalism, and Culture.* Bolton: Manchester University Press, 1985.

Cannon, Moya. "Toam." *Oar.* Galway: Salmon, 1990. 13–14.

Castle, Terry. *The Female Thermometer: Eighteenth-Century Culture and the Invention of the Uncanny.* New York: Oxford University Press, 1995.

Clarke, Thomas. "From *Glimpses of an Irish Felon's Prison Life.*" *The Field Day Anthology of Irish Writing.* Ed. Seamus Deane. Vol. 2. Derry: Field Day Publications, 1992. 280–85.

Cohen, Ed. "The Double Lives of Man: Narration and Identification in the Late-Nineteenth-Century Representation of Ec-centric Masculinities." *Victorian Studies.* Ed. Donald Gray. Bloomington: Indiana University Press, 1993. 353–76.

————. "Writing Gone Wilde: Homoerotic Desire in the Closet of Representation." *Critical Essays on Oscar Wilde.* Ed. Reginia Gagnier. New York: G. K. Hall, 1991. 68–87.

Colley, Linda. *Britons: Forging the Nation, 1707–1837.* New Haven: Yale University Press, 1992.

Comerford, Joe. "The Skeleton in the Garden." *Film Base News,* no. 20 (November–December 1990): 22.

Condren, Mary. *The Serpent and the Goddess: Women, Religion, and Power in Celtic Ireland.* San Francisco: Harper and Row, 1989.

Corbett, Mary Jean. "Public Affections and Familial Politics: Burke, Edgeworth, and the 'Common Naturalization' of Great Britain." *ELH* 61 (1994 Winter): 877–97.

Coughlan, Patricia. "Women and Desire in the Work of Elizabeth Bowen." *Sex, Nation, and Dissent in Irish Writing.* Ed. Éibhear Walshe. Cork, Ireland: Cork University Press, 1997.

Coulter, Carol. *The Hidden Tradition: Feminism, Women, and Nationalism in Ireland.* Cork, Ireland: Cork University Press, 1993.

Craft, Christopher. " 'Kiss Me with Those Red Lips': Gender and Inversion in Bram Stoker's *Dracula.*" *Speaking of Gender.* Ed. Elaine Showalter. New York: Routledge, 1989. 216–42.

Cullingford, Elizabeth Butler. "Gender, Sexuality, and Englishness in Modern Irish Drama and Film." *Gender and Sexuality in Modern Ireland.* Ed. Anthony Bradley and Maryann Gialanella Valiulis. Amherst: University of Massachusetts Press, 1997. 159–86.

————. *Gender and History in Yeats's Love Poetry.* Cambridge: Cambridge University Press, 1993.

Cvetkovich, Ann. *Mixed Feelings: Feminism, Mass Culture, and Victorian Sensationalism.* New Brunswick, N.J.: Rutgers University Press, 1992.

Deane, Seamus. *Celtic Revivals.* London: Faber and Faber, 1985.

————. *A Short History of Irish Literature.* Notre Dame: Notre Dame University Press, 1986.

————. *Strange Country: Modernity and Nationhood in Irish Writing since 1790.* Oxford: Clarendon, 1997.

De Bruyn, Frans. "Edmund Burke's Gothic Romance: The Portrayal of Warren Hastings in Burke's Writings and Speeches on India." *Criticism* 29, no. 4 (Fall 1987). 415–38.

DeSalvo, Louise. " 'This Should Not Be': Iris Murdoch's Critique of English Policy towards Ireland in *The Red and the Green.*" *Colby Literary Quarterly* 19, no. 3 (1983): 113–24.

————. *Virginia Woolf: The Impact of Childhood Sexual Abuse on her Life and Work.* NY: Ballantine Books, 1989.

Devlin, Polly. Introduction. *Two Days in Aragon.* By Molly Keane. New York: Viking Penguin, 1986. v–xvi.

Dinnerstein, Dorothy. *The Mermaid and the Minotaur: Sexual Arrangements and Human Malaise.* New York: Harper and Row, 1977.

Doyle, Damian. "Burning Down the House." A paper presented at "Sub/Versions," a graduate conference at the University of Colorado, Boulder, March 1991.

Eagleton, Terry. *Heathcliff and the Great Hunger: Studies in Irish Culture.* London: Verso, 1995.

———. "Nationalism: Irony and Commitment," Derry: Field Day Pamphlet no. 13, 1988.

———. *The Rape of Clarissa.* Minneapolis: University of Minnesota Press, 1982.

———. *Saints and Scholars.* London: Verso, 1987.

Edgeworth, Maria. *Castle Rackrent.* 1800. Oxford: Oxford University Press, 1969.

Ehrenpreis, Irvin. *Swift: The Man, His Works, and the Age.* Vol. 1. Cambridge: Harvard University Press, 1962.

Eliot, T. S. *"The Waste Land" and Other Poems.* New York: Harcourt Brace Jovanovich, 1988.

Ellman, Maud. *The Hunger Artists: Starving, Writing, and Imprisonment.* Cambridge: Harvard University Press, 1993.

Faderman, Lillian. *Surpassing the Love of Men: Romantic Friendship and Love between Women from the Renaissance to the Present.* New York: William Morrow, 1981.

Fairweather, Eileen, Roisin McDonough, and Melanie McFadyean. *Only the Rivers Run Free: Northern Ireland, the Women's War.* London: Pluto, 1984.

Feldman, Allen. *Formations of Violence: The Narrative of the Body and Political Terror in Northern Ireland.* Chicago: University of Chicago Press, 1991.

Fingall, Elizabeth Mary. *Seventy Years Young: Memories of Elizabeth, Countess of Fingall, Told to Pamela Hinkson.* New York: E. P. Dutton, 1939.

Forbes, Robert P. "Eliade, Joyce, and the Terror of History." *Cross Currents* 36, no. 2 (Summer 1986): 179–92.

Foster, R. F. *Modern Ireland: 1600–1972.* 1988. New York: Penguin, 1989.

———. *Paddy and Mr. Punch: Connections in Irish and English History.* London: Penguin, 1993.

———. "Protestant Magic: W. B. Yeats and the Spell of Irish History." *Proceedings of the British Academy* 75 (1989): 243–66.

Foucault, Michel. *Discipline and Punish: The Birth of the Prison.* Trans. Alan Sheridan. New York: Vintage, 1979.

———. *The History of Sexuality.* Vol. 1, *An Introduction.* Trans. Robert Hurley. New York: Random House, 1980.

———, ed. *I, Pierre Rivière, Having Slaughtered My Mother, My Sister, and My Brother. . . : A Case of Parricide in the Nineteenth Century.* Trans. Frank Jellinek. Lincoln: University of Nebraska Press, 1975.

Freud, Sigmund. "Family Romances." *Complete Psychological Writings of Sigmund Freud.* Ed. James Strachey. London: Hogarth, 1959.

———. *An Outline of Psycho-Analysis.* Trans. and ed. James Strachey. 1949. New York: Norton, 1969.

Friel, Brian. *Dancing at Lughnasa.* London: Faber and Faber, 1990.

Furniss, Tom. *Edmund Burke's Aesthetic Ideology: Language, Gender, and Political Economy in Revolution.* Cambridge: Cambridge University Press, 1993.

Fussell, Paul. *The Great War and Modern Memory.* London: Oxford University Press, 1977.

Gibbons, Luke. "Topographies of Terror: Killarney and the Politics of the Sublime." *Ireland and Irish Cultural Studies.* Ed. John Paul Waters. *South Atlantic Quarterly* 95, no. 1 (Winter 1996): 23–44.

Gillespie, Raymond. "The Image of Death, 1500–1800." *Archaeology, Ireland* 6, no. 1 (Spring 1992): 8–10.

Gilbert, Sandra, and Susan Gubar. *The Madwoman in the Attic: The Woman Writer and the Nineteenth-Century Literary Imagination.* New Haven: Yale University Press, 1979.

Girard, René. *The Scapegoat.* Trans. Yvonne Freccero. Baltimore: Johns Hopkins University Press, 1986.

Glassie, Henry. *Passing the Time in Ballymenone: Culture and History of an Ulster Community.* Philadelphia: University of Pennsylvania Press, 1982.

Goldberg, Jonathan. *Sodometries.* Stanford: Stanford University Press, 1992.

Gonda, Caroline. *Reading Daughters' Fictions, 1709–1834: Novels and Society from Manley to Edgeworth.* Cambridge: Cambridge University Press, 1996.

Gordon, Avery F. *Ghostly Matters: Haunting and the Sociological Imagination.* Minneapolis: University of Minnesota Press, 1997.

Greenblatt, Stephen. "Shakespeare and the Exorcists." *After Strange Texts: The Role of Theory in the Study of Literature.* Ed. Gregory S. Jay and David L. Miller. Tuscaloosa: University of Alabama Press, 1985. 101–23.

Greenfeld, Liah. *Nationalism: Five Roads to Modernity.* Cambridge: Harvard University Press, 1992.

Grossberg, Lawrence, ed. "On Postmodernism and Articulation: An Interview with Stuart Hall." *Journal of Communication Inquiry* 10, no. 2 (Summer 1986): 45–60.

Halberstam, Judith. *Skin Shows: Gothic Horror and the Technology of Monsters.* Durham: Duke University Press, 1995.

Haraway, Donna. *Primate Visions: Gender, Race, and Nature in the World of Modern Science.* London: Verso, 1992.

Harden, Elizabeth. *Maria Edgeworth.* Boston: Twayne, 1984.

Haslam, Richard. "Maturin and the 'Calvinist Sublime.'" *Gothic Origins and Innovations.* Ed. Allan Lloyd Smith and Victor Sage. Atlanta: Rodopi, 1994.

Hill, Christopher. "Clarissa Harlowe and Her Times." *Puritanism and Revolu-*

tion: The English Revolution of the Seventeenth Century. New York: Schocken, 1964. 367–94.

Hilliard, Raymond F. "*Clarissa* and Ritual Cannibalism." *Publications of the Modern Language Association of America* 105, no. 5 (October 1990): 1083–97.

Howes, Marjorie. "The Mediation of the Feminine: Bisexuality, Homoerotic Desire, and Self-Expression in Bram Stoker's *Dracula.*" *Texas Literary Studies in Literature and Language* 30, no. 2 (Spring 1988): 104–20.

Hull, Raymona E. "'Scribbling' Females and Serious Males: Hawthorne's Comments from Abroad on Some American Authors." *Nathaniel Hawthorne Journal,* 1975, 35–58.

Inglis, Brian. *Roger Casement.* New York: Harcourt Brace Jovanovich, 1973.

Innes, C. L. *Woman and Nation in Irish Literature and Society: 1880–1935.* Athens: University of Georgia Press, 1993.

Jacob, Rosamond. *The Troubled House: A Novel of Dublin in the 'Twenties.* Dublin: Browne and Nolan, 1938.

JanMohamed, Abdul R. "Rehistoricizing Wright: The Psychopolitical Function of Death in *Uncle Tom's Children,*" *Richard Wright.* Ed. Harold Bloom. New York: Chelsea House, 1987.

Janowitz, Anne F. *England's Ruins: Poetic Purpose and the National Landscape.* Cambridge, Mass: Blackwell, 1990.

Johnson, Anthony. "Gaps and Gothic Sensibility: Walpole, Lewis, Mary Shelley, and Maturin." *Exhibited by Candlelight: Sources and Developments in the Gothic Tradition.* Amsterdam: Rodopi, 1995. 7–24.

Johnston, Jennifer. *How Many Miles to Babylon?* Garden City, New York: Doubleday, 1974.

———. *The Invisible Worm.* London: Sinclair Stevenson, 1991.

Jones, Ann Rosalind, and Peter Stallybrass. "Dismantling Irena." *Nationalisms and Sexualities.* New York: Routledge, 1992. 157–71.

Kamen, Henry. *The Iron Century: Social Change in Europe, 1550–1660.* New York: Praeger, 1972.

Kaplan, Louise. *Female Perversions: The Temptations of Emma Bovary.* New York: Doubleday, 1991.

Keane, Molly. 1941. *Two Days in Aragon.* New York: Viking Penguin, 1986.

Kershner, R. B. "A French Connection: Iris Murdoch and Raymond Queneau." *Eire/Ireland* 18, no. 4 (Winter 1983): 144–51.

Kiberd, Declan. *Inventing Ireland: The Literature of the Modern Nation.* Cambridge: Harvard University Press, 1996.

———. "The War against the Past," *The Uses of the Past: Essays on Irish Culture.* Newark: University of Delaware Press, 1988. 24–54.

Kilgour, Maggie. *Communion to Cannibalism: An Anatomy of Metaphors of Incorporation.* Princeton: Princeton University Press, 1990.

———. *The Rise of the Gothic Novel.* New York: Routledge, 1995.

Kramnick, Isaac. *The Rage of Edmund Burke: Portrait of an Ambivalent Conservative.* New York: Basic, 1977.

Kushner, Tony. *Angels in America: A Gay Fantasia on National Themes.* Part 1, *Millennium Approaches.* New York: Theatre Communications Group, 1993.

Larner, Christina. *Witchcraft and Religion: The Politics of Popular Belief.* New York: Basil Blackwell, 1984.

Le Fanu, Sheridan. "Carmilla." In *The Penguin Book of Vampire Stories.* Ed. Alan Ryan. New York: Penguin, 1988.

Lloyd, David. *Anomalous States.* Durham: Duke University Press, 1993.

Lockhart, J. G. *Memoirs of Sir Walter Scott.* Vol. 4. London: Macmillan, 1914.

Lojek, Helen. "Myth and Bonding in Frank McGuinness's *Observe the Sons of Ulster Marching toward the Somme.*" *Canadian Journal of Irish Studies* 14, no. 1 (July 1988): 45–53.

Longley, Michael. "Wounds." *Poems: 1963–1983.* Dublin: Gallery, 1985.

Love, Patricia. *The Emotional Incest Syndrome.* New York: Bantam, 1991.

MacCannell, Juliet Flower. *The Regime of the Brother: After the Patriarchy.* New York: Routledge, 1991.

MacLysaght, Edward. *Irish Life in the Seventeenth Century.* Dublin: Irish Academic Press, 1979.

Marx, Karl. *Capital.* Vol. 1. Trans. Ben Fowkes. New York: Vintage Books-Random House, 1977.

———. *Early Writings.* Trans. and ed. T. B. Bottomore. New York: McGraw Hill, 1964.

May, Leila. "The Violence of the Letter: *Clarissa* and Familial Bo(u)nds." *English Language Notes* 32, no. 3 (March 1995): 24–32.

Maturin, Charles. *Melmoth the Wanderer.* Ed. Douglas Grant. 1820. New York: Oxford University Press, 1989.

McCormack, W. J. *From Burke to Beckett: Ascendancy, Tradition, and Betrayal in Literary History.* Cork, Ireland: Cork University Press, 1994.

———. "Irish Gothic and After (1820–1945)." *The Field Day Anthology of Irish Writing.* Ed. Seamus Deane. Derry: Field Day, 1992. 831–949.

McDiarmid, Lucy. "The Posthumous Life of Roger Casement." *Gender and Sexuality in Modern Ireland.* Ed. Anthony Bradley and Maryann Gialanella Valiulis. Amherst: University of Massachusetts Press, 1997. 127–58.

McGuinness, Frank. *"Carthaginians" and "Baglady."* London: Faber and Faber, 1988.

———. *Observe the Sons of Ulster Marching toward the Somme.* London: Faber and Faber, 1986.

McKeon, Michael. *The Origins of the English Novel: 1600–1740.* Baltimore: Johns Hopkins University Press, 1987.

McLoughlin, Dympna. "Exploding the Nuclear Family." *Irish Reporter,* no. 15 (Third Quarter 1994): 7–8.

McVeigh, Joseph. *A Wounded Church: Religion, Politics, and Justice in Ireland.* Dublin: Mercier, 1989.

Memmi, Albert. *The Colonizer and the Colonized.* Boston: Beacon, 1965.

Michals, Teresa. "Commerce and Character in Maria Edgeworth." *Nineteenth-Century Literature* 49, no. 1 (June 1994): 1–20.

Miller, Alice. *Thou Shalt Not Be Aware: Society's Betrayal of the Child.* Trans. Hildegard Hannum and Hunter Hannum. New York: New American Library, 1984.

Moir, David Macbeth. *The Life of Mansie Wauch.* Chicago: A. C. McClurg, 1912.

Montag, Warren. *The Unthinkable Swift: The Spontaneous Philosophy of a Church of England Man.* London: Verso, 1994.

Moore, Christy. *The Christy Moore Songbook.* Cooleen, Dingle, Co. Kerry: Brandon Book Publishers, 1989.

Monter, William. "Protestant Wives, Catholic Saints, and the Devil's Handmaid: Women in the Age of Reformations." *Becoming Visible: Women in European History.* Ed. Renate Bridenthal, Claudia Koonz, and Susan Stuard. Boston: Houghton Mifflin, 1987. 203–19.

Moretti, Franco. "Dialectic of Fear." *Signs Taken for Wonders.* London: Verso, 1983. 83–108.

Morgan, Lady. Patriotic Sketches of Ireland. Baltimore: Geo. Dobbin, 1809.

Moynahan, Julian. *Anglo-Irish: The Literary Imagination in a Hyphenated Culture.* Princeton: Princeton University Press, 1995.

Murdoch, Iris. *The Red and the Green.* New York: Avon, 1965.

Nandy, Ashis. *The Intimate Enemy: Loss and Recovery of Self under Colonialism.* Delhi: Oxford University Press, 1983.

Nussbaum, Felicity. "'Savage' Mothers: Narratives of Maternity in the Mid-Eighteenth Century." *Eighteenth-Century Life* 16 (February 1992): 163–84.

O'Brien, Conor Cruise. *The Great Melody: A Thematic Biography of Edmund Burke.* Chicago: University of Chicago Press, 1993.

O'Donnell, Katherine. "'An Union Not to Be Expressed': Burke and the Advent of the Male Homosexual." Paper presented at the national meeting of the American Conference for Irish Studies, Albany, New York, April 1997.

O'Grady, Timothy. *Motherland.* London: Picador, 1989.

OhEithir, Breandán. *The Begrudger's Guide to Irish Politics.* Dublin: Poolbeg, 1986.

O'Toole, Fintan. Interview with Frank McGuinness, *Sunday Tribune* (Dublin) 17 February 1985: 19.

———. "Little Savageries of Domestic Life: *Two Faced* and *Baglady*." *Sunday Tribune* 10 March 1985: 10.

Paredes, Américo. *With His Pistol in His Hand.* Austin: University of Texas Press, 1958.

Pateman, Carole. *The Disorder of Women.* Stanford: Stanford University Press, 1989.

Patterson, Glenn. *Burning Your Own.* London: Abacus, 1988.

Patterson, Orlando. *Slavery and Social Death: A Comparative Study.* Cambridge: Harvard University Press, 1982.

Perry, Ruth. "Colonizing the Breast: Sexuality and Maternity in Eighteenth-Century England." *Eighteenth-Century Life* 16 (February 1992): 185–213.

Poblacht Na Heireann, Irish Political Documents, 1916–1949. Ed. Arthur Mitchel and Pádraig Ó Snodaigh. Dublin: Irish Academic Press, 1985. 17–18.

Punter, David. *The Literature of Terror: A History of Gothic Fictions from 1765 to the Present Day.* Vols. 1 and 2. New York: Longman, 1996.

Rashkin, Esther. *Family Secrets and the Psychoanalysis of Narrative.* Princeton: Princeton University Press, 1992.

Rich, Adrienne. "Compulsory Heterosexuality and Lesbian Existence." *Blood, Bread, and Poetry: Selected Prose, 1979–1985.* New York: W. W. Norton, 1986. 23–75.

Richardson, Samuel. *Clarissa, or The History of a Young Lady.* 1747–48. Ed. Angus Ross. New York: Penguin, 1985.

Richter, David H. "The Reception of the Gothic Novel in the 1790's." *The Idea of the Novel in the Eighteenth Century.* Ed. Robert W. Uphaus. East Lansing, Mich.: Colleague's Press, 1988. 117–37.

Rubin, Gayle. "The Traffic in Women: Notes on the 'Political Economy' of Sex." *Women, Class, and the Feminist Imagination.* Ed. Karen V. Hansen and Ilene J. Philipson. Philadelphia: Temple University Press, 1990. 74–113.

Sage, Victor. *Horror Fiction in the Protestant Tradition.* New York: St. Martin's, 1988.

Said, Edward. "Swift as Intellectual." *The World, the Text, and the Critic.* Cambridge: Harvard University Press, 1983. 72–89.

Sands, Bobby. "The Voyage." *Skylark Sing Your Lonely Song.* Dublin: Mercier, 1989. 125–26.

Sangari, Kumkum. "The Politics of the Possible." *Cultural Critique* 7 (Fall 1987): 157–86.

Schaffer, Talia. "'A Wilde Desire Took Me': The Homoerotic History of *Dracula.*" *ELH* 61 (Summer 1994): 381–425.

Seccombe, Wally. *Weathering the Storm: Working-Class Families from the Industrial Revolution to the Fertility Decline.* London: Verso, 1993.

Sedgwick, Eve Kosofsky. *Between Men: English Literature and Male Homosocial Desire.* New York: Columbia University Press, 1985.

———. *The Coherence of Gothic Convention.* 1976. New York: Methuen, 1986.

———. *Epistemology of the Closet.* Berkeley: University of California Press, 1990.

———. "Nationalisms and Sexualities in the Age of Wilde." *Nationalisms and Sexualities.* New York: Routledge, 1992. 235–45.

Somerville-Large, Peter. *Dublin.* New York: Granada Publishing, 1981.

Spence, Joseph. " 'The Great Angelic Sin': The Faust Legend in Irish Literature, 1820–1900." *Bullan* 1, no. 2 (Autumn 1994): 47–58.

Stallybrass, Peter, and Allon White. *The Politics and Poetics of Transgression.* Ithaca: Cornell University Press, 1986.

Stoker, Bram. *Dracula.* New York: Bantam, 1989.

Stone, Lawrence. *The Family, Sex, and Marriage in England, 1500–1800.* Abr. ed. New York: Harper Torchbooks, 1977.

St. Peter, Christine. "Jennifer Johnston's Irish Troubles: A Materialist-Feminist Reading." *Gender in Irish Writing.* Ed. Toni O'Brien Johnson and David Cairns. Philadelphia: Open University Press, 1991. 112–27.

Sussman, Charlotte. " 'I Wonder Whether Poor Miss Sally Godfrey Be Living or Dead': The Married Woman and the Rise of the Novel." *Diacritics* 20, no. 1 (Spring 1990): 88–102.

Swift, Jonathan. *Gulliver's Travels.* Ed. Christopher Fox. New York: Bedford St. Martin's, 1995.

———. "A Modest Proposal." *The Prose Works of Jonathan Swift, D.D.* Ed. Temple Scott. Vol. 7, *Historical and Political Tracts—Irish.* London, 1925. 207–16.

Synge, John Millington. *The Playboy of the Western World.* 1907. New York: Dover, 1993.

Taussig, Michael. *The Devil and Commodity Fetishism in South America.* Chapel Hill: University of North Carolina Press, 1980.

———. *Shamanism, Colonialism, and the Wild Man: A Study in Terror and Healing.* Chicago: University of Chicago Press, 1987.

Theweleit, Klaus. *Male Fantasies.* 2 vols. Trans. Erica Carter, Chris Turner, and Stephen Conway. Minneapolis: University of Minnesota Press, 1989.

Thomas, Tammis Elise. "Masquerade Liberties and Female Power in Le Fanu's *Carmilla.*" *The Haunted Mind: The Supernatural in Victorian Literature.* Ed. Elton E. Smith and Robert Haas. New York: University Press of America, 1999. 39–65.

Thompson, E. P. *The Making of the English Working Class.* New York: Vintage, 1966.

Trumpener, Katie. *Bardic Nationalism: The Romantic Novel and the British Empire.* Princeton: Princeton University Press, 1997.

Walshe, Éibhear. Introduction. *Sex, Nation, and Dissent in Irish Writing.* Ed. Walshe. Cork, Ireland: Cork University Press, 1997.

Ward, Margaret. *Unmanageable Revolutionaries: Women and Irish Nationalism.* London: Pluto, 1995.

Watt, Ian P. *The Rise of the Novel.* Berkeley: University of California Press, 1964.

———. "Time and the Family in the Gothic Novel: *The Castle of Otranto.*" *Eighteenth-Century Life* 10, no. 3 (October 1986): 159–71.

Weekes, Ann Owens. *Irish Women Writers: An Uncharted Tradition.* Lexington: University Press of Kentucky, 1990.

Whelan, Kevin. *The Tree of Liberty: Radicalism, Catholicism, and the Construction of Irish Identity, 1760–1830.* Notre Dame: University of Notre Dame Press, 1996.

Wiesner, Merry E. "Spinning Out Capital: Women's Work in the Early Modern Economy." *Becoming Visible: Women in European History.* Ed. Renate Bridenthal, Claudia Koonz, and Susan Stuard. Boston: Houghton Mifflin, 1987. 221–49.

Wilde, Oscar. *The Picture of Dorian Gray. The Portable Oscar Wilde.* Ed. Richard Aldington and Stanley Weintraub. New York: Penguin, 1988. 138–91.

Williams, Anne. *Art of Darkness: A Poetics of Gothic.* Chicago: University of Chicago Press, 1995.

Williams, Raymond. *The Country and the City.* New York: Oxford University Press, 1973.

Wilson, Des. *An End to Silence.* Cork: Royal Carbery, 1990.

Woodward, Carolyn. " 'My Heart So Wrapt': Lesbian Disruptions in Eighteenth-Century British Fiction." *Signs* 18, no. 4 (Summer 1993): 838–65.

Yeats, W. B. "The Rose of Shadow." *The Secret Rose, Stories by W. B. Yeats:* A Variorum Edition. Ed. Phillip L. Marcus, Warwick Gould, and Michael J. Sidnee. Ithaca: Cornell University Press, 1981. 227–31.

———. *Selected Poems and Four Plays of William Butler Yeats.* Ed. M. L. Rosenthal. New York: Scribner, 1996.

———. *The Variorum Edition of the Poems of W. B. Yeats.* Ed. Peter Allt and Russell K. Alspach. New York: Macmillan, 1957.

Index

165, 168, 246; as counterpart to the marital contract, 104. *See also* Burke, Edmund: social contract; Compact(s)

Devorgilla, 27, 177

Diabolism, 53–57

Dinnerstein, Dorothy, 135

Divorce, 218, 265 n.5

Doyle, Damian, 206

Dublin, 104, 107, 164, 206, 207

Eagleton, Terry, 15, 16, 52, 90, 93, 97, 156, 241

Easter Uprising, 156, 172, 179, 180, 192–193, 209, 226

Edgeworth, Maria, 5, 76–77, 79; *The Absentee,* 100, 262 n.3; and anti-quarianism, 97–98, 99–101, 106; *Castle Rackrent,* 80, 98–106, 108, 110, 132; childhood, 96–97; *Ennui,* 98, 101, 262 n.3

Ehrenpreis, Irvin, 82

Eliot, T. S., 239, 248

Ellman, Maud, 50, 73

Engagement(s), 188; broken, 179, 191–194

English literature: field of, 241

Enlightenment: epistemologies, 13, 15; shift from state to family repression during, 44–45

Exchange value, 226; versus use value, 219

Family(ies): of alliance, 45, 48, 73, 78, 89, 102; Anglo-Irish, 19, 51, 75, 77–79, 80, 81, 89, 98, 99, 110, 112, 117–134, 142, 177–178, 195, 228, 236, 239, 241; within Anglo-Irish settler colonialism, 2, 6, 8, 77, 81, 140–141, 143, 175, 183, 196, 217, 223, 231, 237; aristocratic, 57; British, 140; and capitalism, 19, 33–41, 85, 139–

141, 234; destruction of, 8, 178, 194, 213, 219; dynamics, 1, 136, 175, 207, 208; emergence of, 4, 15, 17, 19, 30–31, 35–41, 43, 48–49, 53, 57, 60, 62, 73, 81, 143; eroticization of, 43–46, 50, 51; iconization of, 62, 69, 97–98; intensifying affective bonds within, 43, 46, 57, 70–71; isolation of, 110, 128; middle-class, 3, 45–47, 50, 56, 57, 69, 231; nuclear, 4, 15, 19, 33, 36, 41, 48, 50, 57, 60, 85, 90, 92, 125, 196, 232, 234, 235, 237, 240, 254 n.5; patriarchal, 71, 92, 107, 136, 216, 222–223; of the poor and propertyless, 47, 254 n.5; in relation to colonialism, 16, 31, 137–141, 143, 217, 248; in relation to public/private division, 15, 17, 50, 51, 56, 69, 137–138, 140; reproduction of, 4, 54, 61–62, 67–70, 81, 88, 103, 126, 131, 139–141, 177, 179, 186, 213–214, 216, 232, 234–235, 240, 248; secrets, 113, 175, 177, 196, 201, 232; and the state, 44–45, 50, 69–70, 92, 137–138; working-class, 42, 62, 229–230

Family romance: Anglo-Irish, 77, 106, 172, 195; Freudian, 109; the gothic as a form of, 18; internalization of, 50; Irish, 226, 228; nuclear, 92

Famine, 23; as colonial weapon, 24–25

Farrell, M. J. *See* Keane, Molly

Female sexuality, 213; demonized, 172, 177; as a facade, 187–188; as scapegoat, 207; as undermining national coherence, 177–178, 196

Feudalism, 30, 48, 139

Fingall, Elizabeth (Countess), 214–215

First World War. *See* World War I

Forgiveness, 232, 237

Foster, R. F., 21–22, 30, 131, 246, 256–257 n.1

Fosterage, 21

Margot Backus is Associate Professor of English Literature
at St. John Fisher College.

Library of Congress Cataloging-in-Publication Data

Backus, Margot Gayle
The Gothic family romance : heterosexuality, child sacrifice, and
the Anglo-Irish colonial order / Margot Gayle Backus.
p.   cm. — (Post-contemporary interventions)
Includes bibliographical references and index.
ISBN 0-8223-2380-X (cloth : alk. paper). — ISBN 0-8223-2414-8
(paper : alk. paper)
1. English fiction — Irish authors — History and criticism.
2. Family in literature.   3. Psychological fiction, English —
History and criticism.   4. Domestic fiction, English — History
and criticism.   5. Capitalism and literature — Ireland — History.
6. Repression (Psychology) in literature.   7. Gothic revival
(Literature) — Ireland.   8. Parent and child in literature.
9. Heterosexuality in literature.   10. Imperialism in literature.
11. British — Ireland — History.   12. Colonies in literature.
I. Title.   II. Series.
PR8807.F25B33   1999
823.009'355 — dc21   99-20689